SOUTH-EASTERN EUROPE AFTER TITO

In 1914 the assassination of an Austrian Archduke in the remote Balkan town of Sarajevo precipitated a world catastrophe that involved the death of millions and the collapse of three powerful dynasties. But though the First World War had an obscure beginning in a backward part of Bosnia, deep rivalries underlay the conflict. For the region as a whole had, for many years, been a center of acute instability. The fear today must be that, following the death of Tito, the continuing tensions there could trigger another and maybe even more devastating war in the 1980s. This book contains papers on this theme presented to the International School on Disarmament and Research on Conflicts (ISODARCO).

The unique character of ISODARCO as a non-official international forum is the breadth of opinion it is able to encompass. In the words of a reviewer of a previous conference volume, "Although many readers will find some of the arguments contentious, its main strength is that it covers a very wide range of viewpoints across the ideological spectrum" (*British Army Review*).

Among the contributors are citizens from a variety of rival states in the region: Greece, Bulgaria, Romania, Hungary and Yugoslavia. In addition, participants from many more countries and from a large number of diverse professions were in attendance to discuss the papers in the present volume, including citizens from NATO and Warsaw Pact countries, students, professors, journalists and those with direct military experience.

The range of opinion may be gauged by contrasting the contributions of Professor Ciro E. Zoppo of the United States with that of Dr. György Réti of Hungary. Zoppo, writing about Turkey, discerns hegemonial ambitions on the part of the Soviet Union. Réti, however, categorically denies the existence of any Soviet threat to peace and stability. Moreover, in a piquant contribution, he presents a severe critique, from one Communist standpoint, of another Communist position, namely that embraced by Albania. Yet other sharply distinctive Communist perspectives are provided by a member of the Romanian Institute of Political Sciences, Dr. Ioan Mircea Paşcu, by a member of the Bulgarian Academy of Sciences, Dr. Nansen Behar, and by a Yugoslav Professor of International Relations, Dr. Radovan Vukadinović.

The general reader seeking to make sense of these many conflicting strands of opinion will surely find invaluable the contribution of the British strategist, Professor William F. Gutteridge, formerly of the Royal Military Academy, Sandhurst, and now at the University of Aston, who provides a summary of the intense discussions that followed the presentation of the various papers.

SOUTH-EASTERN EUROPE AFTER TITO

A Powder-Keg for the 1980s?

Edited by
David Carlton and Carlo Schaerf

St. Martin's Press   New York

Library of Congress Cataloging in Publication Data

Main entry under title:

South-eastern Europe after Tito.

Includes index.
1. Balkan Peninsula — History — 20th century —
Addresses, essays, lectures. I. Carlton, David, 1938−
II. Schaerf, Carlo.
DR48.5.S674   1983   949.6   82−7352
ISBN 0−312−74730−6

Contents

Preface

The chapters in this volume were presented to the eighth course of the International School on Disarmament and Research on Conflicts (ISODARCO), held in Venice, Italy, between 26 August and 5 September 1980.

The organisation of the course was made possible by the generous collaboration and financial contributions of many organisations and individuals. For their financial contributions we wish to express our gratitude to:

The Ford Foundation, in particular Enid Schoettle;
The Italian National Research Council — National Committee for Juridical and Political Sciences;
The Italian Ministry of Cultural Affairs;
The University of Rome, in particular Professor Antonio Ruberti and Professor Giorgio Tecce;
The Pugwash Conferences on Science and World Affairs.

We wish to acknowledge the dedicated collaboration, before and during the course, of Mimma Mauro, Gabriella Fascetti, Marzia Mauro, Bruno Pellizzoni and Anna Petrelli. For administrative work our thanks are due to Fernando Pacciani and Luciano Fiore. For hospitality in Venice we are indebted to the Domus Ciliota.

The editors are grateful to Allen Lane for allowing David Carlton to include in Chapter 3 passages first published in his *Anthony Eden: A Biography* (1981). They also wish to thank Kossuth Könyvkiadó of Budapest for permitting György Réti to reproduce in Chapter 12 a translated excerpt from *Mit kell Tudni Albániáról?* (1981).

Chapters 6 and 11 were previously published in *The Arms Race in the 1980s* edited by David Carlton and Carlo Schaerf (Macmillan, 1982).

All opinions expressed in the chapters and in the summary of discussions are of a purely private nature and do not necessarily represent the official view either of the organisers of the School or of the organisations to which the writers may be affiliated.

D. C.
C. S.

List of Abbreviations

ADM	Atomic Demolition Munitions
BALT	Arms and Troop Reduction Talks on the Balkans
BBC	British Broadcasting Corporation
BP	British Petroleum
CBM	Confidence-Building Measures
CCD	Conference of the Committee on Disarmament
CDE	Conference on Disarmament in Europe
CENTO	Central Treaty Organisation
CFP	Compagnie Française des Pétroles
CMEA	Council for Mutual Economic Assistance
COMECON	Council for Mutual Economic Aid
CSCE	Conference on Security and Co-operation in Europe
DC	Developing Country
DMZ	Demilitarised Zone
EEC	European Economic Community
GDP	Gross Domestic Product
GFCF	Gross Fixed Capital Formation
GNP	Gross National Product
IAEA	International Atomic Energy Agency
IAI	Istituto Affari Internazionali
IISS	International Institute for Strategic Studies
IMF	International Monetary Fund
IPC	Iraq Petroleum Company
IRBM	Intermediate Range Ballistic Missile
ISODARCO	International School on Disarmament and Research on Conflicts
LDC	Less Developed Country
MALT	Arms and Troop Limitation Talks dealing with Naval Forces in the Mediterranean
MBFR	Mutual Balanced Force Reduction Talks
MFR	Mutual Force Reduction Talks
MLF	Multilateral Force

MRBM	Medium Range Ballistic Missile
NALT	Northern Arms and Troop Limitation Talks
NATO	North Atlantic Treaty Organisation
NGO	Non-Governmental Organisation
NNWS	Non-Nuclear-Weapons State
NPT	Non-Proliferation Treaty
NWFZ	Nuclear-Weapon-Free Zone
NWS	Nuclear-Weapons State
OECD	Organisation for Economic Co-operation and Development
OPANAL	Agency for the Prohibition of Nuclear Weapons in Latin America
OPEC	Organisation of Petroleum Exporting Countries
PLA	Party of Labour of Albania
QRA	Quick Reaction Alert
SALT	Strategic Arms Limitation Talks
SAS	Special Ammunition Storage Sites
SIPRI	Stockholm International Peace Research Institute
SOE	Special Operations Executive
TNF	Theatre Nuclear Forces
UN	United Nations
UNCTAD	United Nations Conference on Trade and Development
UNSSOD	United Nations Special Session on Disarmament
WTO	Warsaw Treaty Organisation

Notes on the Contributors

Nansen Behar (Bulgarian) is Head of the Economics Department of the Institute for Contemporary Social Studies in the Bulgarian Academy of Sciences. He was formerly Editor-in-Chief of the magazine *International Life* (Sofia). He is author of numerous books and articles published in a number of different languages.

Hans Günter Brauch (West German) is Research Associate at the Institute of Political Science at Heidelberg University and a Teaching Associate at Tübingen University. He was formerly a Teaching Associate at Darmstadt University. He has published extensively in German on problems of international security and of arms control.

David Carlton (British) (co-editor) is Senior Lecturer in Diplomatic History at the Polytechnic of North London. He holds a Ph.D. degree from the University of London. He is author of *MacDonald versus Henderson: The Foreign Policy of the Second Labour Government* (1970); of *Anthony Eden: A Biography* (1981); and of numerous articles on modern international politics. He is co-editor of six previous volumes in this series.

William F. Gutteridge (British) is Professor of International Studies and Head of Political and Economic Studies Group at the University of Aston in Birmingham. He was formerly Senior Lecturer in Commonwealth History and Government at the Royal Military Academy, Sandhurst. He is author of *Armed Forces in New States* (1962); *Military Institutions and Power in the New States* (1965); *The Military in African Politics* (1969); and *Military Regimes in Africa* (1975).

Giacomo Luciani (Italian) is Director of Research at the Istituto Affari Internazionali in Rome. He is author of three books in Italian on international politics. He has also contributed an article in English entitled 'Detente and the New Order: A Difficult Juncture' to *Lo Spettatare Internazionale*, no. 1, 1980.

Daniele Moro (Italian) is an official of the Italian Socialist Party in Rome. He is currently in the Party's International Department. He has also served in Brussels and London on European Economic Community business. He has published many articles on international politics and has also appeared on radio and television both in Italy and abroad.

Ioan Mircea Paşcu (Romanian) is Senior Researcher in the Department of International Relations at the Institute of Political Sciences of the Stefan Gheorghiu Academy in Bucharest. He has visited the United States under the auspices of the Ford Foundation. He is author of an article in Romanian on 'The Non-Use of Force in International Relations'.

Athanassios G. Platias (Greek) is a Fellow of the Peace Studies Program at Cornell University. He is registered as a Ph.D. candidate in the Department of Government at the same university. He was formerly a Fellow at the Center for Science and International Affairs, Harvard University. He is a graduate of the Law Faculty of the University of Athens.

György Réti (Hungarian) is a Researcher at the Hungarian Institute for Foreign Affairs in Budapest. He was formerly a Hungarian diplomat, seeing service in Peking, Tirana and Saigon. He has written several articles on Hungarian–Italian relations. He is also author of a book in Hungarian on Albania: *Mit kell Tudni Albániáról?* (Budapest, 1981).

R. J. Rydell (US) is a political scientist at the Lawrence Livermore National Laboratory and is currently studying the causes and effects of the proliferation of nuclear weapons. He was previously a Research Fellow at the Center for Science and International Affairs at Harvard University. He was educated at the University of Virginia (B.A.), the London School of Economics (M.Sc.), and Princeton University (M.A. and Ph.D.). His doctoral dissertation, entitled 'Decision Making on the Breeder Reactor in Britain and the United States' will be published as a book.

Carlo Schaerf (Italian) (co-editor) is Professor of Physics at the University of Rome. He was formerly a Research Associate at Stanford University and on the staff of the Italian Atomic Energy Commission. With Professor Eduardo Amaldi he founded in 1966 the International School on Disarmament and Research on Conflicts (ISODARCO). He was appointed Director of ISODARCO in 1970. He is co-editor of six previous volumes in this series.

Kosta Tsipis (US) is Associate Director of the Program in Science and Technology for International Security at the Massachusetts Institute of Technology. He was previously associated with the Stockholm International Peace Research Institute. He is author of three books and 42 articles on international security themes.

Radovan Vukadinović (Yugoslav) is Professor of International Relations in the Faculty of Political Sciences at Zagreb University. He was a Senior Fellow in the School of International Affairs at Columbia University during 1970–1. He is Editor-in-Chief of the Yugoslav journal for the Political Sciences entitled *Politiška Misao*. Dr Vukadinović is author of numerous books and articles on international politics.

Ciro E. Zoppo (US) is Professor of International Relations in the Political Science Department, University of California, Los Angeles. He is a former Executive Director of the California Seminar on Arms Control and Foreign Policy. He has contributed numerous articles on Mediterranean problems and on arms control to such journals as *Survival* and *World Politics*.

List of Course Participants

Venice, 26 August–5 September 1980

Abdel-Moneim, Mohamed (Egyptian) Ministry of Foreign Affairs, Tahrir Sq., Cairo, Egypt.

Annequin, Jean Louis (French) Institut Français de Polémologie, Hotel des Invalides, 129, rue de Grenelle, 75700 Paris, France.

Behar, Nansen (Bulgarian) Institute for Contemporary Social Studies, Bulgarian Academy of Sciences, Pionersky put 21, 1635 Sofia, Bulgaria.

Berglund, Gregory (US) Mas Roussier Entremont, 13100 Aix-en-Provence, France.

Bjornerstedt, Rolf (Swedish) SIPRI, Sveavägen 166, S-113 46 Stockholm, Sweden.

Brauch, Hans Günter (West German) Alte-Bergsteige 47, D-6950 Mosbach, West Germany.

Burzynski, Andrzej (Polish) Institute of State and Law of the Polish Academy of Sciences, Nowy Swiat 72, Warsaw, Poland.

Caldéron, Félix (Peruvian) Peruvian Embassy, Wien, Austria.

Calogero, Francesco (Italian) Istituto di Fisica dell'Università di Roma, P. le Aldo Moro 2, 00185 Roma, Italy.

Carlton, David (British) Department of History, Philosophy and European Studies, Polytechnic of North London, Prince of Wales Road, London, Great Britain.

Celentano, Guido (Italian) C. so Vittorio Emanuele 168, 80121 Napoli, Italy.

De Andreis, Marco (Italian) Aviazione e Difesa, Via Tagliamento 29, Roma, Italy.

De La Riva, Careaga Ion (Spanish) Villa Berriz-Emen, c/Bermudez Cañete 1, Madrid 16, Spain.

De Volpi, Alexander (US) Bldg. 208, Argonne National Laboratory, Argonne, Illinois 60439, USA.

Dona' Dalle Rose, Luigi F. (Italian) Istituto di Fisica, Univ. di Padova, Via Marzolo 8, Padova, Italy.

Duffy, Gloria (US) Arms Control Program, Stanford University Bldg. 160, Stanford, California 94305, USA.

Elzen, Boelie (Dutch) Twente University of Technology, PB 217, Enschede, The Netherlands.

Emelyanov, V. S. (Soviet) Leninskiyi Prospect 17, Academy of Science, Moscow, USSR.

Fabiyi, Edwin (Nigerian) Institute of Peace Law and International Department, Université de Nice 9, Av. de Fabrón, 06200 Nice, France.

Feld, Bernard T. (US) Physics Department, MIT, Cambridge, Massachusetts 02139, USA.

Ferm, Ragnihild (Swedish) SIPRI, Sveavagen 166, S-113 46 Stockholm, Sweden.

Frankowska, Maria (Polish) Polish Academy of Science, Institute of State and Law, Noury Surat 72, Warsaw, Poland.

Freedman, Lawrence (British) RIIA, Chatham House, 10 St James's Sq., London, Great Britain.

Ghantus, Wolfgang (East German) Institute of International Politics and Economics, Breite Strasse 11, 102 Berlin, German Democratic Republic.

Gusmaroli, Franca (Italian) Defence Today, Via Tagliamento 29, 00100 Roma, Italy.

Gutteridge, William (British) Political and Economic Studies Group, University of Aston, Birmingham, Great Britain.

Henderson, Robert D'A. (Canadian) National University of Lesotho, Lesotho, Africa.

Kaplan, Richard Alan (US) 1912 Elliott Drive, Vallejo, California, 94590, USA.

Leifer, Jeffrey (US) Yale School of Organization and Management, 135 Prospect St, New Haven, Conn. 06520, USA.

Lellouche, Pierre (French) IFRI, 6 Rue Ferrus, 75014 Paris, France.

Löhmannsröben, Hans (West German) Robert Koch Str. 38(913), 34 Göttingen, West Germany.

Luciani, Giacomo (Italian) Istituto Affari Internazionali, Viale Mazzini 88, Roma, Italy.

Mack, Newell (US) U-Consultants, 100 Leonard St, Belmont,

Massachusetts 02178, USA.

Milstein, M. A. (Soviet) Academy of Sciences of the USSR, Klebny 2/3, Moscow, USSR.

Moro, Daniele (Italian) Direzione Nazionale del PSI, Intern. Dept., Via Tomacelli 146, 00100 Roma, Italy.

Nabil, A. Eissa (Egyptian) Physics Dept., Faculty of Science, Alazhar University, Nasr City, Cairo, Egypt.

Nakai, Yoko (Japanese) USICA, American Embassy Tokyo, 10-5, Akasaka 1-Chome, Minato-Ku, Tokyo, Japan 107.

Ooms, Jack (Dutch) Prins Maurits Laboratory TNO PO Box 45, 2280 AA Ryswyk, The Netherlands.

Pascolini, Alessandro (Italian) Istituto di Fisica, Univ. di Padova, Via Marzolo 8, Padova, Italy.

Pașcu, Ioan Mircea (Romanian) Institute of Political Sciences, 1–3 Armata Poporucui, Sector 6, Bucharest, Romania.

Patania, Annino Aldo (Italian) Johns Hopkins University, 1740 Massachusetts Ave., NW, Washington DC 20036, USA.

Pfeifenberger, Werner (Austrian) Österreichisches Institut für Politische Bildung, A-7210 Mattersburg, Austria.

Platias, Athanassios (Greek) Peace Studies Program, Cornell University, 180 Uris Hall, Ithaca, NY 14853, USA.

Ravi, Komarraju (Indian) Department of Politics and Public Administration, Andhra University, Waltair, Andhra Pradesh, India.

Réti, György (Hungarian) Hungarian Institute of International Affairs, 1016 Budapest, Bérc U23, Hungary.

Schaerf, Carlo (Italian) Istituto di Fisica dell'Università di Roma, P. le Aldo Moro 2, Roma, Italy.

Schmidt, Max (East German) Institute of International Politics & Economics, 102 Berlin, Breite Strasse 11, German Democratic Republic.

Schoettle, Enid (US) The Ford Foundation, 320 East 43rd Street, New York, NY 10017, USA.

Silvestri, Stefano (Italian) L'Europeo, Via della Mercede 37, Roma, Italy.

Skons, Elisabeth (Swedish) SIPRI, Sveavagen 166, S-11346 Stockholm, Sweden.

Smart, Ian (British) Grosvenor Avenue, Richmond, Surrey, Great Britain.

Smit, A. Wim (Dutch) Center for Studies on Problems of Science and Society, Twente University of Technology, PB 217,

Enschede, The Netherlands.

Šuković, Olga (Yugoslav) Institute of International Politics and Economics, Makedonska 25, 11000 Belgrade, Yugoslavia.

Taylor, Trevor (British) Department of International Relations and Politics, North Staffordshire Polytechnic, College Road, Stoke on Trent, Staffordshire, Great Britain.

Thompson, Susan (British) Centre for Disarmament Geneva Unit, UN Office at Geneva, Palais des Nations, 1211 Geneva, Switzerland.

Tromp, Hylke (Dutch) Polemological Institute, PO Box 121, Haren (Gr.), The Netherlands.

Tsipis, Kosta (US) Room 26 402, MIT, Cambridge, Massachusetts 02139, USA.

Vogt, Margaret (Nigerian) Nigerian Institute of International Affairs, GP Box 1727 Lagos, Nigeria.

Wiedmeyer, Hans (West German) Phil.-Theol. Hochschule, St. Georgen Offenbacher Landstr. 224, D-6000 Frankfurt 70, West Germany.

Wright, Steve (British) Richardson Institute, Politics Department, University of Lancaster, Bailrigg, Lancaster, Great Britain.

Ziai, Iradj (Iranian) POB 1512, Tehran, Iran.

Zoppo, Ciro Elliott (US) Political Science Dept., University of California, Los Angeles, California 90049, USA.

OBSERVERS

Castelli, Antonio (Italian) Collegio Navale Morosini, S. Elena 30122, Venezia, Italy.

Elkin, Natan (Argentinian) Pl. Université 1, 1348 Louvain-la-Neuve, Belgium.

Gurevich, Sergio (Argentinian) 27, rue de Luxemburg, 1150 Bruxelles, Belgium.

Jacchia, Enrico (Italian) Piazza dell'Orologio, 7, 00186 Roma, Italy.

Note Two authors of papers were unable to attend the course, namely R. J. Rydell and Radovan Vukadinović.

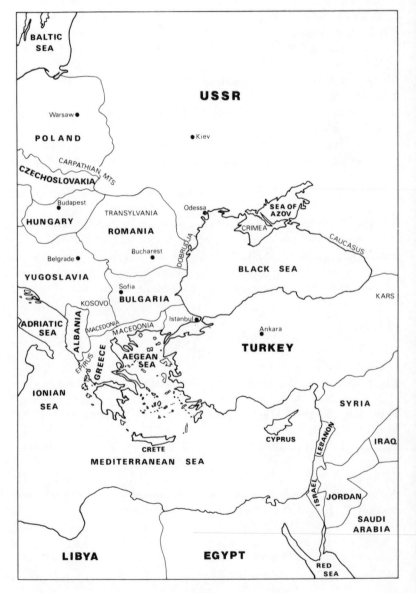

1 Summary of Discussions and Notes on Recent Developments

William F. Gutteridge

Introduction

A number of significant developments has taken place in the Balkans and Eastern Mediterranean since the majority of papers in this volume were written and presented. This introductory chapter seeks first to record the essence of the relevant discussion which took place at the eighth course of the International School on Disarmament and Research on Conflicts (ISODARCO) held in Venice between 26 August and 5 September 1980. The aim was to delineate the key political and strategic problems of the region. Certain of the subsequent developments through the year 1981 are then reviewed and some resultant reassessments are made. The military coup in Turkey in September 1980 and the election in October 1981 which led to the first Socialist government in Greece have shifted the international perspectives and clearly cannot be ignored. There have also been some alterations in the position and political potential of Albania in relation to its neighbours and more widely. (There have, of course, also been many important and arguably relevant developments in the Middle East. But these are not treated here in any detail as most authors of papers decided that the Middle East should be largely disregarded in order that they could sharpen the focus on the Balkans and the Eastern Mediterranean *per se*.)

1

Lines of Discussion

The problems of this rather ill-defined region tend to defy consistent systematic analysis. Various inherently divergent models can be proposed.

One possibility is to see the area in terms of East—West and North—South interests, conflicting largely because their methods and concepts differ according to the axis. In the Eastern Mediterranean and West Asia, in particular, a number of changes are taking place which require interpretation in the light of the lack of coincidence between the East—West and North—South strands in international political economy. The interaction, for example, of Soviet aid to Turkey with European Economic Community (EEC) or American aid programmes in that country clearly has important implications for its development whatever the regime in power at the time. The current (January 1982) differences between American and Western European attitudes towards the military regime add a further complexity to the domestic situation, while at the same time illustrating effectively the difficulties implicit in attempting to use external pressures to induce internal change, thus inviting comparison with Western stances towards El Salvador, Poland or South Africa.

Historically, in spite of the distances involved, the Balkans were never untouched by the problems of North-Eastern Europe, though today what happens in the south is clearly less important to the Russians than what happens in the northern tier of their alliance. But they are inevitably concerned with the problems of their neighbour, Turkey, not only because of the Dardanelles and the southern shore of the Black Sea, but because of Cyprus and the linkages with the Middle East. At the same time the possibility of progress towards Arab regional integration is bound to have repercussions in other Moslem areas in the vicinity including Asia Minor.

Moves towards Balkan integration are clearly inhibited by the existing external relations of the states in the area with Western or Eastern Europe, and especially with the EEC on the part of Greece and Turkey and of those two countries also with the North Atlantic Treaty Organisation (NATO). There is no doubt that Western Europe has for long had a fundamental interest in the security of the region, which the Soviet Union, certainly since the Yalta Conference in 1945, has recognised. Thus regional integration is even in the longer term a doubtful prospect in the face of Western European and Eastern European alliances and possible eventual Arab integration. Such associations of states, whatever the formal arrangements at a given moment, generate strong pressures or pulls on individual countries in the Balkans or Eastern Mediterranean, whether they belong to them or have connections with them.

The military balance in the area is susceptible to change as adjustments take place in the deployment of naval forces in the Mediterranean. A relatively enclosed sea area such as the Mediterranean could well be the subject of at least experimental confidence-building measures relating to the announcement and justification of naval dispositions. Satellite observation is now adequate for maritime intelligence purposes and this means that the adoption of confidence-building gestures would involve little sacrifice. The recent injection of an aggressive Libyan influence into the southern half of the region, culminating initially in American naval exercises resulting in the shooting down of Libyan aircraft, makes such arrangements between the major powers aimed at retaining control of potential conflict more desirable.

The relative lack of stability at the Turkish end of the region has been a matter of continuing international concern. Turkey is seen by some as a country suffering a long crisis in the development of its modern national identity. There are continual tensions arising partly from the interaction between domestic and foreign policies. Turkey's commitment to the Western alliance is a product of its emergence as a secular state and contingent on the direct threat which it perceives from the Soviet Union; and its military position is not as strong as sometimes appears, because its armed forces are essentially dispersed to accommodate its geographical position and range of interests. It has to consider the relationships with and commitments to the West, its involvement in the problem of Cyprus and the fact that it is the only country in the Mediterranean with a common boundary with the Soviet Union. Along with recurrent and indisputable internal security problems these constitute a formidable set of military tasks.

It now seems questionable whether in the event of a future crisis in the region the United States has, through its naval forces in the Mediterranean, the capacity to maintain the strategic balance or indeed actually to provide direct assistance if a conflict developed on the northern frontier of the region. Circumstances are conceivable in which the only military option remaining would be pre-emption. The presence of Soviet divisions in Hungary would be relevant to such a situation. Again in the case of the Mediterranean itself, there is obviously a case for confidence-building measures not only aimed at reassuring the population of a region in which Soviet bloc and non-aligned or Western-oriented states are so closely interlocked.

The preeminence in debate on the future security of the Balkans of military factors is likely to inhibit new forms of scientific and technological co-operation and joint ventures on any scale. The original argument that intra-Balkan arrangements are not a practicable or desirable alternative to integration in the EEC tends to prevail even though the new government of Greece may more effectively question it. The existing military involvements would also seem to preclude serious discussion of the feasibility of a nuclear-weapon-free zone (NWFZ).

Not only are the interests of the Balkans and the Eastern Mediterranean generally subordinate to the NATO—Warsaw Pact interactions but they are still in large measure determined by the legacy which emerged from Winston Churchill's visit to Moscow in October 1944 and from the Yalta and Potsdam meetings in 1945. Nowhere outside central Europe is the recognition of Soviet and Western spheres of influence more explicit. A successful outcome of the continuing Helsinki—Belgrade—Madrid process in the shape of a realistic European disarmament conference would benefit a region whose interest cannot be divorced or seen separately from those of the rest of Europe.

Turkey: Internal Change and External Relations

1981 saw the centenary of the birth of Kemal Atatürk, founder of the Turkish Republic. When, in September 1980, the army, apparently reluctantly, took over the running of the country for the third time within thirty years, it did so in the name of Atatürk. Towards the end of 1981 Turkey was once again endeavouring to draw up a new constitution and to plan for new elections. In the meantime the interim rule by the army had produced a number of revisions in Turkey's relationship with the rest of the world.

It seemed that the military rulers wanted to remain all things to all men; continuing membership of NATO and hopes of joining the EEC, improbable, to say the least, with the military in power, were set alongside increasing eastward links and new relationships with Islam. Once dominant over the Arabs of the Eastern Mediterranean in the Ottoman Empire, Turkey has been for ten years becoming progressively more conscious again of the Arab world.

In 1980–1 Iraq displaced West Germany and the United States as Turkey's principal trading partner. Business connections especially through the activities of Turkish construction firms have rapidly increased. Civil engineering contracts doubled and by the beginning of 1982 approached ten billion dollars in value. Food production and exports to the Near East have also expanded. Diplomatically the shift in emphasis was typified by the military government's downgrading of Turkey's relationship with Israel and much more outspoken support for the Palestinian cause than had ever emanated from Ankara before. A certain caution remained primarily because of the suspicion that the Palestinians have lent some support themselves to Turkish dissidents – to Kurdish separatists and Armenian terrorists.

The original encouragement in Turkish eyes to look East again came out of the Cyprus crisis of 1974 and the assumption that the West was committed to the support of Greece. By 1980 Turkey had already established a new position in international politics through close links with Iran as well as Iraq, Saudi Arabia and Libya. The doubtful stability of the regime of Ayatollah Ruhollah Khomeini, however, symbolised Turkey's need for caution in turning too emphatically towards the East. Apart from the tangible signs of co-operation, such as Iraq's oil pipeline to the Mediterranean and a major loan from Saudi Arabia, Turkey has also re-established a kind of relationship with its neighbour Syria. There are inherent problems, however, in the way of tighter links. The more radical Arab states certainly distrust Turkey's membership of NATO and its close links with the United States. This was certainly not reduced by the sensational clash between American and Libyan forces in the Gulf of Sirte. The Turks on the other hand are no longer really concerned about the possibility of a general slide back on the part of their population towards Islam. Participation in intergovernmental Islamic meetings has become a regular feature of Turkish diplomatic relations. Provided Turkey does not take part in Arab internecine struggles for power in the Middle East, it can take advantage of lucrative markets while enhancing its old claim to act as a bridge between East and West.

Turkey adopts a similarly pragmatic view of its membership of NATO and believes that, because of the West's strategic need of Turkey, it has not much to lose from it and much to gain. Turkey joined NATO thirty years ago and in spite of the usual pressures against it, has become an integral part of the Alliance, which itself has come to affect the ideological stance of the Turkish élite. Turkey has managed to draw on Western — notably West German and American — technological assistance for industrial development, while also relying on the Soviet Union and Romania. It even imports electric power supply from the Soviet Union and Bulgaria.

Important bulwarks of the Western connection in Turkish eyes have proved to be the disturbed conditions further east. The Iranian Revolution created considerable unease but nothing to compare with the alarm generated by the Soviet invasion of Afghanistan in December 1979. Since then Turkey has had to reconcile its appetite for industrial aid and trade with the Communist bloc with the well-documented discovery of Soviet links through embassy officials with terrorist groups in Turkey, to whom arms were being smuggled, apparently from Bulgaria.

The post-Cyprus phase of tension for Turkey within NATO and reactions to the arms embargo imposed by the United States have largely passed, though the attitudes of the new Socialist government in Greece towards NATO provided another complication. The appointment of General Alexander Haig, in particular, as Secretary of State in President Ronald Reagan's Administration stimulated US–Turkish relations and increased American aid to Turkey in 1981 amounted to a total of nearly $800 million. This was, however, accompanied by tensions between Turkey and the EEC members of NATO. Indeed in December 1981 the imprisonment by the Turkish Government of Bulent Ecevit, the former Prime Minister, prompted the imposition of a block on substantial EEC aid for Turkey scheduled for 1982. The European Commission advised against the final approval of the relevant financial protocol on the grounds that Turkey did not seem to be fulfilling her promise to move towards a return of democracy. This put the application of Turkey to move from being a beneficiary associate to being a full member of the Community in serious doubt, but was seen in Turkey as an attempt to interfere in Turkish domestic politics. Elections after a constitutional referendum were in any case unlikely before 1983. This apparent indifference to Western European pressure for democratic reforms also put Turkey in danger of suspension from participation in the Council of Europe and from associate membership of the Common Market.

The arrival of Caspar Weinberger, the American Defense Secretary, in Ankara, more or less simultaneously with Ecevit's imprisonment, seemed to confirm the difference in attitude of the United States and the EEC towards human rights and democracy in practice. The visit in fact led to a speed-up in American aid to Turkey for the modernisation of the army and other purposes and an indication to the Turks that they might be mildly favoured as compared with the Greeks, especially in the light of Andreas Papandreou's reservations about the military wing of NATO.

The suppression of terrorism was the essential reason for military intervention in Turkish politics in 1980, but an implicitly and uncritical — in terms of the actions of the regime — pro-Turkish attitude by the United States was not generally seen, at the beginning of 1982, as the best means of ensuring a balance or stability in the region in the face of whatever threats to it really existed. The division of opinion within NATO on the political situation in Turkey enhanced the importance of any Greek decisions about future military co-operation, but served in Europe further to confirm the importance of EEC insistence on democratic criteria for membership of the Community. It perhaps portended a return to the kind of US — Western European dichotomy of opinion which prevailed over the Greek military dictatorship between 1967 and 1974 and was not likely to stem the growth of anti-Americanism on the continent generally.

While in Turkey the actions of a military government proved the source of tensions in 1981, elsewhere in the Mediterranean elections had potential implications for the military and political balance in the region. In Malta, in spite of prognostications which could have had a positive impact on the EEC and possibly NATO, Dom Mintoff and the ruling Labour Party were returned to power by a small margin. The Nationalists had, however, demonstrated the appeal of a distinctively pro-Western stance by E. Fenech-Adami. In Greece, by contrast, the Socialist election victory of Papandreou heralded a reappraisal of NATO's role at least in the Aegean.

Greece: the International Effect of Domestic Realignment

In the months before the Greek election in October 1981 interest focused on three main aspects of that country's international performance — in the EEC following its accession at the beginning of the year; over Cyprus where in May the United Nations (UN) endeavoured to initiate steps towards a new deal for the island; and on the small relief of economic difficulties resulting from the opening of the Prinos oilfield, in the Aegean off the island of Thassos. The original announcement in 1973 of the discovery of oil in the Aegean prompted Turkey to press claims for the demarcation of the sea's continental shelf. In the mid-1970s a Turkish research vessel intruding in Greek-claimed territorial waters brought the two countries almost to the brink of war. The delimitation issue, however, remains unresolved, perhaps because the oilfield is not as rich as the Greeks first thought. Reduction of dependence on oil remained a Greek objective with the encouragement of a switch to coal with the possibility of assistance from new EEC partners such as Great Britain.

Speculation about the international consequences of a radical change of government in the election of 18 October 1981 was quickly overtaken by actual words and actions. The symbolism implicit in taking a bold historical initiative to abolish official celebrations of the Civil War which ended in 1949 in the defeat of the Communist insurgents was quickly apparent. This was a deliberate act of national reconciliation which even so did not meet with wholehearted support from the Communist Party of Greece, which was evidently disappointed at the scale of electoral success for the Socialists which effectively diminished their own influence. They regarded the new government as failing to grasp the opportunity for radical change by removing the basic centres of power from the control of the Right. The strength of the Socialist government allowed Papandreou at an early stage to modify substantially, towards pragmatism, his original attitude towards Greece's links with the West. But even so the pull of the EEC and the NATO relationship came under scrutiny with a probably inevitable public confrontation between Greek and Turkish representatives.

One main reason why the changes in Greek foreign policy remained a matter of style rather than substance was fear of Turkey. Relations with Turkey and the desire for a revised attitude towards NATO are not necessarily compatible in their implications. Greece became a member of NATO and has accommodated American bases since 1952. Pressure might build up further to remove nuclear weapons from these bases as a condition of the renewal of their leases but closure is unlikely. Even less likely is a decision by Papandreou to pull out of NATO even if the restraints imposed by the conservative, pro-Western President Konstantin Karamanlis could be circumvented. The army too, though not inclined to intervene again in politics at the moment, imposes its own restraints. The Prime Minister promised at an early stage not to interfere with the supply of modern military equipment from the United States. Overriding all these considerations is the unwillingness of Greeks to leave the field in NATO to the Turks. It is in fact the feeling that in the last resort the Americans will support Turkey, confirmed in several senses by the Weinberger mission to Ankara in December 1981, that ultimately keeps Greece in NATO. The failure of the West to prevent the Turkish action in Cyprus and the token American gesture of reduced arms deliveries to Turkey simply served to convince the Greek Government that nothing would be done to stop a seizure of islands in the Eastern Aegean. For some Greeks, however, this does not indicate so much a continued membership of NATO as a total disillusionment with the Alliance.

It is out of this complex of perceptions that there re-emerges a possible Greek initiative towards a Balkan *entente* of the kind which Eleutherios Venizelos used to favour. The possibility of a stance approaching neutrality between the superpowers, and in a way analogous to the Yugoslav position, appeals to many Greeks. Immediately after the election the Bulgarian Prime Minister welcomed the result and, evidently with Soviet approval, put back into circulation the concept of a Balkan NWFZ. Realists in Athens and elsewhere in the region, however, recognise that even if Greece left NATO, Bulgaria could not leave the Warsaw Pact. This makes such a proposition as the NWFZ irrelevant to Greece's position in NATO: her resultant position in fact would be comparable to that of Norway. Greece is more concerned, as a matter of national interest, with Turkish activities than with the great power struggle, and would probably as a result be a party only to superficial categories of Balkan co-operation which did not prejudice her relationship with Western Europe.

A month after the October 1981 election Papandreou made it clear that he took a negative view of Turkish claims to the Aegean continental shelf, arguing that the initiative lay in Ankara with a resort to the International Court in the light of the provisions of the Geneva Convention of 1958 — that in the terms of Greek interest the question was non-negotiable. At more or less the same time he stressed: 'There is no point in belonging to the military wing of an alliance which does not guarantee our eastern borders and which with the unrestrained supply of military equipment to Turkey tends to upset the military balance in the Aegean.' Negotiations with Turkey, he stressed, could not concern any concessions 'of our irrevocable sovereign rights'.[1] Suggestions of a timetable for the withdrawal of American bases, however, brought immediate advice from Helmut Schmidt, the West German Chancellor, to tone down public opposition to these bases. Such a posture, it was indicated, might encourage Italian Socialists to exploit opposition to the siting of US cruise and Pershing II missiles in Western Europe and thus make more sensitive the West German position. At the meeting of the NATO Defence Planning Committee which followed, Papandreou in fact specified as Greece's condition for continued full military membership, control of the Aegean Sea and especially of the disputed air space above it. This claim with reference to the position until 1974 and by the language in which it was expressed indicated a restrained approach to controversial questions. The possibility of partitioning the zone for the purposes of control, however, led to a clash with Turkey over a single clause in the communiqué from the NATO meeting which was not all for internal consumption in Greece. Subsequently the appearance of a Turkish naval vessel apparently on a NATO mission in waters near to the Greek mainland provoked a reaction which faithfully reflected the continuing sensitivity of the Greek Government. The position of Greece in both NATO and the EEC at the beginning of 1982 depended at least partly on the strength of the influence which might be exerted on Papandreou by other European Socialists, notably President François Mitterand and Chancellor Helmut Schmidt. There was little sign of the attractions of a national Balkan zone of co-operation overriding the evident advantages of membership of an established community or alliance, whatever the grounds for disgruntlement.

The Albanian Enigma

Unlike Greece and Turkey, Albania has been one of the most politically isolated countries in the world, and so any signs of activities by Albania which may have implications for its neighbours or the world at large are unusually significant. One factor in its isolation from Communism and Capitalism alike has been Albania's self-sufficiency for most of its raw material needs. Minerals and similar products also account for 75 per cent of the country's total exports and significantly chromite makes the largest contribution, from fourteen mines along the border with Yugoslavia. Elsewhere in the world the main reserves (90 per cent of the total known) are south of the Zambesi (in Zimbabwe and the Republic of South Africa). Though relatively limited in quantity, Albanian chromite has useful refractory applications in industry: output in 1977 was 9 per cent of the world production and in that year Albania overtook the Soviet Union as the world's second largest producer.

In 1978 Albania capped the 1961 ideological break with Moscow with a severing of the Chinese connection, at which point Chinese experts left, destroying or removing as they went the blue-prints of three new ferro-chrome plants designed to supply China's needs. This has left 400 000 tons of Albanian chromite annually planned for the Chinese market, available on the general world market. This may result in an increase in the long-established Albanian chromite export trade with Eastern Europe and extend formal connections with the Council for Mutual Economic Assistance (CMEA) from which, as the Council for Mutual Economic Aid (COMECON), Albania withdrew in 1962. On the other hand, Italy, West Germany, Sweden and Japan are also likely to take large quantities of the additionally available Albanian ore. Because of its essential use in the production of stainless steel, chrome with manganese is in all senses a key strategic mineral and any country able to supply good quality ore is able to exert some international leverage. Albania is one of the cheapest sources of chromite supply in the world, partly because of hydroelectric power; it produces nickel and cobalt as by-products and can compete effectively with South Africa. At a time when EEC countries are not unwilling to distance themselves from South Africa, if they can do so without damaging their own economic interests, the existing situation has possibilities for an Albania which may want, in spite of its Marxist-Leninist principles, further to assert its ideological independence.

In another respect, however, Albania risks an unwanted international entanglement. In 1981 there were Albanian nationalist riots in the Yugoslav province of Kosovo. The Albanian Government accused Yugoslavia of repression and persecution while the

Yugoslavs in their turn claimed that Albanian nationalists wanted nothing less than secession. Charges of political and ethnic discrimination were bandied about and by January 1982 it was apparent that the Yugoslav authorities were trying to prevent a mass exodus of the Serbian minority, from what Serbs regard as the cradle of their nation, in the face of anti-Serbian riots. The suggestion that the Albanian authorities were intent on a break-up of the Yugoslav federation was, of course, denied from Tirana. The fact of an exceptionally high ethnic Albanian birthrate in the Kosovo province, reputedly the highest in Europe, and three times higher than the national Yugoslav average, served dramatically to heighten the tension.

The death from gunshot wounds in January 1982 in Albania of Mehmet Shehu, Prime Minister for twenty-seven years, and associated reports which proved untrue of the death of Enver Hoxha, Albania's leader for nearly forty years, forcibly reminded the world of the potential international dangers of a new struggle for power there. The position of Albania between Yugoslavia and Greece would have, if it became politically destabilised, important implications for both NATO and the Warsaw Pact. A long period in which both were denied specific influence may have assisted the maintenance of peace in the area. The complexion of Albania's government is inescapably a matter of concern to both military blocs as well as to Yugoslavia. The resumption of Soviet diplomatic ties with Tirana could lead to the use of naval bases and affect the maritime balance of power in the Mediterranean and alarm the Italians in particular. The danger of such a transformation might even force a settlement of the long-standing dispute between Great Britain and Albania over Albanian gold. This came into Allied hands in Berlin at the end of the Second World War and has never been returned, because of the subsequently unpaid award of £800 000 by the International Court to Great Britain for the mining in 1946 of two British destroyers in Albanian waters.

An anxiety in NATO for the resolution of differences with Albania is compounded by Albania's difficult relationship with Yugoslavia. This situation and the tensions between Greece and Turkey, as well as the firm continuing alignment of Bulgaria and its northern neighbours with the Soviet Union, demonstrate clearly the unlikelihood of real Balkan co-operation in its own right. The continuance of the competition for influence in the region by external forces seems inevitable: while the desire to contain local tensions is probably strong, it might not be sufficient to restrain opportunism in response to radical changes inside Albania or Yugoslavia.

Note

1. *Guardian*, 23 Nov. 1981.

2 East–West and North–South Interrelationships in the Eastern Mediterranean

Giacomo Luciani

Introduction

Since the Second World War and the explosion at Hiroshima the future of humankind has been threatened by the impending danger of a nuclear holocaust. It is neither surprising nor unwarranted that responsible scientists and intellectuals concentrate their attention on this problem, trying patiently to build on that basis of understanding which made detente possible. Today, however, detente is threatened. Indeed, numerous experts seem to be exceedingly eager to pronounce its death. A complacency in mutual recrimination between East and West is carelessly undermining the basis of understanding which was so difficult to reach.

The reason for such a negative turn in events does not, however, lie in a direct failure of the detente process *per se*. The foundations of that policy still hold. A fundamental balance exists because nuclear arsenals still guarantee mutual assured destruction. Also, no serious crisis is developing in Europe which might lead to the belief that one of the two sides would consider resorting to war.[1] Tensions in Europe have been far worse many times in the past, and even the death of Josip Broz Tito has not precipitated the kind of crisis that many predicted. Still, detente is being temporarily shelved because events which are not directly connected with

14

relations between East and West impinge upon these relations, creating disturbances which increase the perception of vulnerability of *both* sides.

These disturbances are the consequence of two large sets of conflicts. The first set comprises all conflict between countries, or different forces from various countries (ranging from groupings of countries to guerrilla groups), exclusively belonging to the Third World. This type of conflict we shall call 'South−South'. The second set comprises all conflict between countries or other groupings, one of which belongs to the Third World and the other to the industrial world. This type of conflict we shall call 'North−South'. North−South conflict also exists at the global level, as embodied in relations between the Group of 77 on the one side and the Organisation for Economic Co-operation and Development (OECD) and CMEA countries on the other. This definition of North−South conflict is only preliminary. Later elaboration will show that North−South conflict can also occur between two countries both belonging to the Third World, or both belonging to the OECD, given certain circumstances.[2]

Both South−South and North−South conflicts are not necessarily resolved by military means. Some of them might have no strategic implication at all, or just a very marginal one. However, crises are not independent, random events. They interrelate and their simultaneous occurrence hinders any action to solve them. When we consider the reality of the South−South and North−South sets of conflicts as a whole, we cannot but acknowledge that it has very serious implications for East−West relations and balance.

The distinction between South−South and North−South conflict is analytically necessary, although the two are strictly intertwined, one kind of conflict leading almost necessarily to the other. It must be stressed from the outset, however, that South−South conflict is relevant to the East−West balance only inasmuch as it has North−South implications.

The relevance of South−South and North−South conflict to the East−West balance is a result of the growth of global interdependence, which was in the making in the 1950s and 1960s, but was recognised only in the 1970s. Previously, we had a situation in which developing countries were very economically, strategically and politically dependent on the industrial world, while the reverse was not true: the industrial world could do without relations with the developing world or parts of it, but no less developed country (LDC) could survive if deprived of its relations with the industrial world. As a consequence, the industrial countries did not feel threatened by South–South conflict. On the contrary, they sometimes indulged in fanning it in accordance with the philosophy of divide and rule.

In the 1970s, on the other hand, both industrial and developing countries came to recognise the reality of interdependence, that is mutual dependence. Undoubtedly, the interdependence existing between the two sides is still very much out of balance. Nevertheless it is politically important that the vital interests of the industrial world are today controlled by developing countries. Initially, the reality of interdependence was perceived as affecting only a part of the industrial world, the OECD. While it is clear that the OECD is more directly affected, at the same time later events showed that the CMEA as well is to some extent dependent on developments in the developing world.

As a consequence of interdependence, practically any South–South conflict has today North–South implications. At the same time, interdependence opened the way to a more assertive international role on the part of the developing countries. This is most often not confined within East–West codes of conduct and is therefore unsettling to East–West relations.

Finally, interdependence has increased the strategic importance of the developing world in the eyes of both East and West, thus stimulating a competitive approach which is bound to generate mutual distrust and suspicion. At the same time, because of the increased strategic importance of developing countries, it is now more difficult to define an East–West balance. Such a balance must not only apply to the nuclear field globally and to the European theatre with respect to both nuclear and conventional forces; but it must now apply to all the different regional theatres. But as the number of sub-equilibria to which a balance must apply is multiplied, the definition and enforcement of such a balance becomes increasingly elusive.

These considerations suggest that it is not possible to isolate South–South from North–South conflict or to lay the blame for the crisis of detente on one or the other. At the same time, the distinction is necessary both analytically and politically. We must analyse the way in which South–South and North–South conflict interact, because industrial countries are presumably better able to defuse North—South conflicts than South—South ones. It is important to inquire into whether a determined effort to defuse or eliminate North—South conflict would also reduce South—South tensions, and allow a new period of detente. The alternative conclusion, in which many experts explicitly or implicitly believe, is that no effort from OECD countries could reduce instability in the developing world; these same people tend to think that there is no imminent possibility of overcoming the present crisis of detente.

This chapter is an attempt systematically to discuss the interrelations between East—West and North—South questions in the Eastern Mediterranean, which is defined extensively as including the following countries: Libya, Egypt, Saudi Arabia, Jordan, Iraq, Israel, Lebanon, Syria, Turkey and Greece. It is difficult, if not impossible to discuss equilibria in the Eastern Mediterranean without taking into account events in the Balkans as a whole as well as in the so-called Northern Tier, comprising Iran, Afghanistan, and Pakistan as well as Turkey. While it is not intended to offer extensive coverage of all these countries, it will be appropriate to mention them in a wider context.

The chapter is divided into three parts. Since there is not, as yet, an accepted body of theoretical discussion on the interrelationship between East—West and North—South, it is necessary to devote a first section to a partial treatment of these interrelations in a general way. It is, however, only a partial treatment because consideration is given only to those types of linkages of which we have examples in the Eastern Mediterranean. The second section is devoted to an analysis of the Eastern Mediterranean conducted on the basis of categories and concepts introduced in the first part. The third section is devoted to some general policy conclusions with specific attention to the Eastern Mediterranean.

The Eastern Mediterranean is traditionally a region generating impulses that unsettle wider political equilibria. The Balkan question was more than the immediate occasion for the beginning of the First World War, and after the Second World War equilibria in the region have remained unsettled to this day. Since 1945 open conflicts have repeatedly erupted in the Eastern Mediterranean, even if none has led to the direct involvement of outside actors on a scale comparable to Korea or Vietnam. Paradoxically, this points to the importance of the Eastern Mediterranean rather than the contrary. Indeed, it is felt by many that direct superpower involvement in open war in the region would most likely lead to escalation and thus to global conflict. Nevertheless, the superpowers are directly present with increasingly large military forces, though they do not actively engage them in war action. Up to now, their presence has proved a sufficient deterrent to contain conflicts in the region. Containment is not, however, a final solution, and the danger of an explosion which could not be contained leading to the third world war is increasing every day.

Of course within the Eastern Mediterranean events and attention have been concentrated around the Arab–Israeli conflict. The situation of both Turkey and Greece must, however, be discussed at the same time, because events in the 1970s have also drawn in these two countries as well. In many ways, the possibility of containing recurring crises in the Arab–Israeli conflict is dependent on the stability and appropriate behaviour of Greece and Turkey. Events in the 1970s show that this cannot be taken for granted.

East–West and North–South Interrelations: an Analytical Framework

Introduction

The fact that in the long run peace and economic development are convergent goals has been stressed authoritatively many times. Indeed, while the danger of nuclear holocaust hangs over the future of humankind, underdevelopment and starvation take their daily toll, and are a more immediate and dangerous threat than the arms race.

The necessary convergence of the two objectives can easily be argued if we are discussing a long-run perspective. Given projections of population growth to the first decades of the coming millenium, it is indeed difficult to conceive how peace could be maintained without the kind of economic development that would provide a larger share of humankind with human living conditions. At the other extreme, it is difficult to conceive an acceleration of development in a world which experiences nuclear warfare. True, technological progress allows increasing accuracy in weapons delivery and therefore the adoption of smaller warheads. This has led some commentators to think that a nuclear war is feasible, or even that it could meaningfully be won. Still, it is difficult to see how a nuclear exchange could happen without provoking economic damage that would need decades to be offset.

The Differing Logic of North—South and East—West Interrelations

At the same time, convergence of the two objectives — peace and economic development — is not at all evident in the short run. Quite to the contrary, the logic of East—West relations, on which global peace is based, is profoundly different from the North—South logic which reflects the global demand for development.

East—West relations pursue peace through equilibrium. Their logic can be synthetically described by a sequence of steps. First, find an equilibrium. This assumes that such an equilibrium can be defined and agreed upon — an assumption which could easily be challenged. Also, the equilibrium which is sought is a complex one resulting from a sum of partial equilibria on specific classes of armaments and/or on specific regions (theatres). It is not acceptable to 'net' partial disequilibria into an overall equilibrium because of the impossibility of agreeing on weights to be attributed to each partial disequilibrium. Secondly, once an equilibrium is found, even if just a partial one, it should be frozen. The assumption seems to be that the persistence of an equilibrium through time will enhance confidence to the point where both sides will be willing to modify this same equilibrium, de-escalating forces on both sides. This, again, is an assumption that can easily be challenged. Thirdly, once sufficient mutual confidence is built, move to arms reduction and, eventually, disarmament.

This process requires a rigid hierarchical order of nations, in order to allow the definition and freezing of equilibria. Uncertainty over the identity of those with whom the equilibrium should be reached inevitably creates problems. For example, the nuclear balance can look different as a consequence of the means used to account for British and French nuclear forces. Thus East—West relations postulate the existence of blocs, and postulate as well that each country will declare unrestricted allegiance to its bloc. The contrary would not allow a freezing of equilibria because autonomous action on the part of this or that country might change an equilibrium into a disequilibrium. A sufficient equilibrium has been kept in Central Europe because both superpowers have paid maximum attention to unrestrained allegiance on the part of

West Germany on one side and the German Democratic Republic on the other. The situation is, however, sharply different in the Balkans, where allegiance is normally heavily loaded with reservations, with the exception of Bulgaria. If we further extend our consideration to the rest of the Eastern Mediterranean we see a majority of countries which declare no allegiance to either of the two blocs, and the task of defining an equilibrium or freezing it becomes impossible.

If this is the logic of East—West relations, the difference with North—South relations is very sharp. North—South relations, as dynamically pursued by the developing countries, tend to modify existing equilibria rather than freeze them. The goal of global development is interpreted by a majority of LDC governments as meaning a tendency to a reduction in income per capita differentials. It is extremely significant that the so-called basic needs approach has been strongly criticised at the official level. The problem is not so much that of overcoming absolute poverty. It is, rather, equality among nations.

The North—South question is the logical and historical follow-up of the process of decolonisation. The logic of the North—South set of relations is therefore that of nationalism. Economic and political nationalism concur in determining a position which entails repudiation of blocs, of hierarchies, of allegiance to any single foreign nation. Of course, within the Third World we see many different nuances of economic and political nationalism. Some countries maintain economic policies which are open to relations with the international market. Others are aligned and have kept a great deal of constistency in their position in international relations. In the Eastern Mediterranean we see examples of all kinds of behaviour. We see, at the same time, how nationalism is a common denominator of all the different combinations of policies and, given certain conditions, can easily justify a shift from one combination to the other.

The fact that economic nationalism is the logic behind many of the initiatives taken by Third World countries, in pursuance of faster development, is often lamented by those who believe that free trade and, more generally, free international economic intercourse allow all participating parties to maximise benefits. However, it has become clear that, if on one side the development of international economic relations is a positive-sum game, on the other the distribution of the benefits can be uneven to an extreme.

This is not surprising even from a theoretical point of view, given that very often international economic relations take place in conditions of unilateral or bilateral oligopoly, not perfect competition. In most instances economic nationalism is the reaction to the experience of uneven distribution of the benefits of international economic relations. A clear example of this is in the case of oil, which is a fundamental factor in developments in the Eastern Mediterranean. There we witness a nationalistic attitude which leads not only to the assertion of unrestricted national control over natural resources, but utilises such control to limit quantitative production within certain ceilings. This attitude can be understood only in connection with the fact that the international economic system does not provide sufficient reward to stimulate an increase in production. (Such an increase would not necessarily require additional investment: the countries involved are deliberately underutilising existing productive capacity.) Given that there is no agreement on quantities to be produced — this being the main reason for denying that OPEC is a cartel, as it is often inappropriately called — such a manifestation of economic nationalism would never have appeared had the benefits of international oil trade been distributed more evenly. The very fact that this distribution has changed so dramatically since 1973 shows how uneven the distribution was beforehand.

Economic nationalism is not a necessary feature of international relations. It is rather the reaction to a set of rules (Old International Economic Order) which has not allowed an equitable distribution of the benefits of international economic intercourse. The egalitarian logic of North—South relations leads, therefore, along with other individual or collective behaviour, to the demand for a New International Economic Order.

Differences of participation and polarity between North—South and East—West

Further differences between North—South and East—West, leading to short-term conflicts between the two sets of relationships, concern participation and the nature of polarity.

Asymmetries in participation are relevant in determining attitudes at the global level, less so at the regional one. Globally we have on one side a substantial refusal on the part of CMEA countries to participate constructively in North—South negotiations, and to a large extent also a refusal of minor industrialised countries to participate in negotiations on strategic equilibria. While this appears to have consequences at the global level, such as undermining the appeal of the Non-Proliferation Treaty (NPT), it is much less relevant at the regional one. One could hardly say that nuclear proliferation in the Eastern Mediterranean is an effect of non-participation in the preparation of the NPT; and if the Soviet Union does not participate constructively in global North—South negotiations, it certainly has been active on North—South questions in the Eastern Mediterranean providing economic support to most countries in a very significant way.

Far more relevant is a difference in the nature of polarity. Both East—West and North—South relations are polar, and both are *de facto* bipolar. However, the implications of polarity are profoundly different.

In East—West relations, polarity is based on power, and military power is increasingly becoming the distinctive factor because differentials in economic power are gradually fading out. In the past polarity in East—West relations as a whole was also based on ideology: there was a confrontation between a liberal and a Leninist conception of the state and of its role in the economy. But with time, the importance of ideological affinity is decreasing, because national models are proposed on all sides, blurring the boundary between different systems. True, ideology is certainly still important in the European context. For although there are strong differences in economic policy both between the United States and its Western European allies and between the Soviet Union and its Eastern European allies, there is still a high degree of ideological affinity at the institutional level. Indeed, if anything, homogeneity has increased on the Western side during the 1970s because of the termination of dictatorial regimes in Greece, Spain and Portugal.

Outside Europe, however, ideology plays a very small role indeed. A majority of countries in the Eastern Mediterranean cannot be said to follow either of the two ideologies. To a large extent existing alignments are determined more by aversion for one ideology than by sympathy for the other. The Saudi Arabian ruling family certainly hates communism, but at the same time it hardly could be said to stick to the Western principles of individual freedom, democracy and economic liberalism. There are important consequences flowing from this state of affairs, because

ideology is a powerful guarantee of stability of international alignments and allegiance to each bloc. Thus the superpowers,
recognising that ideology no longer plays the same role as before,
are trying to revitalise it. Such a policy has been followed recently
by the Americans stressing the importance of civil rights, and by
the Soviets by stressing the role of the party (and the need to create
one where it does not exist, as in Ethiopia). In both cases, however,
the impression is that the policy has backfired badly (for the superpowers), leading to the fall of the Shah in Iran and precipitating
guerrilla warfare in Afghanistan.

If, however, one accepts the concept that ideology is no longer
an essential factor in international relations, then the door may be
open to an evolution of the bipolar East—West system towards
multipolarity. If France or West Germany or the EEC were superpowers (which they are far from being) their status would be the
consequence of power, not ideology. An evolution towards multipolarity based on ideology is more difficult, principally because no
ideology succeeds in effectively asserting itself in international
relations without a clear leader with sufficient power. In the
Eastern Mediterranean this is clearly shown by the case of Islam.
Islam is the common denominator of all countries in the region
with the exception of Greece and Israel. Nevertheless it has failed
to perform a decisive role because there is no clear Islamic leader.
In the short run the banner of Islam is agitated by this or that
government or party (generally more than one at the same time,
with strongly contradictory consequences).

East—West polarity is, then, essentially the consequence of a
given distribution of power, allowing a potential evolution towards
multipolarity, and also permitting individual countries to stay in a
grey area which is outside the polar system, not just in the middle
of it.

The same is not true for North—South polarity. This turns on
objective economic indicators from which political attitudes are
generally derived. North and South are not groupings, they are
forces, or definitions of relativity. If at the global level these two
forces generate two main groupings, the Group of 77 on one side
and the OECD on the other, the same forces also generate sub-
groupings within each of them as well as among the centrally-
planned economies (CMEA).

Thus it would be wrong to talk about the South and the North to
indicate groups of countries, in the same way as we may well use

East and West. Most countries appear as either North or South depending on the circumstances. Italy appears as North in Mediterranean North–South conflicts, while it belongs to the South whenever similar conflicts arise within the EEC. In the Eastern Mediterranean some countries, such as Israel and Saudi Arabia, belong to the North if we look at regional equilibria and realities; but if we look at global relativities they both belong to the South. The behaviour of each country also depends on the issue under consideration and her specific interests. Saudi Arabia has a Northern approach within the International Monetary Fund (IMF), insisting on financial orthodoxy, and a Southern one within the United Nations Conference on Trade and Development (UNCTAD) supporting all the proposals put forward by the Group of 77. These are not inconsistencies, as they are viewed by those who insist on reasoning on the basis of a taxonomic approach. All attempts to stress contradictions between LDCs have so far failed as a negotiating tool. One can see that these contradictions are easily recognised by the LDCs; but they become irrelevant for international alignments whenever the problem is being discussed at the global level.

The implications of the nature of North–South polarity for the Eastern Mediterranean are extremely important. The region is involved in the global North–South conflict, but is also internally divided by North–South tensions: as a consequence considerations linked to economic development influence the behaviour of individual countries within the region in a complex way. Moreover, regional behaviour crucially affects global developments in at least one respect, namely oil. As a consequence, impulses emanating from the region exacerbate North–South tension *within* both West and East. In the case of the West this has not been true only since 1973 but was true before then. One only needs to recall the role of national oil companies from Italy and France (a typically Southern initiative) in the gradual erosion of the power of the Seven Sisters.

Contradictions between East–West and North–South processes

The differences enumerated above lead to the consequence that the logic of either one of the processes dictates to individual actors behaviour which often has negative consequences on the other process. The North–South logic leads to behaviour which is

East—West destabilising, and the East—West logic suggests policies which are not compatible with co-operative North—South relations. Furthermore, the fact that there is conflict in North—South relations can lead to consequences which are East—West destabilising independently of the behaviour of any one government. On this basis, we can propose a typology of interconnections between East—West and North—South. It is intended to limit the enumeration and general description to those linkages which are relevant to the Eastern Mediterranean region.

First, the existence of North—South conflict negatively affects the process of economic development in almost all LDCs. If it were possible to agree to a New International Economic Order, the conditions of some countries in particular would improve sharply. For some countries — certainly not for all developing countries — the present condition of conflictual North—South economic relations is the major obstacle to politically-stabilising economic development. Their development is either slowed down (and in some instances, stopped altogether) or constrained in such a way that it becomes politically destabilising for the domestic power structure. Because there are some countries whose internal stability is essential to East—West equilibria, if their development is so affected by North—South conflict, they constitute an objective link between the two sets of relations. It must be stressed, however, that:

1. Not all LDCs in critical economic conditions are principally victims of North—South conflict. Sometimes they are victims of bad domestic management of their own economies (as in the case of Zaire).
2. Critical economic conditions do not always lead to domestic instability. Countries become unstable not because they are poor in absolute terms, but because they experience a process of economic development which is either abruptly arrested or inconsistent with socio-political realities.
3. Not all unstable countries are immediately relevant to East—West equilibria. In most cases these equilibria might change, if, following a period of instability, a new leadership emerged which would take East—West destabilising attitudes (thus falling into the case which we will discuss below).

There are only a few countries whose position is such that the opening of a period of instability will *per se* undermine East—West equilibria. In practice, most of these countries are in Central Europe and the Eastern Mediterranean. The only important case outside these regions is South Africa (which is an example of a country whose stability is threatened by the racial nature of her regime, not by North–South conflicts).

Secondly, independently of problems of domestic stability discussed above, governments may adopt East–West destabilising behaviour while pursuing North–South objectives. In this group fall numerous kinds of behaviour. The most obvious example is commuting from one bloc to the other in order to gain direct or indirect economic advantages. As this practice has become increasingly widespread throughout the 1960s and 1970s, the international climate and superpower attitudes have evolved to the extent that today it is most often not necessary actually to commute; all that is necessary is to resort to some flirting with the adversary bloc, such as requesting economic aid without necessarily and officially modifying the country's international alignments. However, this practice is exemplary of allegiance reservations, and it undermines the stability of the blocs, or at least the perception which superpowers have of it. It tends, therefore, to enlarge the 'grey areas' which make it impossible to reach an East–West equilibrium. Again, countries may try to attract superpower attention, or divert domestic attention from economic difficulties, by resorting to regional conflict. We see internationally a growing number of such coincidences: countries become more ready to utilise military strength whenever they need assistance. The logic behind it might not always be the same, and does not need to be explicit. However, the recurrence of this type of behaviour is a fact.

If not to regional conflict, countries might also resort to other East–West destabilising activities in order to increase the perception of their strategic relevance or manifest their displeasure and exert pressure. An example of this kind of behaviour is nuclear proliferation on the part of countries which face neither a nuclear threat nor a conventional threat which could be deterred by the possession of a nuclear weapon. East–West destabilising behaviour with a North–South objective can come from industrial countries as well, because of a perception of dependence in specific sectors considered of strategic importance. Armaments, nuclear energy and electronics figure prominently as examples of sectors in which European countries feel an excessive dependence on the United States. In order to establish viable national industries, these countries are ready to export armaments on a strictly commercial basis, with little or no political strings attached, thus objectively facilitating the development of 'grey areas' and accompanying instability. (There are other possible examples of this kind of behaviour, but they are not relevant for the Eastern Mediterranean.) A final linkage between the two sets of relations concerns the behaviour of exporters of raw materials of strategic significance. Oil is the most important case but not the only one. Absence of an agreement on pricing and production policies is a part of the North—South conflict. Unilateral action on the part of the producers does not evenly affect the two superpowers and their closest allies. It affects for this reason East—West equilibria, or at least the perception of them.

Finally, we may consider North—South destabilising action which is taken for East—West purposes. This falls into two large categories: the global attitude of the superpowers to the North—South problem and the way it is (indeed very strongly) dictated by East—West considerations; and the superpowers' attitudes on problems of a regional nature. Only the latter need to be treated in the present context. We must briefly recall the fact that the process of decolonisation was so managed by the former colonial powers as to lead to the creation of a plethora of formally independent and sovereign states, whose structural basis is such that most of them have little or no chance to develop on their own. There are, of course, significant exceptions: countries which have sufficient population, territory and natural resources independently to sustain their economic development. There are also examples of countries which, lacking one or the other of the indispensable primary ingredients, are successfully integrated in the international economy and aggressively pursue a path of export-led growth. Still, many criticise the experience of the latter countries because it only leads to dependent economic growth. Therefore, regional integration among smaller LDCs is a fundamental aspect of a positive North—South process. Indeed, the difficulties confronting regional integration attempts are possibly the most important cause for the setbacks experienced by the Arab world, by most African countries and by Spanish-speaking Latin American countries. Regional integration among these countries has never received more than lip-service from the superpowers. They have, at the same time, mostly been busy locating some friend or separating friend from foe. For a process of integration, which could not possibly be just economic,

would politically reinforce the regional actors, therefore necessarily involving some loss of control. *De facto*, the Soviet Union has
until recently been kept at the margin of the regions to which these
considerations are relevant, and hence most of the responsibility
for the negative attitude to regional integration must be laid on the
former colonial powers and the United States. However, Soviet
behaviour has consistently proved to be as divisive as possible.

A second way in which East—West consideration can hinder
economic development in specific countries, thus exacerbating
North—South tensions in the long run, is by freezing unsatisfactory
domestic equilibria. Underdevelopment is also due to bad
management (and sometimes more than just that: for example,
corruption and oppressive regimes representing only limited élites)
on the part of national governments of LDCs. At the same time,
the fear that any change in the distribution of political power
could lead to a shift in the international position of a country, has
led both superpowers to support governments which clearly have
no sound political base. The examples on the Western side are so
numerous that it is unnecessary to recall them: notwithstanding
the fact that during the Carter Administration the United States
somewhat modified its attitude. It is important, however, to stress
that the argument is valid for the Soviet Union as well — even if
they like to appear as little more than the obstetrician who helps
history to follow her inevitable course by giving birth to revolution
everywhere. One need only mention Cuba.

The Situation in the Eastern Mediterranean

The present situation may best be analysed under three distinct
headings. First, we shall consider countries whose domestic
stability is in itself relevant to East—West equilibria and which are
threatened by North—South conflicts. Secondly, we shall concern
ourselves with countries that behave in an East—West destabilising
way in order to pursue North—South objectives. Finally we shall
examine cases of North—South destabilising behaviour deriving
from East—West considerations.

*Countries whose domestic stability is relevant to East—West
equilibria and theatened by North—South conflicts*

There are at least two countries in the Eastern Mediterranean
which fall into this category, namely Turkey and Saudi Arabia.

The stability of Egypt is also essential to East—West equilibria, but at the same time it is not threatened by North—South conflicts in the short to medium term. In the longer run, the stability of Egypt, as well as that of Saudi Arabia, would be threatened by the lack of sufficient progress in regional integration. We shall return to this aspect later.

The stability of no other country in the Eastern Mediterranean is in itself essential to East—West equilibria. But immediately outside what we have defined as the Eastern Mediterranean, there are two more countries whose stability is essential: Yugoslavia and Iran. In the case of the latter, the period of instability following the fall of the Shah has indeed rapidly undermined the detente process. Here, however, we shall give detailed consideration only to Turkey and Saudi Arabia.

Turkey Turkey is the clearest of the two cases we shall deal with. A few data on the recent economic development of Turkey are necessary. The record of Turkish economic growth was rather positive until at least 1977 (Table 2.1); thereafter growth was stopped abruptly. If we compare the Turkish record on growth for the period 1973—8 to that of other OECD countries, we find that Turkey was the country that achieved the largest average annual increase of Gross Domestic Product (GDP) in real terms (Table 2.2, column 1). This very high rate of growth had solid foundations in a relatively high rate of Gross Fixed Capital Formation (GFCF) as a percentage of GDP (Table 2.2, column 2), a rate which allowed Turkey to rank third only to Japan and Yugoslavia, well ahead of all the industrialised European countries and of other Southern European countries as well. The fact that such rapid growth was not translated immediately into a higher standard of living is due partly to the exceptionally high rate of

TABLE 2.1   *Turkey: long-term indicators (percentage yearly GDP growth)*

Year	GDP growth (%)
1973	4.1
1974	8.8
1975	8.8
1976	8.8
1977	5.7
1978	3.8
1979	0.9

TABLE 2.2   *Turkey: some international comparisons*

	ΔGDP 1973–78	GFCF / (GDP × 100)	ΔPopulation 1968–78
West Germany	1.9	20.9	0.3
Great Britain	0.9	18.1	0.1
Italy	2.1	19.8	0.7
Japan	3.7	29.9	1.3
Turkey	6.7	25.8	2.5
Portugal	2.4	17.0	0.7
Spain	3.1	20.8	1.2
Greece	3.6	23.0	0.7
Yugoslavia	6.1	34.3	0.9

population growth (Table 2.2, column 3); at the same time it must be recalled that the higher GDP growth allowed an average annual increase of GDP per person of 4 per cent; and a growing population can also act as a stimulus to growth if it does not endanger capital accumulation.

These figures must be recalled because most articles on the Turkish economic crisis stress the negative role of inefficiencies in public industry and the ineffectiveness of government economic policies.[3] While both factors might well be very relevant, the Turkish economy proved that it was capable of growing at a high speed, until it was suffocated by outside events. The increase in the price of oil in 1974 upset the positive equilibrium in the Turkish trade balance. For Turkey depends on imports for more than 75 per cent of her total oil supply (although it has large untapped reserves of domestic energy in the form of coal and hydro-electricity). Turkish imports rose abruptly, while at the same time her exports were damaged by the economic downturn in the in-dustrialised countries. As a result the trade balance deteriorated badly (Table 2.3). The final blow came from the forced reduction of Turkish emigration to Western Europe (mainly to West Germany). This entailed a sharp decline in remittances which, after hitting close to $1.5 billion in 1974, fell by 31 per cent in two years in nominal terms (Table 2.3). As a consequence the Turkish current balance went from a surplus of $484 million in 1973 to a deficit of $3426 million in 1977. Thus North–South conflicts hit Turkey in two ways. First, the price of oil increased too abruptly, after her dependence on it had been magnified by a price which was too low. Secondly, as a new industrialising country, she was

TABLE 2.3   *Turkey: balance of payments — selected items*

	1972	1973	1974	1975	1976	1977	1978	1979
Trade, net	− 678	− 769	− 2245	− 3337	− 3169	− 4044	− 2311	− 2808
Remittances	740	1183	1426	1312	982	982	983	1694
Current balance	− 8	484	− 720	− 1879	− 2301	− 3426	− 1519	− 1349

not provided with sufficient capital inflows and market outlets to pursue her growth path.

The Turkish case is interesting because it illustrates the problems that a large number of countries (including some industrial ones, like Italy) met in the late 1970s. Faced with a deteriorating external situation and mounting domestic demands, most governments were politically unable to react in time. When the reaction came it was too late, and Turkey showed appalling symptoms of stagflation. In 1979 Gross National Product (GNP) growth was down to a mere 1 per cent implying a 1.5 per cent decrease in per capita GNP; inflation, as measured by the GNP deflator, increased 61 per cent over the year; real fixed capital formation dropped by 9 per cent and industrial production fell by 2.8 per cent; and the current balance closed with a deficit of $1.3 million.

The kind of domestic turmoil into which this state of affairs plunged Turkey is well known. The military takeover which ensued in September 1980 cannot be assumed to have provided a solution by itself. Most commentators agree that Turkey cannot be run by military rule on a long-term basis, and the military will need an improvement in the economic situation. But there is no way in which such an improvement can take place without a co-operative approach on the part of the industrialised world.[4]

Saudi Arabia   The case of Saudi Arabia is very different. Turkey is a case of a country whose growth has been arrested by unfavourable North—South developments, whereas Saudi Arabia is a case of a country whose development is far from having been arrested, but nevertheless finds itself constrained to follow a path which is dangerous for domestic stability.

Since the beginning of the Iranian Revolution it has become commonplace to point to Saudi Arabia as a dangerously unstable country.[5] The present writer, however, believes that instability is today being exaggerated. At the same time it is clear that any hope of gradual evolution within Saudi Arabia can effectively be dashed if Western industrial countries continue to confront that country with demands that are incompatible with her own long-term interests and with her perceptions of what constitute regional equilibria. And of course we hardly need to elaborate on the contention that instability in Saudi Arabia might by itself precipitate open conflict between East and West.

The key to the Saudi problem is its oil policy. Saudi Arabia is confronted by what has been called Midas's dilemma,[6] because whichever way she manages her production, prices react, so that her income is necessarily magnified. This goes to the heart of the problem, namely the excess of Saudi Arabia's oil income relative to its development needs. The mechanism at work is however more complicated than Midas's. Saudi Arabia can try to moderate the evolution in oil prices, but in order to do so she needs to have unused productive capacity, on which her ability to influence the Organisation of Petroleum Exporting Countries (OPEC) decision-making depends. Whenever Saudi Arabia is short of unused capacity to produce oil, other OPEC members can announce higher prices and the Saudis cannot discourage them from doing so. This creates a situation in which Saudi oil is sold for less than any other oil (including non-OPEC oil): a situation which can hardly be justified in terms of national interest, and which has an obvious potentially destabilising effect on the Saudi regime. At the same time, Saudi Arabia must increase production whenever the supply from other countries is disrupted (as from Iran since the end of 1978, and both Iran and Iraq since September 1980), because industrial countries may be unable to cut demand. Each increase in Saudi production decreases her available unused capacity and damages the country's influence over OPEC. To avoid this, the Saudis should increase their overall capacity, a difficult decision to take given that the country's long-term economic interest would be best served by a reduction in production to levels somewhere between 5 and 7 million barrels a day (as against 10.4 million at the time of writing), which would allow for a rough balance of exports of oil with the demand for imports of foreign goods.

Therefore Saudi Arabia is the victim of North–South conflict because it has to bear the burden of reconciling the conflicting interests of oil exporters and importers. A New International Economic Order would necessarily involve (or presuppose) a decline in the quantity of oil burned by the industrial world and an agreement on some mechanism to increase oil prices gradually.

The Saudi Arabian Government has been working to have OPEC agree on a long-term pricing formula which would increase prices gradually. The success of the Saudi strategy is, however, dependent on moderation of oil imports of industrial countries which has repeatedly been requested by oil producers. If industrialised countries continue to drag their feet on energy conservation and on the development of energy sources other than oil, Saudi Arabia will be obliged to choose between either increasing production and productive capacity to moderate prices and maintain international equilibria, thereby exposing the country to regional and domestic instability or reducing production within the limits dictated by long-term self-interest, letting prices skyrocket, and running the risk of precipitating a crisis in East—West equilibria which might eventually be fatal to the existence of Saudi Arabia as an independent country.

Countries Contributing to East—West Destabilisation in Order to Pursue North—South Objectives

The most frequent case of linkage between the East—West and North—South axis is that of governments taking initiatives which are East—West destabilising in order to gain North—South advantages. The Eastern Mediterranean offers a great wealth of examples of this phenomenon and here the present writer does not intend to offer an exhaustive treatment of the topic. Rather we shall concentrate on the major examples. A distinction will be made between moves that have a predominantly politico-strategic character and moves of a predominantly economic nature.

Politico-Strategic Moves   The first type of politico-strategic moves that can be made in order to reach a North—South objective and which are unsettling to East—West equilibria, are what has been called 'commuting' and 'flirting'.

Egypt is an important example of a 'commuting' country. The original shift of this country to a pro-Soviet stance was precipitated by a complex of different motivations, largely, though not exclusively, connected to the desire to accelerate the country's economic development. It came at the end of a long process, reaching a climax with the nationalisation of the Suez Canal following the refusal by the United States and Western-dominated international organisations such as the World Bank to provide

finance to build the Aswan Dam. At the same time Gamal Abdel
Nasser never became a wholehearted pro-Soviet, but increased
Egypt's ties with the East in order to reconcile as far as possible
butter and cannons. This is not to say that South–South motivations (the conflict with Israel and the rivalry with Iraq) were
irrelevant. At the same time, it is important to stress that the Soviet
Union had been looking for a client in the region for a long time,
and it was friendship for Egypt that determined her position on
Israel rather than the opposite way round. It was the failure of
Soviet economic aid, its inability to get Egypt's development out of
the doldrums, which set the stage for Anwar Sadat's new reversal
of alliances in 1972. We may thus very well say that the latter was a
move with North–South objectives, and it was undertaken in
order to get economic aid from the United States as well as from
Western Europe. It is quite possible that if the Egyptian economic
situation does not improve within a few years we might witness
a repetition of the past. The only difference might be that this
time some 'flirting' might be sufficient instead of full-scale
'commuting'. For the attitude of the United States on non-
alignment has become far more tolerant in the meantime. Hence a
generic rapprochement with the Soviet Union − which is still an
important economic partner − or a show of displeasure to Washington might be sufficient to gain additional aid for Cairo.

Iraq is a similar story. Her pro-Soviet position is closely connected with the long fight with the former owners of the Iraq
Petroleum Company (IPC), that is all the major international oil
companies.[7] In the modern history of Iraq oil has always been the
central political problem. Furthermore, and in contrast with other
countries in the region, the presence of oil companies in Iraq
attracted the attention of international diplomacy and government interference from the very beginning.[8] Iraq's oil was also
utilised to destabilise the Mohammed Mossadeq Government in
Iran.[9] In the eyes of Iraq's politicians the identification of the IPC
with the West has thus always been evident. And throughout the
1960s this link remained more important than the political and
military ties to the East.

The stubborn resistance on the part of the oil majors to agree on
conditions which, in retrospect, appear to have been very favourable indeed to them, increasingly pushed Iraq towards economic
co-operation with the East. Iraqi production was deliberately kept
at a low level,[10] and with it the government's revenue and ability to

invest in industrial development. The process reached its highest point in the early 1970s, when Iraq turned to the Soviet bloc as an outlet for some of its crude, in order to lay the basis for full nationalisation of the IPC. When this was finally enacted in 1972, the Soviet connection was important in allowing its success, sharply contrasting with the Iranian experience twenty years earlier. Political ties with the Soviet Union reached a peak at the same time, with the signature of a 'Friendship Treaty' in 1972.

During the following years, however, the equilibria in the international oil industry were upset. As more and more exporting countries established production ceilings to conserve their oil, Iraq was able to find new market outlets. Initially the opportunity was utilised to increase overall production, but after the fall of the Shah and the ensuing collapse in Iranian oil exports, it became clear that Iraq was in a position to easily sell all the oil that it could produce.[11] The stage was therefore set for Iraq's return to a more pro-Western attitude, although the reversal was less complete than in the case of Sadat in Egypt. (Iraq did not need to do more than it did, after all.)

Naturally, there were also other reasons that motivated Iraq's new policy. But the willingness to pursue an objective of rapid industrialisation fuelled by the revenue accruing from increased oil exports was an essential factor. At the root of Iraq's intolerance towards the regime of Ayotollah Khomeini in Iran is the incompatibility of their respective economic strategies. In parallel, the alliance with Saudi Arabia was cemented by the fact that Ryadh was compelled by events to produce more oil than it wished, and has welcomed Iraq taking some of the burden off its shoulders (at least until September 1980). Thus Iraq is another example of a country that utilises its foreign policy in order to pursue its development strategy. An alignment with the East was pursued and maintained as long as it allowed Baghdad to reconcile the re-establishment of national control over natural resources with a process of industrialisation. This was abandoned, however, when national control was already a well-established fact, for Western Europe and Japan were able to provide better technology (and arms) than the East.

Egypt and Iraq are the clearest examples of commuting in the Eastern Mediterranean, but one might discuss a variety of other cases. Very often a move is not determined solely by North–South objectives, but these play a role nevertheless. For example, we might consider the case of the abortive Syrian attempt to commute to the West in 1976—7. Although this was abandoned by the Syrians because of political developments (notably the Camp David Agreement), one cannot but note that Syria was, and still is, experiencing grave economic difficulties.

A second type of politico-strategic move relates to the resort to local conflict either to attract superpower attention or to distract domestic attention from economic difficulties. The case of Syria might again provide an example with reference to her intervention in the Lebanon. But by far the most important question one must address in connection with this kind of behaviour is how far the Arab—Israeli conflict with all its ramifications can be considered as an appropriate example of it. The Arab—Israeli conflict was initially politically motivated. It also had a predominantly South—South character, although some Arabs will maintain that the British handling of the Palestinian problem was expressly geared to introduce an element of division (hence dependence) in the Arab world. But one might raise also the question of how far the individual episodes of war were motivated by economic frustrations as well. In the case of Egypt, one might reasonably argue that both in 1967 and 1973 the underlying continuing economic difficulties contributed to tilting the balance in favour of war. In both cases first Nasser and then Sadat must have reasoned that — whatever the immediate outcome of their initiative — it was the only way to break the economic impasse as well as the political one. Had the economy been in a phase of rapid development, the cost—benefit analysis might have led to different conclusions. In 1973 Sadat's initiative must also be seen in conjunction with his subsequent resort to commuting and finally his visit to Jerusalem as a logical consequence geared to creating conditions that would allow an Egyptian economic take-off. It is important to note that Sadat's interest was predominantly in enticing investment from Western Europe and the United States rather than in integration with Israel. The latter belongs to the North within the region — or so it was perceived as being by her Arab neighbours in the past, although this perception might be changing today. Prospects of economic integration between Israel and her neighbours even on a limited scale were thus ruled out not just because of the conflict, but also because the Arabs were unwilling to accept Israeli economic leadership (a North—South relationship vis-à-vis Israel). This is one more element which adds a North—South dimension to the Arab—Israeli conflict, although a fading one.[12]

One further aspect is the role of North—South tensions within the region. After 1973 the Saudi financial assistance to Egypt was beginning to be politically suffocating, without opening significant options for economic development. Sadat's initiative was therefore also a way to escape from excessive dependence on Saudi money by cutting down on the costs of continuing military confrontation and gaining access to alternative sources of finance in the United States. Sadat's visit to Jerusalem is thus a rare case in which peace and development converge, while at the same time it further unsettled East—West equilibria because it led to the exclusion of the Soviet Union from the peace process and killed the conference in Geneva.[13]

What the evolution of the Arab—Israeli conflict tells us is that South—South conflict can be made more complex by the North—South tensions which it may generate; also once superpowers are involved, it acquires East—West relevance, thereby becoming a possible instrument for achieving North—South objectives. Of course, this is not to say that the conflict is kept alive just in order to gain economic benefits. (Some experts doubt that Israel would be economically viable if it had to give up the unilateral transfers which are largely justified by her fight for survival.) At the same time North—South objectives might exacerbate conflictual behaviour within a controversy extended through the years, seriously undermining the chances of ever reaching a solution.

Moves of a Predominantly Economic Nature Sometimes decisions which are fundamentally economic have such implications as to upset the East—West equilibria in a relevant way. The first and foremost case is that of oil prices. Although not all OPEC countries belong to the Eastern Mediterranean, it is in this region that we find some of the most influential members of the group. Furthermore, their behaviour was essential in precipitating oil price increases in 1973—4, and again in 1979—80. In fact, we must ask ourselves why OPEC, which was formed in 1960, repeatedly failed to restrict production in order to get price increases (that is act as a cartel) throughout the 1960s, while in 1973 it succeeded without prior agreement in doing so. The reason is that a number of producing countries decided to limit unilaterally their production — starting with Libya in 1970; or did not allow the kind of increases that the oil companies were looking for (for example Saudi Arabia was seen by them as producing some 20 million barrels a day in the 1980s). The price increase decided by OPEC was thus the final outcome of a series of non-co-ordinated unilateral decisions made by individual key producers in the Eastern Mediterranean.[14]

The fact that these countries decided to put a ceiling on their production was due to the structural conditions of their economies. The decision on the amount of oil which should be produced can be ascribed to a portfolio choice among different assets: oil in the ground is one asset, and it may be traded for industrialisation at home, industrial investment abroad and for such things as real estate or financial investment of various kinds. The decision to keep oil in the ground was taken by those countries that did not have promising opportunities to invest in domestic industrialisation, while international financial investment was becoming less and less attractive both politically and economically. A course which finally upset East–West equilibria was put in motion by the structural conditions of some oil producers and by disturbances in the international financial markets. The existing international economic order did not provide sufficient returns to ensure an appropriate behaviour on the part of these countries. We might say, paraphrasing A. O. Hirschman, that it was a case of 'exit' rather than 'voice';[15] equally it was action to be understood within the North–South context. It was also a case in which one could see very clearly the importance of regional integration, and to which we will return.

North–South economic action which has undermining effects on East–West equilibria can also be undertaken by minor industrial countries, as was mentioned earlier. In the case of the Eastern Mediterranean the most important example is that of arms sales on the part of European countries. The Arab countries in the region have been the largest buyers of armaments in recent years, and the possibility of buying them from European countries under increasingly liberal political conditions has created a situation in which arms supplies are no longer an instrument of political control. Although not all countries in the region have shifted to a different source when confronted with either a general or a specific denial of military hardware from one superpower, some have successfully proved that it is possible to do so.[16] By itself, this development tends to limit the credibility of allegiance, and undermines the solidity of the blocs which is essential to the logic of detente.

Countries Involved in North—South Destabilising Behaviour Deriving from East—West Considerations

Here we shall consider the attitude of the superpowers to regional integration among Arab countries.

The present state of Balkanisation of the Arab world was essentially determined by British and, to a lesser extent, French policy towards the area. The British attitude was explicitly that of creating a large number of weak independent states over which it would be easy to maintain substantial indirect control. Without discussing here the case of Israel, one need only recall that the British unsuccessfully opposed the reunification of the Hejaz and the Nejd, forming what today is Saudi Arabia; and successfully preserved the independence of Kuwait, Bahrain, Qatar, the United Arab Emirates, Oman and the Yemens from possible further Saudi expansion. In the Fertile Crescent as well conditions were created that led to independent Iraq, Syria and Jordan.

After the Second World War the Arab—Israeli conflict further complicated the picture. While British control over the region rapidly faded out, the American commitment to Israeli survival entailed a negative bias against any prospect of Arab political integration which might have paralleled the process which the Americans were favouring in Europe. Strategically it was believed that the Soviet Union could be contained by the countries of the Northern Tier, and the instrument for this policy was to be the Central Treaty Organisation (CENTO). Thus Arab integration was not perceived as being necessary on this account, as was by contrast the case with European integration. Furthermore, any process of Arab integration might have endangered the domestic power structure in the Arab states, finally leading to the emergence of a political entity which might not be controlled as easily.

Being essentially excluded from the region, the Soviet Union concentrated efforts on establishing ties with whatever countries in the region might wish to do so. Although Nasser was certainly a believer in Arab integration, he was, if anything, encouraged by the Soviet Union to take attitudes which were highly divisive within the Arab world. Later, Algeria drew closer to the Soviet Union, and this move was made at the same time as choices in domestic economic policy led to the practical shelving of the idea of Maghreb integration.

Today, the Soviet Unions's closest allies are fighting against the new initiative for Arab integration led by Iraq and Saudi Arabia, which led to the convening of the 1980 summit in Amman. The People's Democratic Republic of the Yemen has become an associ- ated member of the CMEA, while it has also adopted foreign policy positions deeply at odds with the rest of the Arab world. The least that one might conclude is that the Soviet Union is doing nothing to encourage political and/or economic integration among Arab countries, not even among her own allies. This would be a difficult undertaking anyhow; nevertheless it was attempted first by Egypt and more recently, by Libya with respect to Syria (failing in both cases).

The consequences of the negative attitude of the superpowers towards Arab integration are immense. All of the Arab countries in- dividually suffer from the lack of some necessary ingredient for economic growth. They are an almost perfect case of an 'optimal currency area', their factor endowments being largely complement- ary rather than competitive. Still integration has proved impossible on political grounds.[17] No one knows how the economic situation of the Arab world would have evolved in the presence of outside pressure to integrate economically and politically, as it was exerted on Europe. It is difficult, however, to avoid the impression that greater progress would have been possible. For example, had there been a successful process of economic and political integration, it is quite likely that the oil situation would have developed in a different way. The Arab countries would have enjoyed a better bargaining position in the 1950s and 1960s, which would probably have set in motion a process of gradual evolution, allowing the kind of adjust- ment in the industrial countries which was prevented by the stub- born resistence to change displayed by the Seven Sisters. At the same time, the integrative process would have generated a broader spec- trum of investment opportunities, allowing a better utilisation of oil revenues, and shifting the portfolio decision referred to earlier from conservation to greater immediate production. As a consequence we might never have had the oil shock of the 1970s. OPEC might not have been formed, had not the decolonisation process created a number of one-dimensional states (oil being their only political variable), which because they are one-dimensional, cannot com- promise and agree to limits on the utilisation of their only weapon.

In this way the East—West preoccupations which dominated the behaviour of both superpowers combined with the colonial history of the region in creating conditions which did not encourage a positive North—South development (economic integration). In turn, as we have already seen, the frustration of the aspiration to industrialise led to conflictual behaviour, political instability and shifting of alignments, all of which combined in generating tensions which finally ruined detente.

The same line of reasoning may paradoxically be applied to the Balkans. But in that case postwar developments have changed the situation, and today Balkan economic integration could hardly be accepted as the cornerstone of economic development by the countries in the region. The situation was different in the mid-1940s. One might recall that the classical article by P. N. Rosenstein-Rodan, inaugurating the school of thought on balanced growth, was principally aimed at the Balkan situation and stressed the need for regional economic integration. True, the idea of Balkan economic co-operation is not dead, and is often revived by some countries in the region.[18] At the same time, it is clear that while Greece and Turkey have predominant economic ties with the EEC, others have predominant economic ties with the CMEA, while Yugoslavia and Albania lie in between. This state of affairs is nowadays a structural feature of the region, and it is difficult to imagine that it could be radically changed. This does not mean, however, that there is no room for regional economic co-operation in the Balkans; such co-operation is conceivable as a parallel of co-operation between Western and Eastern countries in Central Europe. Both processes should find their institutional framework within EEC—CMEA co-operation.

Thus we might say that East—West considerations ruled out economic integration in the Balkans in such a drastic way and for so long that the idea ceased to be valid. One might add that this was not without some serious consequences. Indeed, we have today in the region some countries whose exact position in terms of regional integration processes is not clear. The problem is most acute for Turkey, which would have been an obvious participant in a process of integration in the Balkans, had there been one. Today Turkey is mainly oriented towards the EEC. But this orientation finds considerable domestic opposition from political forces which would favour integration with the rest of the Middle East. Among EEC members scepticism on the possibility of Turkish membership in the Community is widespread, because of the wide gap in the level of industrialisation which risks turning integration into a negative factor for Turkish development.

Finally, one might note that the Soviet Union has recently changed her negative position on European integration. As a consequence, no objection is being raised to Greece becoming an EEC member, and the same would likely be true for Turkey (while, on the other hand, objections to Spain becoming a member of NATO are explicit). At the same time, it is certainly not by chance that the idea of Balkan economic integration has been revived by CMEA countries in the last few years.

The Problem of Tackling the Intersection of East–West and North–South in the Eastern Mediterranean

Introduction

Thus far an attempt has been made to formulate an organised treatment of the way in which the North–South and East–West dimensions in international relations interrelate in the Eastern Mediterranean. It is now appropriate to try to draw some conclusions, deriving both from the general discussion and from its application to the region. A word of caution is, however, necessary. All of the specific examples are debatable. The interpretation of the behaviour of any country or political system involves a large element of inevitable subjectivity. The objectives of any action are often numerous and diverse, sometimes unconscious, sometimes the total result of the actions of individual forces which pursue different objectives. What is important to the conclusions to be formulated is not the validity of any specific example among those mentioned. For we shall abstain from drawing detailed conclusions related to the many problems of the Eastern Mediterranean. Instead we shall focus on some general indications which are relevant for the region. What is significant is the overall argument which has been presented. It might be useful briefly to summarise it at this point. First, the two dimensions of international relations, East–West and North–South, are contradictory in the short term because of logic, participation and polarity. Secondly, the realities of the North–South dimension (both objective indicators and policy choices of individual countries) prevent progress along the East–West dimension, and vice versa. What, then, is to be done?

Utilisation of Economic Instruments is Insufficient

We might pose the question whether, after all, the foregoing is not merely an argument in favour of utilising economic instruments to supplement political and military ones in crisis management. This conclusion might be a meagre result for our ambitious approach. Its drawback is easily found: economic instruments are costly.

One might agree on the importance of economic instruments while at the same time denying the need to discuss North—South relations in a broad perspective. Neither is it necessary to consider the possibility of a New International Economic Order, as requested by the developing countries within international organisations. Rather, one might, at most, point to the opportunity of taking measures specifically designed to solve well-delimited economic problems, which are evidently and directly leading to undesirable political and strategic consequences. In other words, the superpowers and the West should be ready to buy pieces of political stability or military advantage, and this is what economic instruments are useful for. This line of reasoning is insufficient and possibly even self-defeating. It is insufficient because the episodic utilisation of economic instruments in the way suggested seldom succeeds in buying stability and/or advantage in the long run. Very soon new problems emerge, or expectations change, and equilibria are questioned. This, as has been seen, is the very logic of North—South relations at work. It may be self-defeating because the adoption of such a strategy immediately stimulates East—West destabilising behaviour in order to extract the maximum price for any parcel of stability or any advantage which is sold.

This line of reasoning is in short constrained within the East—West logic. The idea that economic instruments may be utilised to supplement political and military ones has a partisan character. It cannot succeed because, as has been seen, many countries are interested primarily in the North—South dimension and the latter has a different and conflicting logic.

Attempts to Uncouple: Subordinating North—South to East—West

The thrust of the argument is therefore not just that economic instruments should supplement political and military ones. Faced with the contradiction between North–South and East–West one must either try to solve it or to manage it.

Let us first examine the former approach. A solution of the contradiction could be sought through the systematic subordination of one set of relations and priorities to the other. There is very clearly both in the West and in the East a tendency to subordinate the North–South dimension to the East–West one. This tendency probably reached its best expression during the Henry Kissinger years. In that period the superpowers searched for an agreement between themselves, ignoring North–South tensions and demands both at the global level and within each bloc in the belief that ultimately an agreement between superpowers could be imposed on all countries, and that it would allow the containment and/or management of any kind of North–South conflict.

We are not here intending to discuss if this attempt could have succeeded had it been pursued in a different way. The fact is, however, that it failed. One has the impression that this outcome was determined not so much by the poor application of a good strategy. Rather, the superpowers do not have sufficient instruments (including economic, political and military) to deal effectively with all the North–South conflicts at the same time; also, the superpowers were unable to reach an agreement on how to contain or manage North–South conflicts. The will might have been there, but the political gap was too large to be overcome.

The Arab–Israeli conflict is one of the main cases in which the Kissinger doctrine failed. Eventually, it proved impossible to reach East–West compromise on a peaceful solution, this being primarily the result of behaviour from local actors which both superpowers could not control. Thus the bid for peace took a turn which excluded the Soviet Union. Outside the Eastern Mediterranean region many more examples are available. The Kissinger doctrine had good results only in containing the nuclear arms race and in creating a framework favourable to detente between Western and Eastern Europe. In other words, it succeeded whenever actors recognised the preeminence of the East–West dimension. It failed whenever this preeminence was rejected.

The idea that the uncoupling of East–West and North–South is possible by recovering the dominant role of the superpowers is a recurrent temptation, but the inadequacy of instruments available to the superpowers is ultimately the decisive factor. Thus President Jimmy Carter might declare a policy of direct American presence in the non-NATO countries of the Eastern Mediterranean, but then a rapid deployment force does not exist yet. Will it ever become available? President Ronald Reagan promises to make America great again, but he will certainly find it impossible to reconcile the need for a smaller federal budget and lighter taxes with expanded defence expenditure. The Soviet Union appears to have an increasing ability to intervene globally, but this does not mean that her instruments do not have limits. These limits will very soon be demonstrated if Moscow's international commitments grow further.

In the final analysis those favouring the utilisation of economic instruments in co-ordination with political and military ones, but without facing the issue of a New International Economic Order, are also confronted with the problem of its excessive cost. It is a variation, certainly different from the Kissingerian approach, within the same philosophy of subordination of North—South to East—West. It is indeed surprising, along this line, how limited the economic incentives finally provided within the Camp David process were. The negative economic consequences of the Middle East conflict at the global level must obviously be underestimated. Otherwise one would expect industrial countries to be ready to pay a higher price for peace. Certainly they were underestimated in the past: peace might have been bought in the Middle East in the 1950s for a price which today would appear to us very reasonable indeed.

Thus the idea that uncoupling might be achieved by subordinating North—South to East—West cannot be rejected in theory, but fails in practice because insufficient instruments are provided. The Middle East conflict is a very illuminating example of this. Might things change in the future? Yes, but why should they?

Attempts to Uncouple: Subordinating East—West to North—South

Uncoupling is also theoretically possible by subordinating East—West relations to North—South priorities. This way of thinking is increasingly widespread among leading politicians in the Third World. It is also common in some left-wing European circles which are convinced that the only real problem is North—South relations and that once everything is done to eliminate conflicts in these,

conflicts in East–West relations will disappear as well. It is a position which assumes the non-existence of the short-term contradictions which the present writer has tried to underline. It is either
based on the belief that the superpowers (as far as certain Western
political forces are concerned, the Soviet Union in particular) are
not aggressive; or on the belief that they are mere paper tigers. In
both cases it is assumed that North–South progress will accelerate
the crumbling of blocs and that war will not happen as a result.

If the reasoning in this paper is correct, this strategy does not
stand a chance of succeeding. East–West considerations matter,
and if they are ignored in order to favour North–South objectives,
conflicts in East–West relations will multiply until progress is
blocked along the North–South axis as well. Again, the Eastern
Mediterranean provides a good illustration. In the period 1973–9
most countries in the region indulged in East–West destabilising
behaviour in order to pursue North–South objectives. The result
is rapidly increasing direct superpower military presence in the
region and an extremely high level of East–West tension. Ignoring
East–West considerations thus leads to increased regional conflict
very easily. Because North–South polarisation is not active only at
the global level but at the regional one as well, single-minded
attention to North–South problems is divisive. Shelving the
East–West dimension leads to nationalism untamed.

Managing the Interrelationship

If, then, uncoupling does not appear feasible, we can only try to
manage the interrelationship between East–West and North–
South with a goal of minimising short-term contradictions. This
involves a broad spectrum of initiatives, none of which is sure to
succeed.

At the global level, it is necessary to recognise the need for a New
International Economic Order; it is necessary to insist on a mean-
ingful participation from the East in the search and implementation of such an order; and it is necessary to reach agreement
between superpowers on the need to favour regional economic
integration, to limit the arms trade and to reduce or exclude direct
superpower presence in some regions. It is also necessary to reach
some kind of global agreement on raw materials supply, and
utilisation of common resources, along the lines that the new Law
of the Seas would provide for.

Stating the need for a New International Economic Order is not the same thing as accepting all requests of the Group of 77. But the desirability of managing East—West and North—South connections constitutes a criterion for selecting those problems to which priority should be given. The Eastern Mediterranean experience exemplifies this point. If sufficient financial resources had been available from multilateral organisations, countries in the region would not have adopted East—West destabilising behaviour so frequently. An essential feature of the New International Economic Order we should be working for is therefore an expanded role for the World Bank and other multilateral organisations. The multilateral nature of the latter should be reinforced by creating preconditions for Soviet membership in them.

At the regional level a number of suggestions could be spelled out. In the Eastern Mediterranean regional economic integration is a fundamental element, and a broad international agreement on the principle of Arab political unity would be very important. A clarification of the position of some countries — for example Turkey — with reference to regional integration processes would have important stabilising effects. Economic co-operation in the Balkans is not as important but should not be overlooked. Finally, Mediterranean co-operation between the Arab world and the EEC is crucial, because of the objective importance of economic links between the two groupings. The role of the EEC is therefore essentially one of defining and promoting regional economic integration processes.

It is unlikely that the superpowers will be enthusiastic about Arab integration. The United States was a fundamental factor in the beginning of European integration, but later conflicts with the EEC multiplied. And the Soviet attitude towards the EEC has been negative until recently, relations remaining very difficult. A process of Arab integration could thus take off only if the emphasis were laid on economic integration, because present conditions bar any chance of political integration or regional security agreements.[19] At the same time, in the longer run the process of economic integration would spill over into the political and military fields. Although international alignments could remain in place at the beginning, with time they would tend to dissolve. The question is: are the Soviets and the Americans ready to agree in principle that such dissolution should eventually take place?

A further suggestion is that the Soviet Union cannot be excluded from a search for peace in the region. It could be argued that some kind of superpower agreement is a necessary condition to regional integration, which in turn is a necessary condition for peace. Superpower agreement is also necessary to limit the arms race in the region, and arms sales specifically. European countries should be led to accept self-restraint in this field, an objective which can be achieved.

Oil is so important to the Eastern Mediterranean that a global agreement on a few basic points — such as limitations on demand for imports, guarantees on minimum quantities exported and some agreement on prices — would have enormous positive effects on the region. Here, too, the possibility of the Soviet Union becoming a net importer, and the fact that the other Eastern European countries already depend on imports from the Eastern Mediterranean point to the need for responsible participation on the part of these countries in global energy negotiations.

Finally, a few specific initiatives might be taken — some do not require wide international agreement — in order to defuse well-delimited elements of crisis. A possible example is the need to provide alternatives to oil traffic across the Strait of Hormuz. None of these initiatives is easy, of course. Pessimists, will say that there is no chance of managing effectively the interrelationship of East—West and North—South. Success is certainly not assured. But then what is the alternative? The present state of affairs, if not amended, seems inevitably bound to generate war. Finally, it is right to add that even if we succeeded in managing the inter-relationship, not all problems would be solved: South—South conflict would continue to emanate dangerous shock waves. To name just the most important case, what about the Palestinians? There may be no answer to that. But a mismanagement of East—West and North—South interconnections will not help the Palestinians in any case.

Notes

1. As has been made officially clear, NATO would not intervene in the event of a Soviet invasion of Poland although this development would be indeed very critical in the European context.
2. Some clarification is necessary on terminology. Countries of the world can be divided into two large groups: industrial or Developed Countries (DCs) and developing or Less Developed Countries (LDCs). The first group

includes both the OECD and the CMEA (although both groupings have members which are non-industrial). The second is often called the Third World, but this raises the spectre of a Fourth World, opening the door to an unlimited number of subdivisions. The Group of 77 is the diplomatic expression of the developing world within UN organisations.

3. See, among others, the OECD report for Turkey, 1980.

4. Financial assistance was especially provided by a group of industrial countries in 1980. West Germany took the lead in arranging the financial package. Strategic considerations were prominent, and will continue to be, in influencing the attitude of other OECD countries towards Turkish economic needs.

5. A. Hottinger, 'Internal Change and Regional Conflict: the Case of the Gulf', paper submitted to the International Institute for Strategic Studies (IISS) annual conference, Stresa, 11—14 September 1980. See also T. Koszinowski, 'How Stable is the Political system of Saudi Arabia?', mimeo, Istituo Affari Internazionali (IAI), RS/1980—55/STAFF.

6. D. Rustow, 'U.S.—Saudi Relations and the Oil Crises of the 1980s', *Foreign Affairs*, LV (1976—7).

7. N. Sabra, 'Rivalità fra potenze locali e superpotenze nel Golfo', *Politica Internazionali*, no. 6 (1980) pp. 85—6. The partners of IPC were Shell, British Petroleum (BP), Compagnie Française des Pétroles (CFP), Standard Oil New Jersey, Mobil, Texaco, Standard Oil California and Gulf.

8. The saga of international negotiations leading to the formation of the Iraq Petroleum Company is a classic of diplomacy and intrigue. By contrast, in later years the granting of oil concessions as important or even more important than the Iraqi one, in countries such as Kuwait and Saudi Arabia, aroused a minimum of diplomatic attention.

9. Iraqi production was increased to support the boycott of Iranian oil after the nationalisation of assets belonging to the Anglo-Iranian Oil Company (today's BP).

10. Iraq always maintained that IPC was under-investing in the country, ignoring its promising prospects. In retrospect, exploration results confirm the Iraqi potential. Of course, the behaviour of the companies could easily be justified in relation to the negative 'political climate'. The question is whether different behaviour on the part of Western governments might have reassured the owners of IPC and caused an early settlement in the dispute.

11. Iraqi production passed from 67 million tons in 1972, through 115 million tons in 1978, and reached 175 million tons in 1979.

12. It is fading because while the economy in most Arab countries is today rapidly growing, thanks to direct or indirect benefit of oil revenues, Israel is experiencing a very severe economic crisis, with many elements of similarity with Turkey. The economic crisis is affecting Israel's political stability — if not its democratic institutions — and leading to more 'aggressive' foreign policy behaviour, for example over the issue of West Bank settlements.

13. The Geneva Conference was Kissinger's way of taking into account the Soviet Union, because in his eyes after all even a Middle East peace treaty was to be primarily an agreement between the superpowers. It was only after Sadat's visit that the Soviet Union was excluded from the negotiations, and the Camp David process. It is certainly no chance that Sadat's visit was encouraged by such countries as Romania — not by the superpowers.

14. In this and in the following paragraph the present writer is summarising an argument which he developed extensively in *L'Opec nella economia internazionale* (Rome, 1976).

15. A. O. Hirschman, *Exit, Voice and Loyalty: Responses to Decline in Firms, Organizations and States* (Cambridge, Mass., 1970).

16. M. Cremasco has reached the conclusion that in the context of the Eastern Mediterranean regional arms sales are hardly any more an instrument for acquiring political influence over the purchasing country. See his 'I paesi arabi ed il commercio degli armamenti', mimeo, IAI, 19A/80.

17. Rivalries are important both between countries and between personalities within the Arab world. Also, political ideologies are different. Yet, neither rivalries nor ideological differences can be said to be much worse than those that caused two world wars in Europe in a thirty-year span of time. Still, European integration is a reality, even if rivalries and differences are far from being forgotten. Therefore, the present writer rejects the argument that Arab integration is just impossible.

18. Greece has been very active in promoting Balkan co-operation. A first conference with this purpose was held in Athens in 1976. A second conference was held in Ankara at the end of 1979. The long interval was attributed in Athens to Bulgarian reluctance. This was viewed in turn as stemming from Soviet unwillingness to risk a new political grouping emerging in the Balkans. See *Financial Times*, 18 Nov. 1980.

19. This is the indication which emerged from the Arab summit in Amman in December 1980.

3 Great Power Spheres-of-Influence in the Balkans: 1944 and After

David Carlton

The Balkans in the postwar era have differed fundamentally from other major regions of Europe. For the Balkans are the only region that was ever subjected to an informal agreement for partition into great power spheres-of-influence. Even the fate of the area covered by Poland and the two German states was never more than tacitly dealt with at Yalta and in postwar discussions. Thus the Balkan region has differed considerably from, say, Scandinavia in the extent to which a majority of its states have had in practice, at various times, to shape policies that took account of limitations on full sovereignty. The purpose of this chapter is to examine the origins of this state of affairs and to ask whether and to what extent an evolution away from rigid spheres-of-influence assumptions has been taking place.

There has been in the postwar era some lack of recognition, in the West at least, of the full extent to which a spheres-of-influence bargain was struck in the last stages of the Second World War. This arose in large part because it was Great Britain rather than the United States that took the leading role in negotiating with the Soviet Union. At that time this role for London was by no means inappropriate. For Great Britain was acknowledged to be one of the Big Three, a full and equal partner of Washington and Moscow in all discussions if not in military weight: the era of the formal recognition of the existence of *two* superpowers was many years in the future. Moreover, the United States intended to withdraw all its forces from Europe on the surrender of Germany. Indeed, President Franklin D. Roosevelt openly said as much at Yalta – and this policy was not decisively revised until 1947 or even perhaps 1949. Thus Great Britain was expected in the last phase of the war to be the only existing great power directly involved in postwar Europe other than the Soviet Union, with the mere possibility that France in time might again become one. True, Winston Churchill, recognising the facts of British military and economic weakness, regretted Roosevelt's unwillingness to play a larger part in shaping Europe's future. But, as a realist, he had come to the conclusion by the spring of 1944 that the American outlook was unlikely to change and hence he decided to seek the best bargain possible with Moscow. The Americans never openly acknowledged or endorsed the bargain that Churchill struck and at various stages of the Presidency of Harry S. Truman even saw fit to adopt postures suggesting that these bargains had no validity or even that they had not been struck at all.

American commentators have thus been led to play down the spheres-of-influence aspect of the Balkan scene. And they were by no means discouraged from holding this outlook by speeches and writings of British leaders. Churchill himself in his war memoirs deliberately misled the world by implying that his famous 'percentages' discussions with Joseph Stalin related only to arrangements for the military liberation of areas still under German control and that they had no long-term implications.[1] Perhaps he was by then slightly ashamed of his own ruthless treatment of small nations. But more plausible is the explanation that he saw in Truman a great improvement on Roosevelt and sought to draw the former into a more active role in Europe even at the cost of breaking faith to some extent with the bargains he had struck with Stalin. Churchill's Fulton Speech of March 1946 was, for example, not really in keeping with the spirit of his wartime dealings with Moscow – and it came before the Soviets had themselves done much that could have occasioned him great surprise. Churchill was of course by then no longer Prime Minister and the Fulton Speech was not approved by Clement Attlee or Ernest Bevin. Nor was it endorsed by Truman. So Stalin was certainly not entitled to regard Fulton as any breach of faith by the West as a whole – only as cynical conduct by a formerly powerful individual now out of office. The point, for our purposes, however, is that Churchill's postwar conduct served to prevent Western commentators grasping the extent of the wartime bargains struck by Great Britain with the Soviet Union. Indeed, it is only in the last few years, as a result of research in the recently-opened British archives, that it has become possible to establish how far Churchill went in forging long-term spheres-of-influence arrangements with Stalin. This knowledge, even now, has by no means been widely disseminated.

The story began in April 1944 when Anthony Eden, the British Foreign Secretary, went on holiday. In his absence Churchill took charge of the Foreign Office and at once brought to the conduct of Anglo-Soviet relations a greater degree of decisiveness than hitherto. Matters came to a head when the Soviet news agency gave support to the pro-Communist mutineers among Greek forces in Egypt. On 16 April Churchill wrote to Vyasheslav Molotov: 'This is really no time for ideological warfare. I am determined to put down mutiny . . . I wish you all success . . . in your Romanian negotiations in which . . . we consider you are the predominant power.' On 23 April the Prime Minister repeated to Molotov that 'we regard you as leaders in Romanian affairs'.[2] The Soviets took the hint and protested at the presence in Romania of British officers from the Special Operations Executive (SOE). The way was now open for a spheres-of-influence bargain involving Greece and Romania. During May, after Eden's return from holiday, terms for an agreement along these lines were formally discussed between London and Moscow. Surviving British records do not, however, conclusively show whether Eden was wholly in agreement with Churchill about the implications. Possibly the Foreign Secretary saw the Greek–Romanian deal at this stage as being limited to the immediate phase involving military action, whereas Churchill may have realised that Romania was in all probability destined to be permanently Sovietised. Nor did Churchill move towards a spheres-of-influence deal without occasionally thinking aloud about an alternative course, namely that of confronting Moscow. But this was at least as much 'dreaming' as his contemplation of a major Balkan invasion had been during the previous year. His dreams could not be turned into reality without American support, which was not on offer. Hence Churchill's quest for a bilateral bargain with Moscow was pursued with some urgency and a fair degree of consistency during the summer months of 1944.

The Soviets proved surprisingly willing to do business. Their only reservation, reasonably enough, concerned the Americans. How far would any bargain struck with the British be accepted in Washington? Churchill accordingly sought American agreement to the Romanian–Greek arrangement. But the 'high-minded' Roosevelt made great difficulties and eventually consented only with reluctance to a three-month experiment in Anglo-Soviet management of affairs in Greece and Romania. The Soviets were not particularly enthusiastic about this temporary solution but they did not definitely reject it. It was thus now a matter of some urgency for the British to put the 'understanding' with Moscow to a practical test. Hence in July 1944 Eden became almost as anxious as Churchill to prevent Greece, then about to be liberated from German occupation, falling into Communist hands. Pierson Dixon, Eden's Private Secretary, recorded in his diary on 12 July:

> An exhilarating day, during which the plunge was taken which we ought to have taken long ago to support [Georgios] Papandreou and extirpate EAM [Communists] in Greece. In a very racy interview with the Greek Ambassador A. E. [Eden] asserted our whole-hearted support for the Greek Government and promised that we would if necessary withdraw our support and men from EAM, though we 'didn't want to break all the crockery at once'.[3]

In the ensuing months Moscow's reactions on the subject of Greece were ambiguous. Soviet propaganda was muted. But eight Soviet officers were flown in to advise the Communist ELAS forces, leading Eden to minute on 3 August: 'On the face of it this may be a Russian attempt to complete domination of the Balkans and I think we should make it pretty plain that we are not standing for it in Greece.'[4]

Another opportunity for Churchill and Eden to discover whether Roosevelt might not after all be persuaded to interest himself in the fate of the Balkans presented itself in mid-September 1944 when they met him in Quebec. The essentially negative conclusion they reached was reflected in their decision to suggest to the Foreign Office that not only control over Romania but also now of Bulgaria should be offered to Stalin in return for the British being allowed to take the lead in Greece. Officials in the Foreign Office objected to this proposed further concession to

Moscow and subsequently persuaded Eden to put up more of a fight for Bulgaria than Churchill thought prudent.

Once back in London, Churchill resolved to clinch with Stalin a bilateral arrangement for the future of as much of East-Central Europe as possible. Such was his sense of urgency that in his view nothing less than a summit would suffice. Hence on 9 October he and Eden arrived in Moscow. The famous 'percentage agreements' resulted.

Eden initially sought in Moscow to resist Churchill's desire to strike a bargain with Stalin on whatever terms he could get. Hence Churchill told Lord Moran: 'The Foreign Secretary would be obstinate, he must be told that there is only one course open to us − to make friends with Stalin.'[5] Bulgaria became a cause of acute difficulty. Stung by criticisms in the Foreign Office of the 'appeasing' line he and Churchill had agreed upon at Quebec, the Foreign Secretary reversed his position. Because of Bulgaria's proximity to Turkey and the Eastern Mediterranean he wished to see Great Britain have a larger say in its fate than in the case of Romania, with which he was determined that it should not be equated.

Once in conference with Stalin and Vyasheslav Molotov, however, Eden in contrast to his conduct at Quebec, made no serious attempt to prevent Churchill handling matters as he wished. At their first meeting the Prime Minister chose to tackle Stalin with a remarkable bluntness. According to the first draft of the minutes taken by Archibald Clark-Kerr, the British Ambassador in Moscow:

> Prime Minister then produced what he called a 'naughty document' showing a list of Balkan countries and the proportion of interest in them of the Great Powers. He said that the Americans would be shocked if they saw how crudely he had put it. Marshal Stalin was a realist. He himself was not sentimental while Mr Eden was a bad man. He had not consulted his Cabinet or Parliament.

Churchill's precise proposals were:

Romania	
Russia	90%
The others	10%
Greece	
Great Britain (in accord with USA)	90%
Russia	10%

Yugoslavia	50—50%
Hungary	50—50%
Bulgaria	
Russia	75%
The others	25%

Churchill, in his memoirs, claimed that Stalin simply 'took his blue pencil and made a large tick upon it, and passed it back to us'. 'It was all settled,' he added, 'in no more time than it takes to tell.' In fact the discussion was more complicated. For, according to Clark-Kerr's minutes, 'Marshal Stalin reverted to the Balkans and asked for the figures about Bulgaria on the "naughty document" to be amended and suggested that our [British] interest was not as great as the Prime Minister claimed.' There was also some debate about the future of the Montreux Convention which Churchill was in principle willing to see revised; and Stalin tacitly agreed to use his influence to restrain the Italian Communists. Nevertheless Churchill was substantially correct to recall that a rapid under-standing was reached at his first direct encounter with Stalin.[6]

It was probably never intended by Churchill and still less by Eden that a bilateral Anglo-Soviet treaty on postwar arrangements should be drawn up in view of American susceptibilities. But Churchill did consider sending a formal letter to Stalin, of which a mere copy would have gone to Roosevelt. Even this, however, he decided not to do after American Ambassador Averell Harriman had warned him that it would be badly received in Washington. With the 'percentages agreement' thus remaining a wholly infor-mal arrangement too much should not be made of the ensuing Eden—Molotov discussions on details which were in any case technically inconclusive. But they were of some importance in that they convinced the Foreign Secretary that Soviet ambitions were more extensive than he had imagined. Molotov, for example, tried to persuade Eden to accept that the Soviet 'share' in Bulgaria should be increased to 90 per cent as in the case of Romania. Since Churchill's 75 per cent formulation represented a concession by the Prime Minister to Eden's pleas, the Foreign Secretary was unwilling to give way. But, since it was unclear how 75 per cent could in practice have been less decisive than 90 per cent, Eden's stubbornness on this point seems rather academic. On the other hand, he did not discourage Molotov from raising the question whether, if the Soviets agreed to 75 per cent for Bulgaria, they might not increase their 'share' in Hungary from 50 to 75 per cent. But, as stated, these discussions had no decisive or formal outcome.[7] What probably mattered much more was Molotov's clear indication that, though the British and the Americans would be allowed to sign an armistice with Romania and Bulgaria on equal terms with the Soviets, in the post-Armistice phase Soviet troops would remain in exclusive occupation of these countries with a Soviet chairman permanently heading a three-power control commission. That Eden grasped how potentially decisive this was is clear from what he wrote to his Foreign Office critics in London:

> as it now appears that the Soviet government intend to maintain forces in Bulgaria so long as the Control Commission operates, and as neither we nor the Americans are in a position to send troops to the country, I fear we must simply accept the realities of the situation, however disagreeable.[8]

Eden had thus been brought round, as so often happened, to accepting Churchill's realism.

To some observers Churchill's attitude to the Soviets at this period seemed ambiguous. For example, his doctor, Lord Moran, wrote in his diary on 30 October 1944:

> All this havering, these conflicting and contradictory policies, are, I am sure due to Winston's exhaustion. He seems torn between two lines of action: he cannot decide whether to make one last attempt to enlist Roosevelt's sympathy for a firmer line with Stalin, in the hope that he has learnt from the course of events, or whether to make his peace with Stalin and save what he can from the wreck of Allied hopes. At one moment he will plead with the President for a common front against Communism and the next he will make a bid for Stalin's friendship. Sometimes the two policies alternate with bewildering rapidity.[9]

As well as having to bargain about the Balkans Churchill was also of course concerned about the fate of Poland, about which he seemed at times to hold out hopes that Stalin might take a less inflexible view than about, say, Romania or Bulgaria. As evidence of Churchill's capacity for optimism the minutes of the post-Yalta War Cabinet may be cited:

> So far as Stalin was concerned, he was quite sure that he meant well to the world and to Poland. He did not think that there

would be any resentment on the part of Russia about the arrangements that had been made for fair and free elections in that country . . . Stalin, at the beginning of their conversation on the Polish question, had said that Russia had committed many sins . . . against Poland, and that they had in the past joined in the partitions of Poland and in cruel oppression of her. It was not the intention of the Soviet Government to repeat that policy in the future. He felt no doubt whatever in saying that Stalin had been sincere. He had very great feeling that the Russians were anxious to work harmoniously with the two English-speaking democracies.[10]

Hugh Dalton recorded in his diary on 23 February that the Prime Minister had said: 'Poor Neville Chamberlain believed he could trust Hitler. He was wrong. But I don't think I'm wrong about Stalin.'[11] But Churchill's hopeful words probably did not represent his settled conviction about the Soviets. Rather he may have been putting the best face on the bargains struck with Stalin for the benefit of those colleagues who would otherwise have had difficulty in accepting the need for disagreeable surrenders. What Moran saw as 'havering' and 'conflicting and contradictory policies' were merely a reflection of his desperation when faced with the reality of Great Britain's relative military weakness. Indeed on one reading Churchill showed a fair degree of consistency. Three quotations from the Prime Minister during the last year of the war illustrate the argument:

Churchill to Eden, 8 May 1944
I fear that very great evil may come upon the world. This time at any rate we and the Americans will be heavily armed. The Russians are drunk with victory and there is no length they may not go.

Churchill to Lord Cranborne, 3 April 1945
Always remember that there are various large matters in which we cannot go further than the United States are willing to go.

Churchill quoted in Moran's diary, 22 July 1945
The Russians have stripped their zone [of Germany] and want a rake-off from the British and American sectors as well. They will grind their zone, there will be unimaginable cruelties. It is indefensible except on one ground: that there is no alternative.[12]

Eden differed from his chief not so much about the character of the Soviet threat, which, at least intermittently, he had come to accept, but about whether East-Central Europe could be saved without American support. He had to be constantly reminded by Churchill of the limits of British influence, as for example when the Prime Minister minuted on 17 June 1945:

> It is beyond the power of this country to prevent all sorts of things crashing at the present time. The responsibility lies with the US and my desire is to give them all the support in our power. If they do not feel able to do anything, then we must let matters take their course.[13]

In Churchill's view only one substantial prize could be secured by the exertions of Great Britain alone. This was Greece. Hence following his return to London from Moscow the Prime Minister during the remainder of 1944 treated her future as of supreme importance. Eden, while not opposed to trying to save Greece from Communism, showed no comparable sense of urgency. This led Churchill to write to him on 7 November:

> In my opinion, having paid the price we have to Russia, for freedom of action in Greece, we should not hesitate to use British troops to support the Royal Hellenic Government . . . We need another eight or ten thousand foot-soldiers to hold the capital and Salonika for the present Government . . . I fully expect a clash with EAM, and we must not shrink from it, provided the ground is well chosen.[14]

The simmering crisis in Athens, which had been liberated on 14 October, erupted into civil war on 4 December. A Communist takeover appeared imminent. Churchill held that the situation was too urgent to allow time to consult the Americans or even his War Cabinet. He accordingly took drastic action on his own initiative with only the rather passive consent of Eden. Dixon wrote in his diary in an account somewhat at variance with that in Churchill's memoirs:

> Crucial decisions today over Greece. The climax not reached till after dinner . . . we discussed a statement to be made by the PM in the House the following day, and while this was going on

telegrams came in from Rex [Leeper, British Ambassador in Athens] saying that the situation was deteriorating and Papandreou [the Greek Prime Minister] about to resign. We drafted a telegram and a statement which I then took over to No. 10 . . . [and] showed him [Churchill] the Greek telegrams and our proposed instructions to Leeper. He thought them not nearly strong enough, and held that the time had come to order General [Ronald] Scobie to take over law and order and to disarm the ELAS by force. He cleared this on the telephone with Anthony, who was going to bed, and then settled down to draft his instructions, sitting gyrating in his armchair and dictating on the machine to Miss Layton, who did not bat an eyelid at the many blasphemies with which the old man interspersed his official phrases. He was in a bloodthirsty mood, and did not take kindly to suggestions that we should avoid bloodshed if possible – though I couldn't agree more that force must be used if required. Rex was told that there must be no Cabinet-making till order had been restored. Having sent off these tremendous telegrams, he turned to the statement. This, with other matters took till 2.30 a.m.[15]

Thus Churchill alone drafted the famous telegram to Scobie which soon rapidly leaked through American channels into the press: 'We have to hold and dominate Athens. It would be a great thing for you to succeed in this without bloodshed if possible, but also with bloodshed if necessary.'[16]

Even Churchill conceded in his memoirs that this telegram was 'somewhat strident in tone'.[17] It led to bitter recriminations in the House of Commons and, more importantly, to a quarrel with the Americans. Edward Stettinius, the Secretary of State, issued a pointed statement deploring British interference in the internal affairs of Italy and also, by implication, in Greece. This caused Churchill to rebuke Roosevelt, who in turn effectively endorsed Stettinius's line. In the Foreign Office Eden and his officials now became uneasy about Churchill's Greek policy. Dixon's diary is revealing:

5 December 1944
I confess I felt increasingly anxious about the wisdom of our midnight plotting, and was further shaken by a tiresome statement put out by Stettinius condemning our interference in

Italian and Greek internal affairs. The actual military situation in Greece is, as expected, more disquieting every hour. It has yet to reach its climax, which can only be an armed clash between Greek and Briton, unless the ELAS capitulate.

6 December 1944
A.E., very calm, but a bit worried about the PM's position if things get worse in Greece.

11 December 1944
After brooding on Greece during the weekend . . . returned to the FO convinced that we must, without signs of weakening, find some way out before we are really locked in battle with EAM. Found that Moley [Sargent] and the Department's minds were working on the same lines. When A.E. came up at midday we put this to him and he took a plan over to the PM who, however, would agree to no instructions going to Athens for fear . . . of crossing the wires now Harold Macmillan and FM [Harold] Alexander have gone there to find a solution. I feel unhappy about this, as we have given them no lead and with each hour that passes we are more deeply committed to an unnecessary struggle with the Greek irregulars.

19 December 1944
News from Athens no better . . . The great debate is whether there should be a Regency in Greece. There is a divergence on this point between A.E. and the PM the former considering that our military force is not enough to settle the issue and that a political solvent is needed. The PM on the other hand believes that our forces should be allowed to settle the matter, and that raising the constitutional issue would result in a dictatorship or a communist regime. He underrates the ELAS force, overrates our force, ignores the risk to the Italian front of a festering and unpopular crusade in Greece, and above all is swayed by the wish to maintain the King of Greece in power. The feeling is growing ugly in the country, where people see the simple fact that British troops are being made to fight friends. Whether the Regency would help much is perhaps doubtful, but it would help a little, and our situation is so serious that every contribution should now be thrown in.[18]

Churchill, however, kept his nerve and was soon rewarded with the news that the Communists had clearly failed in their bid to take over by the use of armed force. On Christmas Eve the Prime Minister suddenly decided that the time was ripe to visit Athens to investigate at first hand Eden's claim that the establishment of a Regency under Archbishop Damaskinos would best serve British interests. He and Churchill thus arrived on Christmas Day in Greece where they slept aboard *HMS Ajax*. Next day they met a wide range of Greek politicians, including some Communists. The outcome was Churchill's conversion to Eden's view that Damaskinos could be trusted. It was accordingly agreed that the Greek King should invite him to serve as Regent and the Communists tacitly consented in return to end their armed resistance. Both Churchill and Eden thus departed for London on 28 December believing that they had by their differing contributions done much to bring a degree of stability to the country for which they had sacrificed so much to Stalin.

The next expedition for Churchill and Eden came at the end of January 1945 when they visited the Crimea for the Yalta Heads of Government summit. Poland was the dominant issue though the Balkans were no doubt also in everyone's mind. The Soviets insisted that the pro-Communist Lublin Committee should form the core of the Polish Provisional Government but for the sake of appearances they agreed to have discussions about adding some further names 'from within Poland and from abroad'. Eden fought hard to secure better terms in a confrontation with Molotov but he was effectively defeated when Stettinius refused to back him up. Everything now rested on whether free elections would be held under international supervision. The Soviets agreed to elections in which 'all democratic and anti-Nazi parties shall have the right to take part and put forward candidates'. They also signed a document, produced by Roosevelt, entitled 'Declaration on Liberated Europe', which contained vague commitments to the establishment 'through free elections of governments responsive to the will of the people' and to 'the right of all peoples to choose the form of government under which they will live'. But the Soviets' real intentions for Poland were revealed by their refusal to agree to arrangements for Western participation in the supervision or even observation of elections. Churchill wrote in his memoirs that this was 'the best I could get'.[19]

Clearly he and Eden could insist on nothing more with Roosevelt and Stettinius in so irresolute a mood. But perhaps Roosevelt, too, believed that nothing more could be achieved by diplomatic means. William Leahy, for example, claimed that he told the President that the agreement on Poland was 'so elastic that the Russians can stretch it all the way from Yalta to Washington without ever technically breaking it'. Roosevelt is said to have replied: 'I know it, Bill – I know it. But it's the best I can do for Poland at this time.' This has led to speculation that Roosevelt was tacitly of the same opinion as Churchill had been at Moscow in October 1944: suspicious of the Soviets but reconciled to a spheres-of-influence deal. Yet his position also surely differed from Churchill's. First, he had not seen the need to crush the Communists in Greece. Secondly, he had much more military strength at his disposal than Churchill but was quite unwilling to make even the most limited use of it in diplomatic bargaining. On the contrary, at Yalta, in a moment of unparalleled feebleness, he volunteered the information that American forces would leave Europe within two years. Certainly Churchill did not respect Roosevelt's attitude at this time. On 13 March, for example, he wrote a minute to Eden deploring 'the weakness of the United States diplomacy'.[20] Thus Churchill and Eden left Yalta with few positive achievements – but the principal fault was clearly not theirs.

If Churchill and Eden were disappointed, they did not immediately reveal it to their colleagues. As has been seen, the Prime Minister spoke optimistically to the War Cabinet. He and Eden also defended the Yalta arrangements in the House of Commons, where vocal opposition came from a number of Conservative back-benchers, including the future Prime Minister, Lord Dunglass, later Sir Alexander Douglas-Home. Harold Nicolson recorded in his diary: 'Winston is as amused as I am that the warmongers of the Munich period have now become the appeasers, while the appeasers have become the warmongers.'[21]

That Churchill did not set much store by the Yalta Declaration or on the promised elections in Poland is, however, clear from his private minutes to Eden. He remained convinced that the British should try to hold the Soviets to the 'percentages' arrangements of the previous October even at the cost of condoning Stalin's breaches of the Yalta Declaration in the Soviet sphere-of-influence. Eden, on the other hand, was more hopeful that, with American support, the British might yet induce the Soviets to respect the Declaration and hence not seek the Bolshevisation of Poland or even of Bulgaria and Romania. He was thus anxious to engage in active diplomacy contrary to the spirit of the 'percent-ages' agreement when, soon after Yalta, dramatic developments occurred in Romania. Pro-Communist elements, with the support of the Red Army, began openly to persecute and intimidate their rivals. Eventually King Michael agreed, under direct Soviet pres-sure, to dismiss the Prime Minister, Nicolae Radescu, thereby opening the way for a Communist takeover. Churchill, unlike Eden, wished to keep a low profile. Indeed, even before Yalta the Prime Minister had shown remarkable concern for Soviet suscept-ibilities so far as Romania was concerned. On 19 January, for example, he had informed Eden that he positively favoured the Soviets being allowed to deport Romanian citizens to the Soviet Union as forced labour:

> We seem to be taking a very active line against the deportation of the Austrians, Saxons and other German or quasi-German elements from Roumania to Russia for labour purposes. Con-sidering all that Russia has suffered, and the wanton attacks made upon her by Roumania, and the vast armies the Russians are using at the front at the present time, and the terrible condi-tion of the people in many parts of Europe, I cannot see that the Russians are wrong in making 100 or 150 thousand of these people work their passage. Also we must bear in mind what we promised about leaving Roumania's fate to a large extent in Russian hands. I cannot myself consider that it is wrong of the Russians to take Roumanians of any origin they like to work in the Russian coal-fields, in view of all that has passed.[22]

He conveniently forgot how reluctant he had been to make a British declaration of war on Romania in 1941. Now, after the fall of Radescu, the Prime Minister again rebuked Eden, on 5 March, for the excess of zeal in support of the Yalta Declaration shown by the Foreign Office and by British representatives in Bucharest:

> We really have no justification for intervening in this extra-ordinarily vigorous manner for our late Roumanian enemies, thus compromising our position in Poland and jarring upon Russian acquiescence in our long fight in Athens. If we go on like this, we shall be told, not without reason, that we have broken our faith about Roumania after taking advantage of our

position in Greece and this will compromise the stand we have taken at Yalta over Poland. I consider strict instructions should be sent to all our representatives in Roumania not to develop an anti-Russian political front there. This they are doing with untimely energy without realizing what is at stake in other fields.[23]

Eden's response underlined his naive obtuseness. He pointed out that the Americans had protested at developments in Romania and had 'invoked the Yalta Declaration'. 'It seemed to me,' he continued, 'the best we could do was to support the Americans.' Ignoring power political considerations, he piously reminded Churchill that the Yalta Declaration 'applies indifferently to lesser Allied countries which have been liberated and to ex-enemy countries which have been occupied by the Allies'. He concluded:

Although our percentage of interest in Roumania and Bulgaria is small, surely that does not prohibit us from appealing for consultation between the three Powers in accordance with the Yalta Declaration . . .? If we are not allowed to do this in respect of Balkan countries, I fail to see what interpretation we can put on the Declaration or what answer we are to give in public if asked why we did not act in accordance with the procedure laid down in the Declaration . . .

I realise of course, that if we invoke the Yalta Declaration in respect of Roumania we may expect the Russians to do the same in regard of Greece or elsewhere. But you have already offered Russia full inspection in Greece, and I do not think that we have anything to fear, at least so far as Greece is concerned . . .[24]

This argument appeared to be based on the assumption that the Yalta Declaration had miraculously made it safe for Great Britain to abandon the spirit of the 'percentages' agreement. Churchill was unimpressed. For he grasped that over-reliance on the Yalta Declaration, accompanied by a tacit repudiation of the 'percentages' agreement, might lead not to the salvation of Romania but to the loss of Greece. On 13 March, for example, he minuted to Eden:

We must remember
(a) Roumania is an ex-enemy state which did great injury to Russia;

(b) That we, for considerations well known to you, accepted in a special degree the predominance of Russia in this theatre;
(c) That the lines of the southern Russian Army communications pass through Roumania;
(d) The weakness of the United States diplomacy.[25]

Eden had to face similar disillusionment with the effectiveness of the Yalta Declaration in the case of Poland. The Soviets showed no sign of being willing to establish an independent Polish government or to arrange for free elections to be held. And sixteen non-Communist Poles who had gone to Moscow for discussions with the Soviets were rumoured to have disappeared. By 23 March the Foreign Secretary wrote in his diary that he took 'the gloomiest view of Russian behaviour everywhere'. 'Altogether,' he added, 'our foreign policy seems a sad wreck and we may have to cast about afresh.'[26]

Churchill appears to have taken a more relaxed view of matters during the remainder of his Premiership. For the Soviets abstained from making difficulties in Greece. Indeed, even after his retirement from politics, more than a decade later, he looked back on his bargain with the Soviets without regret. He wrote to President Dwight D. Eisenhower reflecting that in the matter of Greece, Romania and Bulgaria Stalin had kept his word.[27]

The bargain struck at Moscow in October 1944 arguably began to fall apart only in 1947 – and even then the main difficulty related to a country in the 50–50 category, namely Hungary. Soon after the end of the war, despite the presence of the Red Army, free elections were held in Hungary – in contrast to what was permitted in Romania, Bulgaria (and also Poland). The Communists won only 16 per cent of the popular vote but joined a coalition government dominated by the Smallholder Party which had won 57 per cent of the popular vote. But early in 1947 the Hungarian Communists set out, with the obvious support and knowledge of the occupying Red Army, to Bolshevise the country. Above all, it is clear that Mátyás Rákosi, the Communist leader, was no Josip Broz Tito, able and willing to act without Stalin's approval.

The drama in Hungary began on 20 January 1947 with the arrest by authority of the Red Army of Béla Kovács, General Secretary of the Smallholder Party, and of seven others among the party's Members of Parliament. All were eventually charged – after delays relating to parliamentary immunity – with complicity in a plot against the Government. The Government was a coalition in which the Smallholders understandably held a majority of posts as they had won 57 per cent of the popular vote in the General Election. By early June the Smallholder Prime Minister, Ferenc Nagy, had sought asylum in Switzerland, agreeing to resign in return for his child being allowed to join him in exile. Within a year the cowed remnants of the Smallholders and the Social Democrats had effectively handed over all power to the Communists. The discovery of the 'plot' of Jauary 1947 thus marked the beginning of a deliberate Soviet plan to break wartime understandings about the future of Hungary.

During 1948 the Communists also seized power in Czechoslovakia, though that country had not of course been part of the bargain struck between Churchill and Stalin and, in any case, the Red Army was not directly involved. Meanwhile during 1947 the British had effectively handed over responsibility for supervising the future of Greece to the United States which, in enunciating the so-called Truman Doctrine, also brought Turkey unequivocally into its sphere-of-influence. The essential battle lines of the European Cold War were duly completed in 1949 with the formation of NATO.

There has only been some limited movement since then so far as countries covered by the Churchill—Stalin bargain is concerned. Bulgaria remains totally loyal to Moscow, while Hungary is almost so. Yugoslovia remains faithful to the non-aligned Communist position it has adhered to since 1948. (Even before that its apparent loyalty to Moscow actually was and was known to be merely Tito's choice and in no way imposed upon Belgrade by Stalin.) Thus the only substantial changes relate to Greece and Romania. The former has clearly now decisively emerged from an era of dependence on Washington. For today in Athens there is clearly more fear of Turkey than of the Soviet bloc. Hence though the Socialist government elected in 1981 may not actually formally leave NATO, Greece has certainly ceased for most practical purposes to be a loyal American ally. The evolution of Romania under Nicolae Ceauşescu is not exactly symmetrical with what has happened in Greece. Nevertheless Bucharest's independent foreign policies must be almost as irritating to the Soviets — given the more rigorous standards they expect of their allies — as Greece's conduct is to the Americans. The unanswered question for the 1980s is whether either superpower will see fit to take steps, whether openly or covertly, to try to reassert their former standing in Athens or Bucharest. It is also of interest to speculate whether, if either should do so, the wartime bargain of October 1944 would be considered to serve as a real or ostensible jusification.[28]

Notes

1. Winston S. Churchill, *The Second World War*, 6 vols (London, 1948–54) vol. vi, pp. 196–7.
2. Prem. 3/211/6, Public Record Office (PRO), London.
3. Sir Pierson Dixon Diary, 12 July 1944.
4. FO 371/43772, PRO.
5. Lord Moran, *Winston Churchill: The Struggle for Survival* (London, 1966) p. 193.
6. Inverchapel Papers, FO 800/302, PRO; and Churchill, op. cit., vol. vi, pp. 196–7.
7. For further details see Albert Resis, 'The Churchill–Stalin "Percentages" Agreement on the Balkans, Moscow, October 1944', *American Historical Review*, lxxxiii, pp. 368–87.
8. Elisabeth Barker, 'British Policy towards Romania, Bulgaria and Hungary, 1944–1946' in Martin McCauley (ed.), *Communist Power in Europe, 1944–1949* (London, 1977) p. 204.
9. Moran, op. cit., p. 206.
10. CAB 65/51, PRO.
11. Hugh Dalton Diary, 23 Feb. 1945, quoted in David Dilks (ed.), *The Diaries of Sir Alexander Cadogan, 1938–1945* (London, 1971) p. 716.
12. Avon Papers, FO 954/20, PRO; and Moran, op. cit., p. 278.
13. FO 371/48193, PRO.
14. Churchill, op. cit., vi, p. 250.
15. Dixon Diary, 4 Dec. 1944; and Churchill, op. cit., vi, p. 252.
16. Churchill, op. cit., vi, p. 252.
17. ibid.
18. Dixon Diary.
19. Churchill, op. cit., vi, p. 337.
20. William D. Leahy, *I Was There* (New York, 1950) pp. 315–16; and Avon Papers, FO 954/23, PRO.
21. *House of Commons Debates* (Hansard), cdviii, cols. 1267–1345; and Nigel Nicolson (ed.), *Harold Nicolson: Diaries and Letters, 1939–1945* (London, 1967) p. 437.
22. Avon Papers, FO 954/23, PRO.
23. ibid.
24. ibid.
25. ibid.
26. The Earl of Avon *Memoirs: The Reckoning* (London, 1965) p. 25.
27. Eisenhower Papers, Abilene, Kansas.
28. Some of the material in this chapter first appeared in the author's *Anthony Eden: A Biography* (Allen Lane, London, 1981). Permission to republish here is gratefully acknowledged. For acknowledgements relating to primary copyright material see the Preface to *Anthony Eden*.

4 Socialist Countries and Some Problems of the Eastern Mediterranean

György Réti

Alvin Z. Rubinstein, an American Professor, has written:

> The Soviet position in the eastern Mediterranean has greatly improved over the past decade or so partly because of the sharp increase in Soviet naval power and military capability, but mainly because of the changed perceptions of the Soviet threat by regional actors and the political skill with which the Soviet Union has responded to regional instability. Moscow has resorted to diplomacy – not power – to weaken NATO's southern flank, it has taken advantage of troubles in the alliance and shifts in the attitudes of ruling elites . . . The oft-expressed fear that the Soviet navy is somehow on the verge of interdicting the maritime routes in the Mediterranean, the Red Sea or the Gulf in order to cut the West's oil supply, needs to be put in perspective: there is nothing to suggest that the Soviets are about to start a war in such a way – for that is what would happen – and the reasons that would motivate Soviet interdiction are never specified. Scenarios, like actors, should not be taken too seriously.[1]

The present writer, while not agreeing with all his conclusions concurs with Rubinstein's objective method of thinking which differs from general Western thinking about the Soviet threat all over the world, including the Mediterranean. Rubinstein believes in the 'Soviet threat' but 'doesn't take it too seriously'. The present writer does not believe in it at all. Nor does the present writer believe in the possibility of a localised war between the two blocs in the Mediterranean. This area involves such great interests of the two blocs, including alliance obligations and oil supplies, that a conflict between them would surely cause a new world war.

Concerning the so-called 'Soviet threat' in the Eastern Mediterranean another American expert, H. L. Chambers, has written:

> The current US military presence is related to the NATO commitment and is justified on the basis of the need to deter Soviet aggression against Greece and Turkey . . . The Soviet naval threat seriously constrains US freedom of action to conduct operations in the Mediterranean area and in the Middle East.[2]

But why should the United States have more major freedom of action than the Soviet Union in an area which is much nearer to Moscow than to Washington!

The present writer agrees with Rubinstein that 'Moscow appreciates that overmilitarizing the environment in the eastern Mediterranean can be detrimental to its political aims'. That is why Greece and Turkey 'tend to take a far more relaxed view of the Soviet military presence than their partners in Western and Northern Europe and for the moment none of NATO's southern members sees any immediate Soviet threat to its vital national interests'. He continues:

> Greece and Turkey, the keys to eastern Mediterranean, have reason of their own for downgrading the Soviet threat. Their historical animosity exploded in July 1974 over Cyprus and has simmered ever since. Preoccupied with each other, at odds with Washington, disappointed in Western Europe's assistance, though hardpressed for alternatives, each casts about for supporters. At present neither fears a Soviet attack. Instead both are engaged in serious efforts to respond to Moscow's overtures for improved relations: witness the visits by high-ranking Turkish and Greek officials to the Soviet Union . . . For almost two decades, Greece and Turkey have experienced steadily improving relations with their Communist neighbours. The borders have been quiet . . . Athens's generally pro-Arab position on the Arab–Israeli conflict predisposed it to view the

suddenly expanded Soviet naval deployments more as a function of the Soviet–American rivalry in the Middle East than a
threat to Greece. A similar attitude, to a lesser degree, marked
Ankara's position.[3]

The present writer also agrees with the following conclusions
also drawn by Rubinstein:

(a) political reasons account for the improved Soviet position in
    the Eastern Mediterranean;
(b) political considerations more than military ones underlie
    Soviet moves and strategy in the Mediterranean;
(c) NATO's southern flank has been weakened primarily as a
    result of strains within NATO itself;
(d) the Soviet military build-up may not pose as immediate and
    direct a threat to the future of the alliance as the profound
    economic, social and political problems currently facing the
    members of the southern flank, to which must be added Italy
    and Portugal.[4]

The present writer disagrees, however, with Rubinstein's final
conclusions that 'the key to a secure Mediterranean lies in a stable
southern flank'.[5] As Soviet columnist Lev Bezimensky wrote in
Moscow's *New Times*, 'what the Mediterranean can and must be is
not the "southern flank of NATO", not a "theatre of operations",
but the southern flank of the process of detente'.[6] The Soviet
Union and other socialist countries have made many proposals
pointing in this direction. That is why Greece and Turkey have no
fears of a Soviet threat!

Rubinstein wrote that Moscow has helped its own policy by skilful diplomacy.[7] The culmination of this skilful diplomacy was the
visits of the Turkish and Greek Prime Ministers to Moscow in June
1978 and in October 1979. The joint communiqué, published
after Konstantin Karamanlis's visit, stated:

The 'two sides', exchanging opinions on questions concerning
the situation in the Mediterranean, emphasised the need to do
away with the sources of conflict and tension in the area and
expressed their readiness to undertake constructive efforts to
strengthen peace, security and cooperation there. They expressed particular anxiety over the situation in Cyprus and stressed

the need for a just solution to the problem in the interests of its population, of security in the Eastern Mediterranean and of international détente. The Soviet Union and Greece confirmed the urgent need for the speediest settlement of the Cyprus issue on the basis of respect for the independence, sovereignty and territorial integrity of the Republic of Cyprus and its policy of non-alignment and for the implementation of the relevant decisions of the UN General Assembly and Security Council.[8]

Apart from the allusions to UN decisions, similar views were expressed during the Soviet–Turkish talks too. It is not the fault of the Soviet Union that Greece and Turkey cannot agree on the same basis among themselves!

The security of the Eastern Mediterranean is strongly correlated with the security of the whole Mediterranean and of Europe. Limitations of space prevent the listing here of all the initiatives of the Soviet Union and of other socialist countries aiming at this goal. It is only possible here to recall the declaration of the latest summit of the leaders of the Warsaw Treaty states, held on 14 and 15 May 1980. Concerning Mediterranean issues, the declaration stated:

> The states represented at the meeting of the Political Consulta-tive Committee consistently advocate realization of measures in the sphere of military détente also in other parts of Europe as well as in the Mediterranean. Relevant steps for the Mediterranean area could envisage the extension to it of confidence-building measures, reduction of troops in that area, withdrawal from the Mediterranean Sea of warships with nuclear weapons on board, renunciation of the deployment of nuclear weapons on the terri-tory of Mediterranean European and non-European non-nuclear states, which would accord with the spirit of the Helsinki Final Act. The Warsaw Treaty states are ready for serious and business-like negotiations on all these issues.[9]

For ensuring reliable and unimpeded use of the principal inter-national sea lanes, the declaration proposes 'to start examining, for example within the UN framework, the question of limiting and scaling down the level of military presence and military activity in the areas concerned, be it in the Atlantic, Indian or Pacific Oceans, the Mediterranean Sea or the Persian Gulf'.[10] It is now NATO's turn to give a positive and constructive response to these intiatives!

The present writer's country, Hungary, being very close to the Mediterranean, is much interested in this region becoming one of peace, good-neighbourliness and co-operation. Hence Hungary − as a member of the Warsaw Treaty Organisation − took an active role in promoting the aforementioned and other intiatives aiming at these goals.

The Hungarians are very anxious about the fact that this area is more and more over-militarised, and has become a hot-bed of many international tensions, for example the Arab−Israeli and the Greek−Turkish conflicts. Precisely because this is the case the present writer considers it is not worth linking the very complicated question of European security with the problems of the non-European Mediterranean countries. Nevertheless there is clearly a very strong correlation between security in Europe and in the Mediterranean. Hence the strengthening of security in the Mediterranean area will be an important contributory factor to the process of European security (and vice-versa).

Concerning the question of Cyprus, on many occasions − among them Premier György Lázár's visit to Turkey and Karamanlis's visit to Budapest − the Hungarian side stressed the urgency of finding a settlement for this question on the basis of respect for the independence, sovereignty, territorial integrity and non-alignment of the Republic of Cyprus, and the implementation of the relevant resolutions of the United Nations.

Within the framework of bilateral relations, fruitful co-operation has been established between Hungary and the Mediterranean countries, in political, economic, commercial, cultural and scientific fields. In the past decade the volume of Hungarian commerce with Italy, Greece and Turkey has been nearly tripled, and there is a growing number of joint economic undertakings.

For promoting mutual acquaintance Hungary exchanges cultural works on a regular basis and creates interest in increased mutual knowledge of various cultural heritages. In Hungarian universities provision is made for the teaching of languages used in the Mediterranean countries. Co-operation between scientific institutions of Hungary and these countries has also intensified. An increased tourist traffic has contributed to a better understanding and acquaintance between the Hungarians and the Mediterranean peoples.

Hungary's co-operation with the Mediterranean countries is based on a whole series of interstate agreements and treaties. The present writer accordingly considers that Hungary's fruitful co-operation with the Mediterranean countries is a modest contribution to better understanding and building confidence between Mediterranean and non-Mediterranean countries, and between countries belonging to various social systems.

After the Western summit in Venice, the Italian weekly *Relazioni Internazionali* published an article with the title 'Occidente in Gondola' ('The West in a Gondola'). The present writer believes that one of the main conclusions of the ISODARCO meeting in Venice should be that now — at a time of all-round interdependence — all of humankind is in one gondola called 'Globe'. He hopes — but he is not sure — that this gondola will not sink in the blue waters of the Mediterranean or in other seas of this world.

Notes

1. Alvin Z. Rubinstein, 'The Soviet Union and the Eastern Mediterranean: 1968–1978', *Orbis*, XXIII (1979–80) pp. 299–300.
2. See US Army War College, *National Security and Détente* (New York, 1976) pp. 101–4.
3. Rubinstein, op. cit., pp. 302–6.
4. ibid., pp. 313–14.
5. ibid., p. 315.
6. *New Times*, no. 20 (1979) p. 6.
7. Rubinstein, op. cit., p. 312.
8. *International Affairs*, no. 12 (Moscow, 1979) p. 94.
9. *New Times*, no. 21 (1980) p. 29.
10. ibid., p. 31.

5 Confidence-Building Measures in the Balkans and the Eastern Mediterranean

Hans Günter Brauch

Introduction

The Balkans or South-Eastern Europe have been known for centuries as the powder-keg of Europe. For the purpose of this chapter we include the territories of Bulgaria, Romania, Albania, Yugoslavia, Greece and Turkey as well as Cyprus and parts of the south-western and southern military districts of the Soviet Union (Carpathia, Odessa, Kiev, North Caucasus and Transcaucasus).[1] Hungary may be included either in an arms control regime for Central Europe or for South-Eastern Europe. According to Stephen Larrabee:

> The Balkans . . . have historically been one of the most volatile areas in world politics. In contrast to the Nordic area, geographic proximity has not led to historic affinity. Whereas a homogeneity of peoples, languages and cultures has produced a common heritage on the Scandinavian peninsula that has inspired and facilitated close regional co-operation, in the Balkans such elements have been sorely lacking. Here ethnic, linguistic, religious and cultural diversities have impeded efforts at regional co-operation and have bred deep-seated hatreds that have smouldered beneath the surface, periodically erupting to threaten security in the area.[2]

For centuries the Balkans have been a battle-ground for rival empires, religions and ideologies: between Greeks and Romans, the Ottomans and the Habsburg Empire, Western capitalism and Eastern state socialism. After the First World War the national boundaries of the Balkan states were drawn ignoring the ethnic identities of the Balkan peoples. No single Balkan country emerged as a mono-ethnic entity. In the interwar period and after the Second World War major powers have sought to exploit irredentist goals and local tensions in order to enlarge their own influence in the region.

After the Second World War, the Balkan region became a microcosm of the world, reflecting the superpower and bloc rivalries between East and West, the Soviet Union and the United States, but also the ideological schism within the socialist camp between Stalin and Tito in 1948 and between the Soviet Union and China and the traditional rivalry between the NATO members Greece and Turkey.

Soviet pressure on Turkey to revise the Montreux Convention of 1936 and territorial claims against the Turkish provinces of Kars and Ardahan and a civil war in Greece (sponsored by Titoist Yugoslavia from 1946 to 1949) prompted US President Harry Truman to replace Great Britain as the dominant Western power in the Eastern Mediterranean, and with the Truman Doctrine he established the United States as the major military factor in the region, effectively dividing the Balkans into two spheres of influence.[3] With the emergence of a major joint enemy, the Soviet Union, the two former rivals, Greece and Turkey, joined NATO in 1952 and co-operated on military and political issues within the framework of a multilateral alliance. With the emerging dispute over Cyprus in the 1960s and 1970s and the erosion of Cold War tensions, a process of disintegration on NATO's southern flank developed after 1974: Greece abandoned military integration in NATO and Turkey closed down American military installations on its territory after an American weapons embargo against Turkey in 1975. Both Greece[4] and Turkey[5] tried to balance their one-sided military and political dependence on the United States by improved relations with the Soviet Union, closer economic co-operation with the European Economic Community and by improved political ties with the Arab world.

Within the socialist camp, the process of disintegration started as early as 1948 with the split between Stalin and Tito that led to an independent Yugoslav way to socialism and to Belgrade's close foreign policy orientation with the non-aligned movement. Albania denounced Tito's ideological betrayal in 1948 and turned to the Soviet Union becoming a full member of the Warsaw Treaty Organisation (WTO) in 1955. With the emerging ideological schism between the Soviet Union and China, however, Enver Hoxha broke with Nikita Khrushchev in 1961 and formed an alliance with China in 1962, although Albania did not formally leave the WTO until 1968. After Hungary's search for greater independence had been stopped by Soviet tanks in 1956, Romania started its search for greater autonomy in foreign and military affairs after 1964, becoming a major proponent of a more independent, national way to socialism within the framework of closer multilateral political and economic co-operation in the Balkans. This has left Bulgaria as the only reliable Soviet ally in an area that was once a bulwark of Soviet influence.

With the increasing processes of disintegration, both within NATO and the WTO, two contradictory trends emerged in the Balkans during the 1970s. First, there was an intensification of ethnic conflicts and irredentist claims, such as those involving Yugoslavia and Bulgaria over Macedonia, Yugoslavia and Albania concerning the Albanian minority in Kosovo, Romania and Hungary about the Hungarian minority in Transylvania and Greece and Albania over the Greek minority in Epirus. Secondly, there were efforts aiming at closer Balkan co-operation and inter-Balkan relations that led to the first all-Balkan conference in January 1976 in Athens.[6]

The Balkans has been an area of utmost strategic importance for the Soviet Union, United States and Western Europe. With the emergence of the Middle East and the Persian Gulf as major trouble spots in East–West relations and in world politics in general, the strategic importance of the Balkans has even increased. For centuries, access to the Mediterranean waters via the Dardanelles has been a permanent interest of Russia and the Soviet Union. In the nuclear age, the importance of the Straits for the Soviet navy and for its strategic naval forces has increased. For both superpowers, the Balkans serve as important air and naval supply lines to the Middle East. During the October War in 1973 both superpowers had to obtain permission to overfly certain Balkan countries in order to supply their Middle East allies.

Following the Iranian Revolution the strategic importance of

Turkey for the United States and for NATO has increased: 'All the natural routes (land, sea, and air) from the Black Sea to the Mediterranean and from the Balkans to the Persian Gulf lead across Turkey, and in some cases through the Straits. Because of her very location, Turkey has always protected and is still protect-ing the Middle East–Persian Gulf area against the threats coming from the north.'[7] American intelligence-gathering facilities in Turkey provide NATO 'with information about Soviet long-range systems, theater nuclear weapons systems, movements of Soviet forces within the Soviet Union and in Eastern Europe, and the Soviet naval and air operations in the Black Sea area'.[8] Both from Turkey and Greece, American fighter bombers with nuclear weapons (F-4 and F-104)[9] can successfully hit Soviet targets along the Black Sea and in the Caucasus.

As a bordering land power, the Soviet Union in times of crisis and conflict has a considerable advantage both in land and air operations. But without control of the Straits, the flexibility of its navy, even in the Mediterranean, is severely hampered. Though the United States has a severe disadvantage in any potential land operation in South-Eastern Europe, given the many naval bases in the area, NATO's naval advantage in the Mediterranean to some observers still appears to be considerable.[10]

Given the many unresolved ethnic, territorial and political conflicts and the ideological disputes in the Balkan region, may a subregional arms control regime be contemplated that may have some chance for gradual political implementation? Though the homogeneity of the Northern region is certainly lacking, joint efforts for intra-regional functional co-operation in such matters as tourism, medicine and folklore developed during the 1970s, leading to a first all-Balkan conference in Athens in January 1976 with all countries – with the exception of Albania – participat-ing. But, given deteriorating Soviet–American and East–West relations in general, it may take several years until some of the con-ceptual suggestions contained in this paper may be realistically tested.

Two approaches to decrease the conflict potential within the region and to induce intra-regional co-operation may be con-sidered for the 1980s. First, we may see bilateral efforts at conflict resolution, for example between Greece and Turkey over Cyprus and the Aegean disputes or between Yugoslavia and Bulgaria over the Macedonian question. Secondly, there may be multilateral efforts at confidence-building, stabilisation, conflict prevention, arms limitation and troop reduction. Here our focus will primarily be on the latter, though we shall not neglect the potential of confidence-building for the solution of bilateral conflicts such as that between Greece and Turkey in the Aegean Sea. Within the framework of a European Disarmament Conference, a subregional negotiation structure for South-Eastern Europe and specific militarily-relevant measures for the Balkan region will be developed. The suggestions in this chapter are primarily of a conceptual nature and they may become of political relevance in the medium term, as steps towards the longer-term goal of a region of cooperation and peace which will contain no weapons of mass destruction.

The present paper is based on three general premises. First, arms control in its present form focusing on quantitative imbalances has essentially failed. Secondly, continuation both of the present trends in arms procurement and deployment and of the present arms control approach may either lead to financial bankruptcy or to a major military confrontation. Conflicts in the Third World, or even on the southern flank of NATO, may spill over to Central Europe with the potential to escalate to an all-out nuclear war. Thirdly, both confidence-building measures and a European Disarmament Conference are being suggested as elements of a conceptual alternative and as a new framework for a regional strategy of conflict resolution, war avoidance, troop reduction and arms limitation in Europe.

The Present Military Balance in South-Eastern Europe

Military balances may be developed both for illustrative or legitimatising purposes. Basic to each effort to compare the military potential within a region are the open and tacit assumptions, the definitions and the reliability of the sources. In our comparison we rely exclusively on Western sources in the absence of generally available sources from WTO states. Besides the six genuine Balkan states (Albania, Bulgaria, Greece, Romania, Turkey and Yugoslavia) we also include the armed forces of Hungary and Cyprus and we provide, to the extent that this is possible, data on Soviet forces in the adjacent military districts in the Soviet Union and data on American naval forces in the Mediterranean. Our

South-Eastern Europe after Tito

data are based on recent issues of the Stockholm International Peace Research Institute (SIPRI) *Yearbook,* of *The Military Balance* from the International Institute for Strategic Studies (IISS) and on *World Military and Social Expenditures* by Ruth Sivard.[11] In our general comparison we use the category of military expenditure in absolute terms and as a percentage of government expenditure, of the gross national product, the number of soldiers and the cost of each soldier. And we shall also provide data on forces of the superpowers stationed in the vicinity of the potential area of conflict (see Tables 4.1–4.3).

TABLE 4.1   *Military Expenditure and Military Manpower in the Balkans*[12]

	Bulgaria	Romania	Hungary	Albania	Yugo-slavia	Cyprus	Greece	Turkey
Military expenditure in billion $								
IISS (1980)	1140	1470	1080		3634		1770	2591[a]
SIPRI (1979)	(666)	(1064)	791	204	(2416)	(174)	(2281)	(1968)
Sivard (1977)	599	972	738	137	2097	25	1523	2700
Military expenditure per capita in $								
IISS (1980)	128	66	101		164		236	58[a]
Sivard (1977)	68	45	69	55	96	41	164	63
Military expenditure as % of government spending								
IISS (1980)	6.0	4.0	3.8		56.9		19.8	15.6[a]
Military expenditure as % of gross national product								
IISS (1979)	2.1	1.4	2.1		5.6[b]		6.9[b]	9.0[b]
SIPRI (1975)	3.0	1.7	2.4		5.9	2.8	6.5	(4.6)
Soldiers in thousand								
IISS (1980)	149.0	184.5	93.0		264.0		181.5	567.0
Expenditure per soldier ($)								
Sivard (1977)	4020	5400	7165	2915	8065	2500	7615	5807

Notes: a = Data for 1979 not 1980
        b = Data for 1975 not 1979

TABLE 4.2 *Deployment of Soviet forces in adjacent European military districts*[13]

Soviet Army: 1 825 000 soldiers; 46 tank divisions; 119 motor rifle divisions; 8 airborne divisions.

Soviet divisions deployed in:

Central and Eastern Europe	30 divisions
European USSR Military Districts	67 divisions
Central USSR	6 divisions
Southern USSR	24 divisions
Sino-Soviet border	46 divisions
Afghanistan	6 divisions

Soviet forces deployed in military districts neighbouring the Balkans:
Carpathia: (11 divisions) 2 tank, 9 motor rifle divisions
Odessa: (7 divisions) 6 motor rifle and 1 airborne division
Kiev: (11 divisions) 7 tank and 4 motor rifle divisions
North Caucasus: (6 divisions) 1 tank and 5 motor rifle divisions
Transcaucasus: (12 divisions) 11 motor rifle, 1 airborne divisions

About half of the Soviet divisions in European USSR are in category 1 or 2. Most of the divisions in southern USSR are in category 3.

Soviet Navy: 433 000 troops; 289 major surface ships; 257 cruise missile and attack submarines.

Black Sea Fleet: 25 submarines; 85 major surface combat ships; 90 bombers.

Soviet Air Force: 475 000 troops.
Tactical air force: 195 000 troops, some 5000 combat aircraft (16 air armies)
Military transport aviation: 125 000 troops, 1550 aircraft
Long-range air force: 45 000 troops, 850 combat aircraft.
Five air armies are deployed in the five military district neighbouring the Balkans.

TABLE 4.3 *Deployment of US forces in the Mediterranean*[14]

US Army: 774 000 troops
US Army deployed in:
Europe: 206 400

Greece:	800
Turkey:	1000
Italy:	4000
(Mediterranean)	5800 troops

US Navy: 528 000 troops, 173 major combat ships, 81 attack submarines.

US Navy deployed in Mediterranean: Sixth Fleet, 5 submarines, 2 aircraft carriers, 12 surface combatants.

US Air Force: 555 100 troops

US Air Force deployed in Europe: 75 400
The 16th Air Force is deployed in the Mediterranean (Spain, with units in Italy, Greece and Turkey).

A. G. Platias and R. J. Rydell provide the following figures for nuclear-capable delivery systems presently deployed in the Balkan region:[15]

Greece: about 56 F-4 and 31 F-104G fighter bombers (long-range TNF); about 240 155mm howitzers; an unknown number of 8 inch howitzers; about 8 Honest John (surface-to-surface); and an unknown number of Nike-Hercules surface-to-air missiles (short-range TNF).
Turkey: about 49 F-4 and 30 F-104S fighter-bombers (long-range TNF); about 190 155mm howitzers; an unknown number of 8 inch howitzers; 18 Honest John and 170 Nike-Hercules missiles (short-range TNF).
Romania: 30 FROG SSM and 20 SCUD SSM (short-range TNF).
Bulgaria: 36 FROG and 20 STUD (short-range TNF).

Not included in this comparison is the number of carrier-based nuclear-capable aircraft belonging to the US Sixth Fleet cruising in the Mediterranean. There are no figures available on the number of nuclear launchers and warheads presently deployed in the five adjacent Soviet military districts.

Political efforts at arms limitation and troop reductions focusing on the Balkan region cannot focus solely on the forces of the six to eight countries in the region. They will have to take into account both the Soviet forces deployed in the military districts: Carpathia, Odessa, Kiev, North Caucasus and Transcaucasus and the American forces stationed in the Mediterranean region as well as the present nuclear balance in the Balkans.

Past Arms Control Efforts in the Balkan Region

In the period of the Cold War (1946–62) the conflict between East and West, between those countries belonging to WTO (Bulgaria, Romania, Hungary and Albania) and those belonging to NATO (Greece and Turkey) did not permit subregional arms control negotiations. In September 1957 Romania proposed a meeting of the heads of state of all Balkan countries to conclude a treaty on the 'transformation of the Balkans into a zone of peace and collaboration'. Although this so-called 'Stoica-Plan' appeared consonant with Khushchev's desire to restore an atmosphere of peaceful coexistence in the aftermath of the Soviet intervention in Hungary, Gheorghe Gheorghiu-Dej's primary goal was securing the withdrawal of Soviet armed forces from Romania.[16] In June 1959, after NATO's decision to deploy long-range theatre nuclear forces in Europe, Romania suggested a denuclearisation of the Balkans. As a tactical reaction to NATO's decisions on the deployment of TNF in Greece and Turkey, the Soviet Union reiterated its call for a nuclear-weapon-free zone (NWFZ) in the Balkans on several occasions between 1959 and 1963. The Soviet proposal of 1959 for a NWFZ in the Balkans and in the Adriatic Sea was supported by Albania, Bulgaria, Romania and Yugoslavia, but for obvious reasons it was rejected by the United States and its NATO allies. During the Conference of the Non-Nuclear-Weapons States in 1968, Bulgaria and Yugoslavia supported the Romanian proposal for a NWFZ in the Balkans and in the Mediterranean. In 1972 Romania tabled the proposal for a conference of Balkan states to deal with a NWFZ in the Balkans at the Conference of the Committee on Disarmament (CCD) in Geneva. Again, these proposals were rejected by all NATO countries. The motives behind these repeated suggestions for a denuclearisation of the region were not identical. While the Soviet Union had a deep security interest in removing those long-range theatre nuclear forces from the territory of Greece and Turkey that could hit its own territory, Romania fostered the same suggestions as an element of a more independent national foreign policy. Although the United States withdrew its long-range theatre nuclear missiles (Jupiter) from Turkey after the Cuban missile crisis, it rejected all proposals that would have inhibited its flexibility in Turkey and in the Eastern Mediterranean. After Hoxha's alignment with China in 1962, Albania refused to participate in all bilateral and multilateral efforts for arms limitation in Europe. Albania was the only European country not participating in the Conference on Security and Co-operation in Europe (CSCE) and was the only Balkan country to refuse to send a delegation to the all-Balkan conference in Athens in January 1976.

Since the first suggestion of 1957 and since the gradual emergence of its more independent foreign policy after 1964, Romania has become the major proponent of a multilateral approach to intra-Balkan co-operation both on the economic and on the politico-military level. After Romania's refusal to participate in the intervention in Czechoslovakia in 1968, Ceauşescu intensified relations with Yugoslavia, with the European neutral and non-aligned states, with the members of the EEC and with non-aligned countries in the Third World. In February 1976 Romania was granted membership of the Group of 77.[17] After August 1968, Romania and Yugoslavia co-ordinated their foreign and military policies in the face of a potential Soviet aggression against both countries. Stephen Fischer-Galati has written:

> These policies have included mapping of military strategy, development of economic and technological relations . . ., devising means of resistance to Russian interference in internal affairs . . ., and working out common tactics for opposing the reunification of the international communist movement under the leadership of the Kremlin. In practical terms, however, these intimate relations with Yugoslavia have offered primarily psychological solace to Romania. This deterrent force of pos-sible Yugoslav–Romanian resistance to Soviet aggression is certainly of greater psychological than military significance.[18]

Though the relations between Romania and Bulgaria have been friendly and bilateral co-operation increased on the economic and technological level, 'the Bulgarians shied away from all proposals which would have lessened their unflinching loyalty to Moscow and thus facilitate the consolidation of Romania's plans for in-dependence and search for security . . . Since Helsinki and the Twenty-fifth Soviet Congress, the Bulgarians, in co-ordination with Moscow, have been trying to undercut Romania's leadership in the search for initiatives designed to woo Greece and Turkey away from Romania and Yugoslavia.'[19]

Not only was Romania a major proponent of a multilateral approach to intra-Balkan co-operation in the context of the preparation of the Helsinki Final Act, but it has also pursued a strategy on military affairs and especially on confidence-building measures similar to that of the neutral and non-aligned European countries (including Yugoslavia): 'it was highly active in putting forward concrete and ambitious proposals, in supporting the pro-posals made by the delegations from the non-aligned countries and, although a member country of the Warsaw Pact, it did not hesitate, sometimes fairly bluntly, to dissociate itself from the theories of the countries of the East'.[20] During the Belgrade CSCE-Follow-Up Conference (1977–8) and during the Madrid Review

Conference (1980–1), Romania and Yugoslavia became the major supporters of an extension of confidence-building measures.[21]

The bilateral relations between Yugoslavia and its neighbours Bulgaria and Albania have not been without problems, because of the unresolved ethnic conflicts on the Macedonian minority in Bulgaria and the Albanian minority in Kosovo. During the conflict on Cyprus, Yugoslavia condemned the Turkish intervention and supported Makarios and the re-establishment of Cyprus as a non-aligned country in the Mediterranean.[22]

Bulgaria has been reluctant to participate in any close political co-operation among the six Balkan states that may somewhat modify its special relationship with the Soviet Union. Bulgaria prefers bilateral economic relations to a multilateral framework. Bulgaria obviously has been reluctant to participate in a second all-Balkan conference after the first meeting took place in Athens in 1976.[23]

The relations between Greece and its Slavonic neighbours in the Balkans and with Turkey have undergone several changes. While Yugoslavia supported the Greek Communists during the Greek Civil War, after the split between Tito and the Soviet Union, Greece, Turkey and Yugoslavia pledged in 1954 in the Balkan Pact to come to the defence of each other in the event of an outside attack. After the Soviet intervention in Czechoslovakia and after the Greek–Turkish conflict over Cyprus and the Aegean, the relations between Tito and Karamanlis improved. After Greece abandoned military integration in NATO in 1974 (it returned in 1980), its relations with the United States became more complex. At the same time the political climate between Greece and the Soviet Union improved gradually. Together with Romania and Yugoslavia, Greece became one of the major sponsors of closer intra-Balkan co-operation. After the first meeting in Athens in 1976, a second all-Balkan conference was held in Ankara in December 1979 on transport and communication problems.

As a member of NATO and of the Baghdad Pact (established in 1955 among Great Britain, Turkey, Iran, Iraq and Pakistan) Turkey played a major role in the Western strategy of containment directed against the Soviet Union. In the 1960s, however, Ankara's close co-operation with the United States deteriorated and after 1974 the conflict with Greece over Cyprus and over the control of the air space and of the territorial shelf in the Aegean intensified, leading to the brink of military confrontation between two NATO countries. Still resenting a very blunt letter from President Lyndon Johnson to the Turkish President Ismet Inonu in June 1964 and following the weapons embargo by the United States against Turkey in 1975, Turkey, as a counter-measure, ordered that twenty-six US military installations on its territory had to be closed, among them several intelligence-observation stations that were to monitor Soviet activities. When the US Congress withdrew its arms embargo against Turkey in the summer of 1978, Ankara agreed in October 1978 that four American observation stations could resume their activities.

Since the mid-1960s economic relations between Turkey and the Soviet Union have improved. During the October War in 1973 Turkey permitted the overflight of its territory by Soviet transport aircraft. In July 1976 Turkey permitted the Soviet aircraft carrier *Kiev* to cross the Straits into the Mediterranean. In April 1978, General Orgakow, the Chief of the Soviet General Staff, visited Turkey and in June 1978 Prime Minister Ecevit went to Moscow to discuss possibilities for improving bilateral economic relations. Since 1966 Turkey has initiated a process of normalisation with Albania, Bulgaria and Romania on the diplomatic and on the economic level. During the conflict with Greece over Cyprus, however, Turkey's neighbours in the Balkans were closer to the Greek position, supporting an independent Cyprus free of Turkish troops. But after returning to power, Prime Minister Ecevit started in 1978 once again to improve Turkey's bilateral relations with the other Balkan nations.[24]

Two meetings between Karamanlis and Ecevit in March and May 1978 contributed to a relaxation of tensions between the two NATO countries. In July 1978 formal bilateral talks started on the controversial issues of Cyprus and the Aegean. In October 1980 a compromise over the Aegean was reached between Greece and Turkey that satisfied the Greeks on the control of the air space in the Aegean and the Turks on naval command arrangements in the region. As a consequence, Greece rejoined the integrated military structure of NATO.[25]

This rather complex set of bilateral relations among the six Balkan nations has not so far permitted a multilateral approach to security and arms control. However, the careful initiatives for closer intra-regional co-operation on the functional and on the economic level together with the first two all-Balkan conferences in Athens (1976) and Ankara (1979) indicate an increasing interest in closer co-operation. Whether these careful initiatives on the functional and economic level may lead to a joint regional approach to arms control and security in the 1980s, either on the basis of the existing military alliances or in a completely different security framework, cannot be foretold. It must also be borne in mind that given that Greece became a full member of the EEC in 1981, given the conclusion of a specific arrangement between Yugoslavia and the EEC in 1980 and given the application of Turkey also to become a member of the EEC, the closer economic integration of a major portion of the Balkans with Brussels will increasingly become a factor also in intra-Balkan co-operation.

Confidence-Building Measures: a Conceptual Element for a New Arms Control Approach

Two decades of arms control negotiations between East and West did not contribute to mutual trust and confidence in East–West relations. Arms control did not lead to disarmament but, in the view of many observers, rather stimulated the qualitative arms competition. Arms control negotiations, most notably the SALT process, did not enhance confidence, they rather became a consumer of trust. In the view of Leslie Gelb, a former Director of the Bureau for Politico-Military Affairs in the US State Department: 'Arms control has essentially failed. Three decades of US–Soviet negotiations to limit arms competition have done little more than to codify the arms race.'[26] Many arms control experts expressed doubts whether arms control could realistically achieve its three traditional objectives: to reduce the likelihood of war by increasing stability, to reduce the damage of war if deterrence should fail, and to reduce the economic burden of preparing for war.[27] Differences in deployment, weaponry and size of forces of NATO and Warsaw Pact countries reflect different military strategies. Arms control negotiations that neglect these strategic differences and that are based on the assumption of a numerical balance of forces in possibly all segments of troop strength and weaponry may eventually provide a means of justifying a permanent drive for armaments. Because a regional numerical military balance may not be negotiable, those structural conditions of East–West relations that continuously make the military balance a restrictive element of arms control have to be changed.

Greater flexibility in negotiating positions does not require a total change of the strategies of both alliances. Alternative security options and a new arms control approach must not reduce the security of the nations concerned. Therefore, confidence-building measures (CBMs) to reduce the level of military confrontation must not interfere with security considerations. CBMs are no substitute for arms control and disarmament but rather a supplement and one of its preconditions. CBMs may even become a conceptual element for a new arms control approach for Europe as a whole.[28]

CBMs do not directly affect the size, weaponry and structure of military forces. Instead, CBMs aim at increasing trust and confidence between two hostile sides, making the intentions and actions of each clearer and more predictable to the other. This usually involves restrictions on the availability of armed forces, their actions and deployment in certain areas. Since confidence-building between enemies is a slow process, CBMs involve many small steps taken over a long time. CBMs in dealing with the causes and the intellectual foundations of worst-case thinking in military affairs should perform at least three functions:

> improve the general international climate with a view to facilitating different forms of progress in the striving for arms control and disarmament, e.g. by the reduction of tensions in the international system;
> reduce the risks of war by increasing communication and predictability in an international system so as to lessen the risks of acute conflicts being sparked off by misunderstandings or misinterpretations of the military and political behavior of states;
> contribute to arms control and disarmament by reducing the importance of various factors accelerating the arms race.[29]

Though the term 'confidence-building measures' was already introduced by President Dwight D. Eisenhower in 1955 in the context of his 'Open Skies' proposal, it took another twenty years until CBMs became a part of the Final Act of the Conference on Security and Co-operation in Europe. The Document on CBMs of the Helsinki Final Act of 1975 includes two measures entailing a high degree of obligation: prior notification of major military manoeuvres, involving more than 25 000 troops; and exchange of observers, voluntarily and on a bilateral basis. Measures involving a relatively low degree of commitment include: prior notification of smaller military manoeuvres; prior notification of military movements; and other confidence-building measures.[30]

On a subregional level, CBMs were introduced as associated measures into the Mutual Balanced Force Reduction Talks (MBFR) by NATO countries as early as 1973. On the global level, at the 1978 UN Special Session on Disarmament (UNSSOD), a number of CBM proposals were introduced. These included a working paper by West Germany which suggested the establishment of regional CBMs as a first step to a global convention on CBMs. In May 1978, at the UNSSOD, France tabled a proposal for a Conference on Disarmament in Europe (CDE) which would 'aim in the first stage at building trust among all countries of Europe by instituting measures to provide appropriate information and notification and in the second stage at achieving a genuine reduction in weaponry within the geo-strategic complex of Europe from the Atlantic to the Urals'. After the UNSSOD, France reformulated its proposal slightly and placed it into the context of the CSCE. At the first stage, the CDE, the following CBMs should be considered:

Measures of mutual information (exchange of data on force structures and on the deployment of forces; exchange of data on military budgets; exchange of military observers to manoeuvres, visits of navies; exchange of military instructors and better working conditions for military attachés).
Measures to prevent surprise attacks (prior notification of manoeuvres and movements for land, air and amphibious forces involving one or two divisions more than a month in advance).
Stabilising measures (limitation of manoeuvres for air and land forces involving more than 40 000 to 60 000 men).[31]

During the Second CSCE-Review Conference in Madrid five proposals were introduced that support the idea that a European Disarmament Conference should be established in the context of the CSCE to deal with extended CBMs for the whole of Europe.[32]

Among the Balkan countries Romania and Yugoslavia have been the most fervent supporters of CBMs in the context of the CSCE. During the Madrid conference both introduced proposals for a European Disarmament Conference that differed from both the Western (French) and Eastern (Polish) proposals. In October 1979 three of the six Balkan nations, namely Greece, Romania and Yugoslavia, reported their interpretations of CBMs to the

Secretary General of the United Nations. Greece supported the regional approach to disarmament suggesting that the convening of such a regional conference 'should be left to the initiative of the States in the region' who should 'determine by themselves and on a regional basis the level of disarmament'.[33] The Romanian Government, in its detailed response, considered it necessary 'to agree on a series of transitional measures to facilitate the process of bringing about a substantial reduction in armaments and achieving the ultimate objective, namely disarmament and, primarily, nuclear disarmament'. It therefore suggested a set of political and military measures both at the international and at the regional level and principles for the identification and negotiation of CBMs. For Romania the CBMs in the Final Act of Helsinki 'represent an initial phase in the establishment of a climate of peace and security, detente and co-operation in Europe'. 'Their implementation has, however, proved that they are insufficient to bring about real progress with regard to the strengthening of European security.' Romania suggested negotiations on the following proposals:

(a) The freezing of military expenditures, military establishments and armaments.
(b) No additional deployment of foreign troops in other countries, the gradual reduction of foreign troops and the dismantling of military bases.
(c) The establishment between the two military blocs of a zone, on both sides, in which no foreign armies or weapons of any kind may be stationed, where no military manoeuvre or show of force may take place and which should only contain limited forces belonging to the countries in whose territory the demilitarised zone would be established.
(d) A continuous reduction in the activities of the military blocs and the creation of conditions for their simultaneous liquidation.
(e) Non-use of nuclear weapons by nuclear weapons states against non-nuclear weapons states.
(f) Reduction and discontinuance of military manoeuvres and, in general, of any show of force in the proximity of the national frontiers of other countries.
(g) The notification of troop movements and of naval and air manoeuvres.
(h) The establishment of nuclear-weapon-free zones of mutual

understanding and peaceful co-operation in various parts of Europe. In this respect, Romania, in association with the other states of the Balkan region, is working for the transformation of this zone into a zone of peace, good-neighbourly relations, confidence and mutually advantageous co-operation.

(i) The conclusion of a general European treaty whereby all the signatories of the Final Act of Helsinki would undertake to renounce the use or the threat of the use of force and not to be the first to use either nuclear or conventional weapons against the others.[34]

The Yugoslav Government proposed four groups of CBMs: (1) information on military activities; (2) restraint from military activities that can cause suspicion; (3) limitation of military activities; and (4) the thwarting of terrorist activities. As far as information measures are concerned, 'with some of its neighbours, Yugoslavia has developed a practice of mutual notification of military manoeuvres and other activities, particularly in border regions'.[35] While Greece and Turkey supported the proposals of their NATO allies, Bulgaria gave full support to the suggestions by the Soviet Union and the WTO states. However, so far no multilateral meeting has taken place on the application of specific CBMs for the Balkan region.

A European Disarmament Conference: the Structure for a Regional Arms Control Approach

The foreign ministers of the WTO states responded in May 1979 to the French proposal for a Conference on Disarmament in Europe, suggesting a Conference on Disarmament and Military Detente in Europe. In November 1979 the member states of the EEC accepted a somewhat modified version of the French proposal and in June 1980 the NATO Council at its Ankara meeting agreed on four conditions for a mandate for a Conference on Disarmament in Europe to be negotiated at the second CSCE-Review Conference in Madrid: the CDE should deal in its first phase with CBMs that should be militarily significant, binding, verifiable and covering the whole of Europe from the Atlantic to the Urals. On 16 February 1981 the Reagan Administration dropped the previous reservations of the Carter Administration on the French proposal and on 23 February 1981 Brezhnev indicated the readiness of the Soviet Union to extend the area of application of future CBMs up to the Urals.

At the end of the first session in Madrid, France, Poland, Sweden and two Balkan states, Yugoslavia and Romania, tabled five different proposals for the establishment of a European Disarmament Conference and for future types of CBMs to be negotiated in this new European framework. The French proposal for a CDE reiterated the previous NATO proposal for a CDE that should deal with three types of CBMs: information, stabilisation and verification measures. The Eastern counter-proposal tabled by Poland remained rather vague and avoided any specification of conditions for a mandate. According to the Swedish proposal the CDE should deal in its first phase with CBMs that should satisfy the following criteria: they should be controllable, politically binding and militarily significant. In the CDE's second phase dealing with the limitation of conventional weapons, however, the nuclear factor should be also considered. According to the Yugoslav proposal, the CDE should focus in its first phase on limitations of military activities, on efforts to end the arms race and on contributing to military disengagement. In its second phase the CDE should deal with disarmament measures focusing both on conventional and tactical nuclear weapons. Romania, in its proposal for a conference on confidence-building and disarmament, suggested that this conference of all thirty-five CSCE members should start in its first phase with measures of confidence-building and stability, progressing gradually to efforts for military disengagement and disarmament.[36] Neither of these five conference proposals offered specific recommendations for a subregional approach to arms reduction.

Considering the structure of the proposed CDE we distinguish among three different models:

1. the *two-phase model* initially introduced by the French President in May 1978 and now accepted in all five proposals mentioned above;
2. the *model of different baskets* that was introduced first by François Mitterrand in December 1977 when he suggested five baskets of a European Disarmament Conference dealing with CBMs, reduction of troops, limitation of military budgets and of conventional and nuclear weapons;

3. the *model of different levels* that combines the security interest of the European region with the specific arms control potentials and security interests of subregions, such as Scandinavia, Central Europe, the Balkans and the Mediterranean.

In previous articles the present writer has preferred the third model.[37] The Conference on Disarmament in Europe should consist of a plenary of all thirty-five CSCE signatories and Albania and of three or four subregional bodies dealing with the Northern, Central, South-Eastern and Mediterranean regions. On the plenary level all CDE-member states should aim at the development of rules of political behaviour (general principles of international law) and of military behaviour (such as confidence-building measures, rules on crisis management, protection of civilians in war). The plenary level could develop basic rules for a European security policy and it could establish European institutions for verification and crisis management. Arms control or arms reduction talks, however, should take place on the second subregion level. We distinguish among four subregional forums:

1. NALT: Northern Arms and Troop Limitation Talks;
2. MBFR: Mutual Balanced Force Reductions for Central Europe;
3. BALT: Arms and Troop Reduction Talks on the Balkans (South-Eastern Europe);
4. MALT: Arms and Troop Reduction Talks dealing with the Naval Forces in the Mediterranean.

While it may be advantageous for the European Disarmament Conference to be located in Geneva to permit a close co-ordination of the global disarmament discussions in the framework of the Conference on Disarmament (CD), the subregional arms reduction talks should take place in capitals of neutral and non-aligned countries. Thus NALT may meet in Stockholm, MBFR in Vienna, BALT in Belgrade and MALT in Malta.

NALT could either cover the territory of the littoral states of the Baltic Sea (narrow alternative) or the territory of the littoral states of the Baltic Sea and of the North Sea as well. NALT I could cover the territory extending from the 4th degree of longitude up to 40th degree of longitude and from the 54th degree of latitude to the 75th degree of latitude. The following countries should participate in NALT I − on behalf of NATO: Norway, Denmark, West Germany, Great Britain and the United States; on behalf of the Warsaw Pact: the Soviet Union, Poland and the German Democratic Republic; and for the neutral and non-aligned countries: Sweden and Finland. The territory of NALT I should include the Baltic military district and a portion of the Leningrad military district of the Soviet Union. NALT II could cover the territory extending from the 45th longitude west of Greenwich up to the 50th longitude east of Greenwich (the Urals) and from the 50th degree of latitude to 80th degree of latitude. The following countries should participate in NALT II − on behalf of NATO: Norway, Denmark, West Germany, the United States, Great Britain, Iceland, the Netherlands, Belgium, France and Canada; on behalf of the Warsaw Pact: the Soviet Union, Poland, and the German Democratic Republic; the the neutral and non-aligned states: Finland, Sweden and Ireland. NALT I and NALT II could deal both with constraints for land, air and naval forces and with reductions of arms and troops deployed within the specific region. One longer-term negotiation goal could be the establishment of a nuclear-weapon-free zone covering Norway, Denmark, Sweden, Finland and the Baltic Military District of the Soviet Union.

In Central Europe the territory of MBFR (present NATO Guidelines area covering all forces deployed in West Germany, the Netherlands, Belgium, Luxembourg, the German Democratic Republic, Poland and Czechoslovakia) should be extended to include the two neutral states, Austria and Switzerland; Hungary, as well as the Soviet military districts of Carpathia (Lvov), Byelorussia (Minsk) and the Baltic (Riga); and the northern part of France from Geneva, Dijon, Paris to Le Havre. However, it is doubtful whether the Soviet Union or France will agree to such an extension.

The arms and troop limitation talks dealing with naval forces in the Mediterranean (MALT) should include all fifteen littoral states: Morocco, Algeria, Tunisia, Libya, Egypt, Israel, Lebanon, Syria, Turkey, Greece, Albania, Yugoslavia, Italy, France and Spain, the two island states Cyprus and Malta as well as the four naval nuclear powers, the United States, the Soviet Union, France and Great Britain. MALT may be only of heuristic interest for the next few years, given the many bilateral conflicts among its North African (Morrocco versus Algeria, Libya versus Egypt) and Asian (Middle East conflict) littoral states.

A Proposal for a Conference on Arms Limitation and Force Reductions in South-Eastern Europe (BALT)

The suggested conference on arms limitation and force reductions in the Balkans could either focus only on the territory of the six Balkan states, Albania, Bulgaria, Greece, Romania, Turkey and Yugoslavia (narrow alternative) or it could include the five neighbouring Soviet military district of Carpathia, Odessa, Kiev, North Caucasus, Transcaucasus (wide alternative).

The following countries should participate in either version of BALT – on behalf of NATO: Greece, Turkey and the United States; on behalf of WTO: Romania, Bulgaria and the Soviet Union; for the non-aligned states: Albania, Yugosolavia, and possibly Cyprus. BALT should focus on more restrictive CBMs (namely constraints) that seriously inhibit military flexibility for offensive operations. In the medium term, geographical restraints, such as the disengagement of offensive military capabilities, the establishment of buffer zones and of zones of reduced armaments as measures to reduce the probability of surprise attack should be considered. In the longer term, the establishment of a nuclear-weapon-free zone covering the territory of Hungary, Yugoslavia, Albania, Romania, Bulgaria, Greece, Turkey and Cyprus could be considered. Efforts at arms reductions in the Balkan region should initially focus on ground and air forces and they could include modest naval forces at a later stage.

While reductions of arms and troops may be limited to the six to eight Balkan states, all far-reaching CBMs should include the neighbouring Soviet military districts, especially the out-of-garrison activities (manoeuvres and movements) of the forty-seven Soviet divisions presently deployed in the five neighbouring Soviet military districts. However, the Soviet strategic forces should be excluded in any subregional arms control negotiation context, because they will be covered in the context of the SALT process.

A multilateral subregional arms control forum for the Balkan region should contribute to the prevention of bilateral (ethnic) conflicts or of a military confrontation between countries belonging to opposing military alliances. To be successful they would have to be complemented by bilateral solutions to existing problems. At present it may be doubtful whether both superpowers or their allies in the region would be interested in a multilateral forum that could develop a dynamic of its own if supplemented by multilateral intra-Balkan co-operation in other issue areas, especially in the field of economic co-operation. BALT would be the ideal forum for the consideration of proposals for a nuclear-weapon-free zone in South-Eastern Europe.[38]

Suggestions for Far-Reaching Confidence-Building Measures for the Balkans

CBMs for the Balkans may be applied both bilaterally and multi-laterally in order either to contribute to the resolution of existing conflicts or to facilitate efforts at arms reduction. Among the four possible options, we shall discuss the two most likely ones, namely bilateral efforts at conflict resolution and multilateral negotiations for arms reductions.

The Role of Confidence-Building Measures in Bilateral Efforts for Conflict Resolution

Platias and Rydell have counted at least eight dyadic conflicts among the six to eight Balkan states. As main bilateral conflicts they have referred to the disputes between Greece and Turkey over Cyprus, over the Aegean Sea (the continental shelf, military and civilian air traffic control, territorial waters and militarisation of the Greek Islands)[39] and over national minorities; and between Yugoslavia and Bulgaria on the status of Macedonia (territorial disputes and minorities). As potential conflicts they mentioned the disputes between Albania and Yugoslavia on the Albanian minority in Kosovo; and between Greece and Yugoslavia on the minorities in Macedonia. Less important old conflicts that might escalate to a minor confrontation are those between Bulgaria and Romania on territorial claims in the Dobrudja; between Greece and Albania on the Greek minority in Northern Epirus; between Hungary and Romania on the Hungarian minority in Transyl-vania; and between Hungary and Yugoslavia on the Hungarian minority in Voyvodina.

   The establishment of a demilitarised buffer zone in the Sinai between Israel and Egypt[40] — a geographical CBM to inhibit surprise attack operations by land forces — had a positive impact on the improvement of bilateral relations between the two former enemies. In the case of Korea, the potential merits of a CBM regime to reduce tensions and mutual fears are vitiated by the proximity of Seoul to the demilitarised zone.[41] Jonathan Alford, writing in 1980, suggested various measures by which the Aegean tension between Greece and Turkey could be reduced in order to clarify intentions and to avoid misperceptions:

> There are three flash points: Thrace, the Dodecanese and the Aegean Sea itself. Although both countries are signatories of CSCE, the rather general provisions of the Final Act need considerable refinement in the context of the Graeco-Turkish dispute. Turkey has certainly notified exercises under CSCE rules (in each case in a NATO context) but Greece is not recorded as having done so, presumably because she does not normally exercise ground forces nationally at strengths above the threshold now that she is no longer part of the NATO integrated military structure.[42]

After the agreement between Turkey and Greece in autumn 1980, hopes rose that CBMs could play a major role in a comprehensive Aegean settlement. According to Alford, the Turkish initiative in 1980 'to resolve the air traffic control dispute carries with it CBM overtones because it will inevitably cover the passage of information concerning military flights in the contested zone, but the linked questions of the fortification of the Aegean islands close to Turkey and the Turkish "Army of the Aegean" cry for some reduction of tension by CBMs which should not be difficult to design specifically for the region'.[43] For each of the eight bilateral conflicts in the Balkan different elements of political and military confidence-building efforts could contribute to peace and stability in South-Eastern Europe, a major precondition for any multilateral arms control approach.

The Role of Confidence-Building Measures in Multilateral Efforts for Arms Reduction

CBMs in Europe as a whole and more specifically in the Balkans region should be gradually extended both by unilateral steps and by subsequent contractual agreements. Some experience with specific CBMs, such as zones of limited armaments, tank-free zones or even a zone free of weapons of mass-destruction, may be made first in the Balkan region that both for historical and strategic reasons may not be applicable in other regions of Europe. In a sub-regional context for South-Eastern Europe constraints such as a limitation of the size of manoeuvres might be easier to accept than in Central Europe. Subregional CBMs as associated measures should be closely linked to efforts for arms and troop reductions.

Supplementary Confidence-Building Measures

Some of the following suggestions for short- medium- and longer-term confidence-building measures might be considered as supplements to a subregional strategy for arms and troop reductions in the Balkans.

Short-Term Confidence-Building Measures for the Balkans

Two sets of short-term CBMs for South-Eastern Europe can be distinguished.

1. *Notifications:*
   of smaller military manoeuvres and movements involving more than 10 000 or 20 000 troops;
   of naval manoeuvres and movements near territorial waters;
   of aerial manoeuvres and movements;
   extension of the date of prior notification from 21 to 30, 45 or 60 days;
   prescription of additional information to be included in the manoeuvre notification and establishment of clearly defined requirements for the notification of manoeuvres and movements and for the treatment of observers;
   publication of an annual register of planned military manoeuvres in Europe.
2. *Limitations:*
   of the size of manoeuvres to 40 000 or 60 000 troops;
   of multinational manoeuvres in border areas;
   of military manoeuvres or exercises within clearly defined border areas or even prohibition thereof.

Medium- and Longer-Term Confidence-Building Measures

In the medium-term perspective, CBMs may be extended in the context of a subregional arms control treaty. For conceptual purposes, five types of CBMs may be considered.

1. *Measures to enhance transparency and openness*   One primary goal of CBMs is an increase in openness and transparency about military activities and an increase in the exchange of information. Procedures might be developed to ensure mutual information on military budgets, on the composition of force structures and on the major objects of military research and developments. The general goal could be achieved by the following measures:

(a) agreements on standardised defence budgets as a precondition of agreements for a freeze or for proportional reductions of military expenditures;
(b) agreements on the exchange and possible publication of detailed data on the composition of forces, of command structures and of military equipment;
(c) agreements dealing with military research and development programmes by the publication of annual arms control impact statements that analyse the longer-term possible effects of ongoing programmes on the prospects for arms limitation and for detente in Europe.

Longer-term CBMs might extend these measures even further by more rigid reporting and publication requirements for military data.

2. *Geographical considerations: steps towards the establishment of buffer zones*   Geographical considerations, such as the disengagement of military alliances and of offensive military capabilities, the establishment of buffer zones and of zones of reduced armament were debated in the 1950s and 1960s as politico-military measures to reduce the probability of surprise attack options. First steps towards the establishment of buffer zones could be the limitation of manoeuvres in border areas. From the vantage point of war prevention various geographical measures might be considered as medium-term and long-term CBMs, such as limitations on the deployment of weapons in certain areas (tank-free buffer zones, NWFZs) and thinning out of forces.

3. *Efforts at institutionalisation: elements of a crisis management and verification structure*   Various unwritten rules of crisis management have been developed in the postwar period between the United States and the Soviet Union, and at least nine crisis

management agreements aimed at the reduction of the risk of a nuclear war involving the four European nuclear weapon powers have been signed. The existing crisis management regime should be extended to the non-nuclear arms control regime in Europe. The establishment of 'hot lines' (jamproof communication links) between various capitals of a region would be a step that should be supplemented in the medium term by:

(a) the establishment of a multilateral crisis management structure (the Standing Consultative Commission of SALT may provide a model of the institutionalisation);
(b) the development of procedures for the peaceful settlement of disputes (such as the Swiss proposal tabled during the first CSCE-follow-up meeting in Belgrade).

Extension of trust by the reduction of risks depends to some extent on knowledge about the implementation of agreed measures. Several steps towards that end were proposed in the 1950s, such as the establishment of observation posts at geographically important points (large ports, railway centres, motorways and airfields). These measures might be supplemented by the establishment of a European Satellite Observation Agency.

4. *Limitation of military options and agreements on military doctrine*   The previous suggestions substantially question the existing military doctrines: NATO's frontal defence and the Warsaw Pact's forward defence. In the longer term, the military doctrines generally, and certain military options specifically should become negotiable. The political goal should be the reduction of surprise attack options by increasing warning time by improved national and international reconnaissance and effective verification systems. Furthermore, joint rules should be developed on the following aspects of military behaviour:

(a) not to interfere with national technical means of verification and the inauguration of co-operative verification techniques;
(b) on 'firebreaks' in the process of escalation and on improvement of mutual communication;
(c) on the limitation of the use of military power in peacetime.

5. *Rules limiting the use and the deployment of weapons*   If the changes resulting from new conventional weapons technologies

should favour the defence over the offence in the late 1980s and early 1990s, present advantages resulting from a superiority in the number of tanks may lose their military attractiveness. As a consequence, NATO's first-use nuclear options may lose their rationale and hence their present deterrence function may be relinquishable. As longer-term CBMs the following rules appear to be negotiable:

(a) a mutual declaration of non-use and no first-use of nuclear weapons;
(b) limitation of the areas for the deployment of nuclear weapons and the declaration of nuclear-weapon-free zones;
(c) limitations on the deployment of all nuclear battlefield systems;
(d) limitations on the deployment of land-based Eurostrategic nuclear missiles.

Conclusion

Both proposals for a two-level approach to European arms control and disarmament negotiations − a Conference on Disarmament in Europe and three or four subregional forums (NALT, MBFR II, BALT and MALT), and for confidence-building measures either on a bilateral level to ease political efforts for conflict resolution or on a multilateral level to supplement subregional efforts for arms and troop reductions − require further conceptual and political refinement. Both the structural arrangement and the substantial suggestions have been introduced as conceptual elements of a new arms control approach that focuses more on the most likely military options and political scenarios that may lead to war and that avoids the over-emphasis on balances of forces and arms that have often been used in order to legitimise a levelling up as a bargaining chip in arms control negotiations.[44]

Notes

1. Although the Soviet Union is no Balkan country, the Soviet troops deployed in the five military districts bordering the Balkan region directly affect the military balance and arms control negotiations in South-Eastern Europe.
2. F. Stephen Larrabee, *Balkan Security*, Adelphi Paper no. 135 (London, 1977) p. 1.

102   *South-Eastern Europe after Tito*

3. For historical background see Robert Lee Wolf, *The Balkans in our Time* (New York, 1967); L. S. Stavrianos, *The Balkans since 1453* (New York, 1961); Charles and Barbara Jelavich (eds), *The Balkans in Transition* (Berkeley, 1963); John Gimbel, *The Origins of the Marshall Plan* (Stanford, 1976); and Thomas G. Paterson, *Soviet–American Confrontation: Postwar Reconstruction and the Origins of the Cold War* (Baltimore, 1973).
4. Klaus-Detlev Grothusen (ed.), *Handbook on South Eastern Europe*, vol. iii, *Greece* (Göttingen, 1980).
5. Duygu Bazoğlu Sezer, *Turkey's Security Policies*, Adelphi Paper no. 164 (London, 1981).
6. Larrabee, op. cit., pp. 34–7.
7. Ali L. Karaosmanoglu, 'Turkey's Defense Policy: Restraints and Choices', paper prepared for the 22nd International Studies Association Convention, Philadelphia, March 1981.
8. ibid.
9. See Athanassios G. Platias and R. J. Rydell, 'International Security Regimes: the Case of a Balkan Nuclear-free-zone', Chapter 6 in this book, pp. 105–30.
10. Wolfgang Hager, 'The Mediterranean: A Further Mare Nostrum?', *Orbis*, xvii (1973–4) pp. 231–51; Robert A. Friedlander, 'Problems of the Mediterranean: A Geopolitical Perspective', *The Yearbook of World Affairs* (London, 1978); Stefano Silvestri, 'Military Power and Stability in the Mediterranean', *Lo Spettatore Internazionale*, xiii, no. 1 (1978) pp. 5–28; Franca Gusmaroli, 'The Role of European Fleets in the Mediterranean', *Lo Spettatore Internazionale*, xiii, no. 1 (1978) pp. 67–76; Ciro E. Zoppo, 'Arms Control in the Mediterranean and European Security' in David Carlton and Carlo Schaerf (eds), *International Terrorism and World Security* (London, 1975) pp. 248–76; Ken Booth, 'Superpower Naval Disengagement in the Mediterranean', *Journal of the Royal United Services Institution for Defence Studies*, cxxiv, no. 2 (1979) pp. 28–35; Marion Smettan, 'Probleme und Politik der NATO im östlichen Mittelmeer', *Deutsche Aussenpolitik*, no. 2 (1979) pp. 49–62; Andjelko Kalpic, 'Der Mittelmeer unter dem Druck der Militärmacht', *Internationale Politik* (20 March 1973); and Lothar Ruehl, 'Entspannung und Sicherheit in Europa: Auswirkungen auf das östliche Mittelmeer' in Deutsche Gesellschaft für Friedens-und Konfliktforschung, *Jahrbuch 1979–80* (Baden-Baden, 1980) pp. 213–28.
11. SIPRI, *World Armaments and Disarmament: SIPRI Yearbook 1980* (London, 1980) pp. 19ff.; International Institute for Strategic Studies (IISS), *The Military Balance 1980–1981* (London, 1980) p. 96; and Ruth Leger Sivard, *World Military and Social Expenditures* (Leesburg, 1980).
12. For definition of exchange rates see sources listed in note 11.
13. IISS, op. cit., pp. 10ff.
14. ibid., pp. 6ff.
15. See Chapter 6, pp. 105–30.
16. Stephen Fischer-Galati, 'Foreign Policy' in Klaus-Detlev Grothusen (ed.), *Handbook on South Eastern Europe*, vol. ii, *Romania* (Göttingen, 1977) p. 211.
17. Dietrich Frenzke, 'Die rumänische Haltung zur Sicherheit und Zusammenarbeit in Europa', *Friedenswarte*, no. 1–4 (1974) pp. 55–64; and

Dietrich Frenzke, *Rumänien, der Sowjetblock und die europäische Sicherheit: Die völkerrechtlichen Grundlagen der rumänischen Aussenpolitik* (Berlin, 1975).
18. Fischer-Galati, op. cit., pp. 225–6.
19. ibid., p. 225.
20. Luigi Vittorio Ferraris (ed.), *Report on a Negotiation: Helsinki–Geneva–Helsinki, 1972–1975* (Geneva, 1979).
21. Hans Günter Brauch, *Vertrauensbildende Massnahmen und Europäische Abrüstungskonferenz: Materialen und konzeptionelle Reformüberlegungen* (Frankfurt, 1983).
22. Klaus-Detlev Grothusen, 'Die Aussenpolitik' in Klaus-Detlev Grothusen (ed.) *Handbook on South Eastern Europe*, vol. I, *Yugoslavia* (Göttingen, 1975) pp. 150–87.
23. Emil Hoffmann, *Bulgariens Balkanpolitik nach dem Zweiten Weltkrieg* (Frankfurt, 1979); and Viktor Meier, 'Bulgariens Interesse an einer Balkan-Politik', *Frankfurter Allgemeine Zeitung* (10 June 1979).
24. Udo Steinbach, *Kranker Wächter am Bosporus* (Freiburg-Würzburg, 1979).
25. *The Times*, 24 and 28 Oct. 1980.
26. Leslie Gelb, 'The Future of Arms Control – A Glass Half Full . . .', *Foreign Policy*, no. 36 (fall 1979) p. 21.
27. Christoph Bertram, *The Future of Arms Control*, Part II, *Arms Control and Technological Change: Elements of a New Approach*, Adelphi Paper no. 146 (London, 1978).
28. H. G. Brauch, 'Confidence Building Measures and Disarmament Strategy', *Current Research on Peace and Violence*, no. 3–4 (1979) pp. 114–45; and H. G. Brauch, 'The Conference on Security and Cooperation in Europe: CBMs and the CSE', *Arms Control Today* (Nov. 1980) pp. 1–4.
29. 'Building Confidence in Europe: An Analytical and Action-Oriented Study', *Bulletin of Peace Proposals*, no. 2 (1980) pp. 150–66.
30. 'Document on confidence-building measures and certain aspects of security and disarmament, including the Final Act of the Conference on Security and Cooperation in Europe' in SIPRI, *World Armaments and Disarmament: SIPRI Yearbook 1976* (London, 1976) pp. 359–62.
31. Jean Klein, 'Continuité et Ouverture dans la Politique Français en Matière de Désarmement', *Politique Étrangère*, no. 2 (1979) pp. 213–48.
32. For a German translation of the texts see Brauch, *Vertrauensbildende Massnahmen und Europäische Abrüstungskonferenz*.
33. United Nations, General Assembly, 34th Session, 1978, *Report of the Secretary-General*, p. 26.
34. ibid., pp. 38–42.
35. ibid., pp. 59–62.
36. H. G. Brauch, 'Vertrauensbildende Massnahmen: Element einer neuen Rüstungskontroll-und Abrüstungsstrategie für Europa' in *Aus Politik und Zeitgeschichte: Beilage zur Wochenzeitung das Parlament* (Bonn, 1982).
37. ibid.; and Brauch, *Vertrauensbildende Massnahmen und Europäische Abrüstungskonferenz*.
38. See Chapter 6, pp. 105–30.
39. ibid.; and Andrew Wilson, *The Aegean Dispute*, Adelphi Paper no. 155 (London, 1979–80).

40. Yair Evron, *The Role of Arms Control in the Middle East*, Adelphi Paper no 138 (London, 1977).
41. Jonathan Alford, 'Confidence Building Measures', paper for the Pugwash Symposium on New Directions in Disarmament, Wingspread, Racine, Wisconsin, 1980.
42. ibid.
43. ibid.
44. H. G. Brauch, *Entwicklungen und Ergebnisse der Friedensforschung (1969–1978): Eine Zwischenbilanz und konkrete Vorschläge für das zweite Jahrzehnt* (Frankfurt, 1979).

6 International Security Regimes: the Case of a Balkan Nuclear-Free Zone

Athanassios G. Platias and R. J. Rydell

Introduction

That the study of international regimes is undergoing a renaissance should come as no surprise to the informed observer of contemporary world affairs. The irony lies in its timing. The superpowers appear to be arming for yet another phase of the Cold War; the developing world is increasingly challenging the political and economic terms that have governed postwar North–South relations, and prolonged domestic economic hardships are threatening a resurgence of protectionism within the industrialised world. Yet despite this apparent throwback of world politics to its older semi-gladiatorial mode, students of international relations are giving renewed emphasis to the study of international co-operation as manifested in the creation and growth of regimes.

An everyday definition of a regime is 'a mode or system of rule or government'.[1] In contemporary theory of international relations, however, regimes consist of procedural and normative guides to state behaviour. These include rules, procedures, norms, principles and institutions – all artifacts of co-operative actions of nation states – which constrain the inherent tendency of countries to act exclusively in the light of short-term perceived self-interests.

Although *Realpolitik* may often lead a state to join a regime or regulate its behaviour after becoming a member, it is the Grotian rather than the Machiavellian tradition of international relations that accounts for the growth of regimes in the modern era.

International regimes have grown most recently in the areas of outer space, the oceans, telecommunications, weather modification, trade in commodities, and the protection of natural wildlife. Various types of international regimes have existed for centuries in such areas as the law of the sea, monetary affairs, trade and communications. But the technological, political and economic forces which have brought nations into these more recent 'webs of interdependence'[2] have extended deeper than ever before into provinces that had once been within the exclusive jurisdiction of national governments: arms control, domestic economic policy, export controls, collective security arrangements, foreign economic assistance and energy policy are all issue areas that are increasingly becoming co-ordinated by international regimes. It is not the existence of regimes *per se* but their incredible geographical and functional diversity that are hallmarks of world politics in this century.

According to the logic of international functionalism pioneered by David Mitrany the root causes of war and disharmony could be extricated if neglected welfare tasks could be managed on an international basis. Hence international co-operation in the relatively 'non-political' areas of health, education, environment and natural resources would develop national habits of acting with others to solve common problems; once the beneficial results emerged for all to see, 'spill-over' would occur as national political and security interests would progressively be incorporated into this liberal vision of a global 'harmony of interests'.[3] In fact, however, functionalists observed that few areas are truly non-political: national rivalries continued, albeit in different forums.

The failure of the functionalist 'spill-over' hypothesis has spawned other approaches to international regimes, including one which turns functionalism on its head and suggests the incremental development of regimes in areas that bear directly upon core security interests of states. Alliance systems, one variant of such a regime, are as old as the city-state. Other 'adversary regimes'[4] are represented in such arrangements as regional defence pacts, the SALT process, non-proliferation agreements and measures taken to restrict national development of chemical and biological weapons. Like all regimes, security regimes serve the interests of their parties by reducing uncertainty, stabilising expectations, and encouraging the 'routinisation' of conflict. Moreover, both types of regimes are shaped both by structural characteristics of international society and by the emergence of shared beliefs about the ends and means of participation in the regime.[5] Regimes will differ, however, in the extent to which these various features are balanced.

This chapter represents an effort to analyse the notion of a nuclear-weapon-free zone (NWFZ) as an adversary security regime. By selecting a regime dealing intimately with sensitive national and international security interests and by assessing the applicability of this regime to the Balkans (included in this region are Bulgaria, Romania, Yugoslavia, Albania, Greece and Turkey), a politically volatile area once known as the 'powder-keg of Europe', the authors seek to shed some light on the wider problems of forming and maintaining security regimes. The Balkans represent an excellent area for research on regime-building because of the extent to which the region mirrors conditions existing in international society. The globalist ideologies of Maoism, Titoism, Marxism−Leninism, Stalinism, capitalism, democratic socialism and Islamic revivalism are all prominent in the Balkans. The heterogeneity of the region also extends to the governmental structures, including past or present parliamentary democracies (Greece and Turkey), socialist governments (Yugoslavia and Romania) a centralist pro-Soviet communist state (Bulgaria), and a hybrid (Stalinist−Maoist) socialist people's republic (Albania). To the extent that the region in many ways represents a microcosm of international society, we believe that it represents a classic case for research on security regimes.

The chapter thus represents an attempt to create the conditions for what Harry Eckstein has called a 'critical case study'[6] − that is a case selected specifically for the purpose of building generalisations or testing hypotheses about some wider universe of activity. In sum, the chapter sheds some light on questions concerning the creation of new international regimes where great 'complexity' prevails, namely conditions of cultural and ideological diversity, interstate rivalries, mutual distrust, the existence of non-state actors, heightened perceptions of security interests at stake, and great political uncertainty and risk.

Security Regimes for Nuclear Arms Control in the 1980s

International efforts focused on controlling the use or effects of nuclear weapons in the 1980s will be concentrated in three diplomatic areas. The regulation of competition in strategic weaponry will continue to be a relatively high priority of the United States and Soviet Union. In the European context, the modernisation of theatre nuclear weapons by both East and West will provide opportunities for talks on the disposition and possible reduction of such weapons. Lastly, further international proliferation of nuclear weapons poses dangers that will continue to attract a great deal of attention by countries which supply and consume nuclear power technology.

Yet there are some enormous difficulties ahead. The future of the SALT process is clouded by the erosion of detente following the Soviet invasion of Afghanistan and the pending collapse of the SALT II Treaty during the Reagan Administration. If the prospects for immediate reductions of strategic arsenals appear dim, so are the chances for reductions in European-based nuclear and conventional forces, given the current international climate of East—West mistrust and suspicion. Moreover, efforts to arrest the spread of nuclear weapons are likely to encounter difficult problems as many non-nuclear-weapons states develop technical capabilities and political motivations for manufacturing nuclear explosive devices. Analysts of non-proliferation are thus increasingly shifting their attention away from stopping proliferation to a greater concern for slowing its rate or scope, or as one analyst put it, 'managing nuclear multipolarity'.[7]

Parties to the NPT, assembling in August 1980 in Geneva for the NPT's quinquennial Review Conference, failed to reach a consensus on the foundations of the international regime for nuclear power. Unlike the 1975 conference, participants at the 1980 Review Conference could not even agree on a joint final communiqué. Both conferences reveal the outlines of what is becoming a schismatic international dialogue about the non-proliferation regime, where non-nuclear-weapons states (NNWSs) attempt to link non-proliferation to wider themes relating to the structure of international society such as the New International Economic Order while the nuclear weapons states (NWSs) and their allies try to decouple non-proliferation from these themes by narrowing the discussion to technical issues associated with the nuclear fuel cycle. In this and in virtually all other fora on arms control and non-proliferation, the notion of a NWFZ has been obscured by this diplomatic *pas de deux* between advocates of technical fixes and proponents of a restructured nuclear world order.

The 1980 Review Conference gave very little attention to NWFZs, focusing instead upon the treaty's provisions on disarmament and its promise of open access to peaceful nuclear technology. Among the non-governmental organisations (NGOs) attending the Review Conference, both Pugwash and the World Without War Council submitted memoranda that included NWFZs among other proposals for strengthening the regime.[8] The Secretariat of the agency monitoring the Tlatelolco Treaty (the Latin American NWFZ) also advocated continued extension of the NWFZ concept.[9] All of these memoranda stress the importance of both positive and negative security assurances (discussed below), the continuing utility of safeguards, and support of the Great Powers as conditions encouraging the formation of NWFZs. The Netherlands and Bulgaria submitted working papers that stressed security assurances and NWFZs as 'effective means of curbing the spread of nuclear weapons . . . [which] contribute significantly to the security of those states [which participate in them]'.[10]

In terms recently developed by Ernest Haas, the recent NPT Review Conference is rich with examples of 'fragmented issue linkage',[11] especially in the efforts of OECD nations to maintain an international consensus on the discriminatory premises of the non-proliferation regime articulated in the NPT and the attempts by less-developed nations to harmonise their positions on nuclear disarmament and access to peaceful technology. Thus, despite little agreement about the causes and effects of proliferation, each bloc conceptualised issue-linkages in accordance with perceived security and economic interests. Little 'substantive issue linkage' occurred: the level of intellectual coherence evident in the debates was very low.

Nuclear-Weapon-Free Zones: Concept and History

In brief, a NWFZ is a spatial area (land, sea, air, extraterrestrial) defined by international treaty wherein nuclear weapons may be neither developed nor stored. Implicit in this brief definition are

TABLE 6.1   *NWFZ dates*

2 October 1957	Rapacki proposal in UN General Assembly for NWFZ covering both Germanies, Poland and (later) Czechoslovakia
8 January 1958	Soviet Premier Bulganin proposes Nordic NWFZ to Norwegian Premier Gerhardsen
25 June 1959	Soviet Union proposes Balkan NWFZ
1 December 1959	Antarctic Treaty
28 March 1962	Second Rapacki Plan
20 May 1963	Soviet Union proposes Mediterranean NWFZ
28 May 1963	Finnish President Kekkonen proposes Nordic NWFZ
5 August 1963	Partial test ban treaty in air, space, sea
21 July 1964	African NWFZ proposed in declaration by Heads of African Governments
30 November 1965	Soviet Union proposal for African NWFZ
14 February 1967	Tlatelolco Treaty creates Latin American NWFZ
10 October 1967	Outer Space Treaty
11 February 1971	Seabed Treaty
16 February 1971	UN General Assembly resolution for Indian Ocean as 'Zone of Peace'
15 October 1974	Soviet President Podgorny promises Soviet Union will guarantee non-nuclear status of Nordic NWFZ if established
9 December 1974 and 11 December 1975	UN General Assembly resolutions on NWFZs for South Asia, Africa, Middle East, South Pacific and Definition of NWFZ
30 May 1975	NPT Review Conference approves NWFZ concept
13 November 1980	Israel proposal in UN for Middle East NWFZ

four essential concepts: initiative from the parties themselves; means of verification; international recognition; and consonance with the regional and strategic military balance and security perceptions. From a legal point of view, the notion of a NWFZ is thus entirely consistent with UN Charter provisions dealing with sovereign equality, the proscription of the threat or use of force, the right to collective self-defence, the peaceful settlement of disputes and co-operation among states.[12] The significance of the concept as a security regime comes from its close association with vital interests of the parties to the agreement. In essence, the NWFZ can serve the interests of the NNWSs by reducing regional suspicions and risks of attack while also promoting the collective interest in halting the spread of nuclear weapons.

As indicated in Table 6.1, NWFZs have been proposed repeatedly in the postwar period. When a comparison is made between the claims and results of other proposals of arms control and disarmament in this period, it is clear that NWFZs are one of the few concrete achievements to which reference can be made. First, geographical denuclearisation has been accomplished in the following uninhabited areas: Antarctica (1959), outer space including the moon and other celestial bodies (1967), and the seabed (1971).[13] Secondly, the Treaty of Tlatelolco established in 1967 a NWFZ covering most of South America; although Argentina, Brazil, Chile and Cuba are not yet full parties, the Tlatelolco Convention has established the largest NWFZ yet attempted in an inhabited area.[14] Other regions where NWFZs have been proposed include: the South Pacific, Africa, the Middle East, South Asia, the Indian Ocean, Central Europe, Scandinavia, the Balkans, and a 'worldwide NWFZ'.[15]

Despite this long-standing international interest in NWFZs as instruments of arms control, the last major effort at analysing the concept and its implementations was completed in 1975.[16] Since then, arms control literature and policies have dealt with non-proliferation by examining the civilian nuclear fuel cycle, tightening up safeguards, imposing strict conditions on nuclear exports and emphasising conventional arms transfers and security guarantees as 'incentives' not to proliferate. Thus despite a growing consensus that proliferation is a political not a technical problem there is an evident tendency for public policies and arms control literature, especially in advanced countries, to concentrate on narrow technical and economic issues, such as 'proliferation-resistant' fuel cycles, criteria for nuclear exports and economic disincentives against early decisions to reprocess. This is fragmented issue linkage, *par excellence*.

One of the foremost reasons why NWFZs are greeted with scepticism is that they have often been used as instruments of policies that have little to do with arms control or non-proliferation. As seen in Table 6.2, for example, many NWFZs have been proposed as political responses to a particular disturbing event rather than as a studied, analytical move aimed at the narrow objective of controlling proliferation. Warsaw Pact countries have in particular shown a predilection for calling for the establishment of a NWFZ

TABLE 6.2   *NWFZs as responses to events*

Date	NWFZ region	Precipitating event
1957	Central Europe	US missiles into West Germany
1959	Adriatic and Balkans	Jupiter IRBMs proposed for Italy, Greece, Turkey
1961	Africa	French Algerian nuclear tests
1963	Mediterranean	MLF Proposal: NATO Polaris submarines in Mediterranean
1963	Nordic Area	Multilateral force
1967	Latin America	Cuban missile crisis
1974	South Asia/Indian Ocean	Indian nuclear test
1974	Middle East	1973 Yom Kippur War and evidence of Israeli bomb
1974	Africa	Nigerian proposal, upon reports of South African bomb
1980	Middle East	Israeli proposal upon reports of Iraqi and Pakistani efforts to acquire the bomb

when perceived security interests were jeopardised. In the terminology developed by Haas, this corresponds to 'tactical issue linkage', where policies are pursued with the aim of securing *ad hoc* advantages rather than the reconstruction of regimes along the lines of substantive rationality.[17]

Thus in 1957, Poland proposed a NWFZ for Central Europe after a NATO decision to instal American IRBMs in West Germany; the Soviets favoured an Adriatic and Balkan NWFZ in 1959 after the installation of Jupiter IRBMs in Italy and Turkey; and the Soviet Union also favoured a denuclearised Mediterranean in 1965 when NATO was considering a nuclear multilateral force (MLF) in the region. Similarly, Iran proposed a Middle East NWFZ shortly after the 1973 Yom Kippur War when it was evident that Israel had the bomb; and Pakistan proposed a South Asian NWFZ after the May 1974 Indian nuclear explosion. In each of these cases, a NWFZ was used as an instrument for attaining tactical policy goals which often had little to do with the wider objectives of non-proliferation, world peace and national economic development.

Although both NWFZs and the NPT share a common objective of curtailing the geographic (or horizontal) spread of nuclear weapons, both also serve other national security interests of member states. By reinforcing a diplomatic commitment of the peaceful uses of nuclear energy, both of these instruments enable a state to shape an environment more conducive to international trade in nuclear power technology. Many NNWSs also like the idea of their neighbours relinquishing the option of developing nuclear weapons which could be used in local conflicts. Whereas the 'NPT bargain' consists of NNWSs giving up their weapons option in exchange for peaceful nuclear technology transfers and reductions of strategic arsenals, NWFZs extend this deal to include a ban on the possession of foreign-controlled nuclear weapons on NNWSs' soil. By agreeing to this arrangement, NNWSs stand to gain security benefits in the form of reduced risks of direct involvement in nuclear war and Great Power security assurances. Opportunities thus abound in NWFZs for fragmented and tactical issue-linkages; the deeper problem of the relationship between NWFZs and world peace (the problem of substantive issue-linkage) remains non-consensual.

The NWFZ concept also relates to some additional themes in the theory and practice of international relations and regime-building. The intellectual heritage of the NWFZ includes past experience with demilitarised zones (DMZs).[18] For example, the need for verification, international recognition, consent of local parties, Great Power acquiescence, and legal codification are shared by all such zones. The possible breakdown of NWFZs will therefore be likely to occur for reasons similar to those which account for the end of other DMZs: termination through negotiation, unilateral abrogation, incomplete verification, covert action, or military responses to changes in regional power balances.

The NWFZ concept is also related to a wider debate over the question 'whether arms cause conflicts, or vice versa?' Those who, like Norman Angell, Philip Noel-Baker, and Prince Kropotkin[19] feel that arms *per se* are causes of war would have great sympathy for NWFZs since the absence of nuclear arms logically prevents their use by local countries. Those who place conflict before arms, however, are likely to remain sceptical about the ability of NWFZs to remain non-nuclear in all conflicts. With respect to nuclear war, proponents of this view posit that it is the nature of the local conflict that will determine whether nuclear weapons are used. They can point to the ill-fated interwar disarmament conferences organised by the League of Nations as illustrations of the fatuity of seeking peace through simple quantitative restraints on arms. The longevity of security regimes thus depends critically upon some measure of substantive issue-linkage; the long-term effects of clashing interests and cognitive disunity increase the likelihood that the regime will be, as Thomas Hobbes might have put it, 'nasty, cruel, mean, brutish and short'.

A Prototypical NWFZ

With this background, we can outline the features of a composite of the various NWFZ regimes surveyed above. Although variations will clearly occur in different regional contexts due to different political military and social conditions, a prototype NWFZ can be sketched to serve as a benchmark for analytical reference.

With respect to the *timing* of NWFZ proposals (in populated areas), the following conditions contribute to fruitful international negotiations: prior existence of a disturbing (or potentially disruptive) international event of political–military significance; local perceptions of security advantages from a NWFZ; forceful and persistent advocacy in international arenas; and Great Power acquiescence.

With respect to the *substantive content* of this prototypical NWFZ, the following characteristics are suggested from past experience:

1. Legal status: international recognition; treaty of unlimited duration; voluntary and initiative consent of local parties; verification by *ad hoc* regional organisations.
2. Membership: geographically contiguous but without any requirement for all-inclusive membership; include all major regional powers and other states within regional perimeter of zone.
3. Political–military: NWFZ must not destabilise existing military security managements including alliances; support by superpowers and other nuclear states (nations developing nuclear technology and weapons); selective conventional arms assistance sufficient to lessen incentives in selected nations to develop nuclear options; regime should not discourage peaceful uses of atomic energy.

4. Obligations: no development, deployment, or storage of nuclear weapons of any sort; NWS security guarantees against threats of using nuclear weapons against any NWFZ member; agreement with UN Charter and other international obligations.

Lastly, the establishment of a NWFZ requires the resolution of a number of collateral issues. They include the problems of transit rights, 'peaceful nuclear explosions', effects on alliance commitments, and the colonial territories of NWSs.

A Balkan NWFZ: Geopolitical Considerations

The Balkan region has historically been characterised by chronic strife at both intra- and inter-state levels, often involving conflicting Great Power interests. As one historian once put it, the Balkans were where 'the politics of British Empire, Russia, France and Germany were practised before their extension to the Afro-Asian continents'.[20] In the nineteenth century and the first half of the twentieth century the Balkans were one of the most explosive areas of the world. From the outbreak of the First World War at Sarajevo (1914) to the continuing disputes between Greece and Turkey, the area has been characterised by great political, social and military instability.

In many respects, the collapse of the Ottoman Empire produced historical consequences resembling those following the collapse of the British and French colonial empires at the end of the Second World War. National boundaries were carved before and after the First World War that often ignored the ethnic identities of the Balkan peoples and conformed primarily to the administrative and political convenience of the Great Powers.[21] The Balkan map was consolidated in its present form at the Paris Peace Conference of 1919. Consequently not a single Balkan country emerged as mono-ethnic, and practically all Balkan states have entertained irredentist notions against one another.[22]

Much is now being written about the instability of NATO's southern flank. In the aftermath of the 1974 Turkish invasion in Cyprus, Greece withdrew from the military structure of the Atlantic Alliance and ended home-porting rights to the US Sixth Fleet. Turkey responded to an American arms embargo of 1975 by closing 25 American bases. Thus, despite recent events, including Greek reintegration into the military sector of NATO, and the re-opening of US bases in Turkey, regional politics have reached the point where, in Stephen Larrabee's words, 'Greece and Turkey have better relations with most countries in the Warsaw Pact than they do with each other or with some members of the Atlantic Alliance'.[23]

With the recent demise of Josip Tito, the disputes within the southern flank of NATO and the continuing suspicions and mis-trust in the area, the whole situation increases the long-term risk that nuclear weapons might some day be developed or used either as nationally controlled devices or via introduction by outside powers. The capability of Balkan countries to do the former is a function of the nuclear technology in the region, both current and planned. One index of this capability is the number of power and research reactors in the region (see Table 6.3) which could conceivably be geared to the production of bomb-grade fissile material.

TABLE 6.3   *Nuclear reactors in the Balkans (in megawatts)*

	Current and past	Planned
Romania	1 research reactor (3 MW)	9 (at 600 MW)
Bulgaria	2 power reactors (at 408 MW) 1 research reactor (1 MW)	2 (at 408 MW)
Yugoslavia	3 research reactors (all <7 MW)	3 (at 1000 MW), 2 (at 1200 MW), 1 (at 632 MW)
Greece	1 research reactor (5 MW)	1 (at 600 MW) 2 (at 900 MW)
Turkey	3 research reactors (<6 MW)	2 (at 1000 MW), 1 (at 600 MW)
Albania	—	—

SOURCES: 1. Nuclear Assurance Corporation, 'Nuclear Megawatt Status Report', October 1981 (Atlanta: NAC, 1981). 2. IAEA, *Research Reactors in Member States*, 1980 edn (Vienna: IAEA, 1980). 3. US Congress, Senate Committee on Governmental Affairs, *Nuclear Proliferation Factbook* (Washington, DC: GPO, September 1980).

The data suggest rather ambitious nuclear development plans, especially in the region's Warsaw Pact countries. Romania, for example, has recently contracted for four 600 MW CANDU reac-tors worth over $3 billion, making it Canada's 'best power reactor export market to date'.[24] According to *Nuclear News*, the Canadians have authorised licensing agreements for an eventual 16 units.[25] By 1990 Romania plans to rely on nuclear power for 18 per cent of its energy capacity, while progressively assuming more of the manufacturing work from Canada. The CANDU, moreover, produces about twice the amount of plutonium per year as conventional light water reactors.[26] Similarly, Turkey, a country now under martial law, announced in June 1979 that it was purchasing its first nuclear power plant as part of an industrial deal with the Soviet Union valued at $8 billion; in addition, the Swedish firm ASEA-ATOM is now negotiating with the Turkish Electricity Authority for the building of another 600 MW nuclear plant. Although Sweden, Canada and the Soviet Union all require strict safeguards on their exports, it is clear that by the end of the century several Balkan nations will have the skills, equipment and materials to manufacture a nuclear explosive and/or to export sensitive components, if such a decision is made.

The mere stockpiling of an ally's nuclear weapons also poses some risks that through theft, sabotage, accident, military capture, or a variety of additional means (such as terrorism and host-country capture) nuclear weapons might be deployed or used in the area. Moreover, given some local fears that external nuclear weapons could be targeted for the Balkans (such as pre-emptive attack or retaliation), there might well be some 'substantive' grounds for all local parties to reach some basic agreement on the need to exclude such weapons from the region. Yet such an agreement would be vacuous unless external NWSs agreed to respect the integrity of the regime through positive and negative security assurances.

Continuing instability in the region also produces some perceived incentives to permit and even encourage the presence of nuclear weapons in the area, or at least the perpetuation of the option of their introduction if strategic circumstances require them. In particular, it seems highly unlikely that NATO will discard its nuclear options given the superiority generally conceded to conventional Warsaw Pact forces in the area. As one State Department Desk Officer for Turkish politics once commented when asked about a possible Balkan NWFZ, 'such a proposal would knock a hole in the southern flank of NATO'.[27]

There are a variety of specific bilateral conflicts that continue to work against regional co-operative efforts for a NWFZ. The two areas of major conflict (actual or potential) remain the ongoing disputes between Greece and Turkey over Cyprus,[28] the Aegean Sea, and over national minorities. Another possible area of serious military conflict is between Yugoslavia and Bulgaria over the status of Macedonia (boundaries and minorities).

TABLE 6.4 *Local conflicts*

	Countries	Subject
Main conflicts	Greece and Turkey	Cyprus*
		Aegean Sea†
		Continental Shelf
		Military and civilian air traffic control
		Territorial Waters
		Militarisation of the Greek Islands
		National Minorities
	Yugoslavia and Bulgaria	Status of Macedonia‡
		Territorial disputes
		Minorities
Underlying or potential conflicts	Albania and Yugoslavia	Albanian minority (in Kosovo)
	Greece and Yugoslavia	Minorities (Macedonia)
Less important conflicts that might escalate under the right conditions	Bulgaria and Romania	Territorial disputes (Dobrudja)
	Greece and Albania	Greek minority (in Northern Epirus)
	Hungary and Romania	Hungarian minority (in Transylvania)
	Hungary and Yugoslavia	Hungarian minority (in Voyvodina)

* The issue is the Turkish invasion and continued occupation of approximately 38 per cent of Cyprus.
† The main dispute is over the Aegean Sea Continental Shelf and territorial waters. With regard to the Continental Shelf, the issue is whether the Greek Islands possess their own Continental Shelf (Greek position) or are merely extensions of the Turkish Continental Shelf and have no rights in the seabed of the Aegean Sea (Turkish position). The dispute on the territorial waters arises from the possibility that Greece might extend her 6-mile territorial waters to 12, an extension that Turkey considers *casus belli*.
‡ The origins of the Macedonian dispute lies in the nineteenth century. Currently it constitutes a most divisive issue between Yugoslavia and Bulgaria (and to a lesser extent between Greece and Yugoslavia). Yugoslavia recognises a *unique* Macedonian nationality (and encourages the use of the Macedonian language). This is against Bulgarian policies which claim that Macedo-Bulgarians are indistinguishable by historical or cultural tradition from the Bulgarians. This makes Yugoslavs suspicious of Bulgarian ambitions to annex part of the Macedonia and/or to use the Macedonia quarrel as an instrument for the advancement of the Soviet aims in the region.

In addition to the many disputes cited in Table 6.4, a number of uncertainties continues to affect regional security, including: the future of post-Tito Yugoslavia; the resolution of the Cyprus problem; the direction of policy in Albania after Enver Hoxha; and the long-term effects of continued deterioration of the Turkish economy. All of these instabilities must be seen in the context of the numerous crises currently under way in the Middle East region, whose escalation would directly or indirectly affect the area. The close proximity of Greece and Turkey to Middle East oil accounts for a considerable degree of NATO's interest in restraining these disputes.

Uncertainties extend also to the future of the NPT regime for countries in the region. At the 1975 NPT Review Conference, for example, Romania and Yugoslavia[29] expressed strong reservations about the discriminatory nature of the NPT bargain, with Belgrade threatening to reconsider its continued adherence to the treaty. Although Turkey has recently ratified the NPT (leaving only Albania outside the NPT regime), several leaders in both Greece and Turkey have spoken of the possibility of indigenous development of nuclear weapons.[30]

A Balkan NWFZ and the European Theatre Nuclear Balance

As Table 6.5 shows, there has been a variety of proposals for a Balkan NWFZ. All of these proposals have originated in Warsaw Pact countries, all have been unilateral initiatives from the statesmen who advocated them, all have been proposed at a high level of generality and all were announced without prior consensus between the superpowers. A brief look at the history of those proposals illustrates the relationship between calls for a Balkan NWFZ and local concerns about the stability of the wider balance of power in Europe.

The Romanians, at the level of Prime Minister, proposed in September 1957 that a 'peace zone' be established in the area; in June 1959, they made explicit reference to denuclearisation, a position supported diplomatically by the Soviet Union.[31] In 1959, 1963 and on numerous occasions in the UN the Soviet Union has reiterated its call for a Balkan NWFZ; in each case, however, the proposal has been preceded by some action by NATO that stimulated

TABLE 6.5 *Proposals for a Balkan NWFZ*

Date	Country	Proposal	Forum	Result
10 September 1957	Romania	NWFZ: Balkans as an area of peace with no foreign military bases	Official	Reiterated
May 1959	Soviet Union	Balkans as region of peace	*Isvestia* 29 May 1959	Romania supported and urged treaty on NWFZ with Great Power guarantees
25 June 1959	Soviet Union	Notes to Balkan states, United States, and Great Britain regarding Balkan and Adriatic	Diplomatic Notes	Yugoslavia, Romania, Bulgaria, Albania supported. United States rejected
17 May 1963	Soviet Union	NWFZ of all Mediterranean	Diplomatic note to the 18-nation Committee on Disarmament	United States rejected
1968	Bulgaria Yugoslavia	Balkans and Mediterranean NWFZ	1968 Conference of NNWSs	NATO rejected
1972	Romania	Proposal for conference of Balkan states to deal with Balkan NWFZ	Conference of the Committee on Disarmament	NATO rejected

some diplomatic response by the Warsaw Pact. These actions have included new missile deployments, the MLF proposal, and force modernisation efforts. American responses to these proposals for a Balkan NWFZ have come in the form of summary dismissals. In particular, NATO countries have stressed the necessity for a nuclear means of countervailing Soviet conventional forces, the threats posed by long-range tactical nuclear weapons deep in the Soviet Union, and the alleged propagandistic and hypocritical nature of these proposals.

There are three basic reasons why tactical nuclear weapons have been justified as being in the interest of NATO. The first reason is political: these weapons help reinforce the American commitment to defend Europe in the event of a massive military attack from the Warsaw Pact. Secondly, they allegedly help reduce the economic burden of mobilising a European conventional force sufficient to deter a Warsaw Pact ground offensive. Thirdly, according to the military doctrine of 'flexible response', NATO must retain the capability to escalate to the nuclear level if necessary to counterbalance alleged Soviet advantages in conventional forces.

The United States has been estimated to possess roughly 31 000 nuclear weapons of all types; roughly 9000 of these are strategic and 22 000 are tactical.[32] About 7000 of these tactical weapons are based on European territory, while another 1000 are deployed in the Atlantic fleet. NATO theatre weapons in Europe are stored in over 100 Special Ammunition Storage Sites (SAS) that consist of igloos and protective facilities; the location of these sites is presumed to be known by the Soviet Union.

The authors were unable to obtain data on the number of SAS in Greece and Turkey, the proportion of the 7000 European tactical nuclear weapons that are based in the Balkan area (if any) and future modernisation plans. Although the exact number and location of nuclear weapons based in the area remains classified, it can be surmised from available data that these weapons are small in number, antiquated and incapable of striking targets deep in the Soviet Union. One index of the actual number of warheads is provided by existing information on the types of equipment that could be used to deliver a nuclear explosive. Table 6.6 summarises the current deployment of nuclear-capable delivery vehicles in the area. When these modest capabilities are compared to the 7000 aggregate total of European theatre nuclear weapons it is apparent that the Greek and Turkish nuclear contribution to NATO is minimal. Furthermore, the modest Soviet deployment of short-range Scud and Frog missiles in Romania and Bulgaria could probably be removed without seriously jeopardising the required balance. No regular Soviet troops are currently stationed in Balkan member states of the Warsaw Pact.

TABLE 6.6   *Nuclear-capable delivery systems in the Balkan region*

Country	Weapon system	Number	Range (miles)	Yield (KT)	Year of initial development
Greece	F-4 fighter-bomber	56 (est. 1985)	1400(+)	—	1960
	F-104G fighter-bomber	31	1450(+)	—	1968
	155 mm howitzer	240	$4-30 \times 10^3$ metres	2	1942
	8 in. howitzer	n.a.	$14-16 \times 10^2$ metres	1	Early 1950s
	Honest John (surface-to-surface)	8	$5-22$	20	1951
	Nike-Hercules (surface-to-air)	n.a.	84	1	1958
Turkey	F-4	49 (1978)	As above		
	F-104S	30 (1978)	As above		
	155 mm howitzer	190	As above		
	8 in howitzer	n.a.	As above		
	Honest John	18	As above		
	Nike-Hercules	170	As above		
Romania	Frog SSM	30	$10-45$	1	Early 1960s
	Scud SSM	20	50	1	1965
Bulgaria	Frog	36	As above		
	Scud	20	As above		
Yugoslavia	155 mm howitzer	n.a.	As above		
	Frog-7	n.a.	As above		

SOURCES: IISS, *The Military Balance, 1979–1980*; *Jane's Weapons Systems, 1979–1980*; *Defense and Foreign Affairs Handbook, 1980.*
n.a. = not available.

Even without serving as depots for nuclear weapons, both Greece and Turkey would still contribute invaluable benefits to NATO in the form of overflight and base rights, intelligence and communications facilities, command and control systems, radar installations, ammunition and supply storage, and manpower. Moreover, ever since the Truman Doctrine was announced in 1947 the United States has given a commitment to the security of both countries concerning Soviet bloc aggression. These security assurances were reaffirmed after the Cuban missile crisis and the subsequent withdrawal of Jupiter IRBMs from Turkey. It is thus by no means clear that a treaty establishing a NWFZ would *ipso facto* constitute a security threat to Greece, Turkey or NATO. Indeed, a report from the US Congressional Budget Office has argued that the retirement of outdated theatre nuclear force (TNF) systems could yield some added security to both countries and Europe as a whole. According to that study, 'it may be desirable to increase US and NATO efforts to . . . reduce or eliminate marginally or highly vulnerable and destabilising theater nuclear systems such as Honest John, ADM (atomic demolition munitions), nuclear Nike Hercules and QRA (Quick Reaction Alert) forces'.[33] These are precisely the systems which now remain in Greece and Turkey.

The Rôle of Security Assurances

Countries will join together to create NWFZs when it is in their apparent interests to do so. Countries will not join when great uncertainty exists with respect to internal compliance or recognition of the zone by nuclear-armed states. Certification of compliance can be arranged through a variety of means, ranging from inspections by the IAEA or some regional organisation (such as OPANAL, the Agency for the Prohibition of Nuclear Weapons in Latin America), to national means of verification including bilateral agreements and pooling of intelligence data. The Tlatelolco Treaty states have approached the problem of recognition by seeking assurances by all NWSs (in Protocols I and II) that the zone and all colonial territories therein will remain free of nuclear weapons. Hence, although a group of countries could declare a *de jure* NWFZ, such a declaration would in itself amount to little unless the NWS agreed to respect the zone. Countries are reluctant to relinquish the same instruments with which they may be attacked.

Considerable attention has recently been given in such fora as the UN Special Session on Disarmament, the 1975 and 1980 NPT Review Conferences and in Conferences of Non-Aligned Nations, to superseding the relatively legalistic approaches offered above with more concrete policy statements by the NWSs regarding the non-use of nuclear weapons. In particular, UN Security Council Resolution 255 (19 June 1968) has called for 'immediate' international assistance for any NNWS that is the victim of a nuclear attack by a NWS; such assistance − known as 'positive security assurances' − is currently supported in principle by all the NWSs.[34] Pledges of no first-use of nuclear weapons under any circumstances against a NNWS, or 'negative security assurances', have so far only been issued by the Chinese.[35] Conditional assurances of this variety have been issued by the following countries:[36]

Soviet Union:	non-use against any country which neither possesses nuclear weapons nor seeks to acquire them;
United States and Great Britain:	non-use against any NNWS party to the NPT, or any other binding agreement not to acquire nuclear weapons, *except* in the event of an attack on the United States/Great Britain or its allies by NNWSs 'allied to' or 'associated with' a NWS;
France:	non-use pledge offered only for members of NWFZs.

The inability of the NWSs to agree on a common position on negative security assurances reveals the prevalence of tactical and fragmented issue linkages and the absence of major substantive international agreement on the rules of the game of weapons development and use. Thus the Soviet position would permit an atomic attack on Europe, the American and British positions would allow first-use in South Korea and the Middle East, and the French position would permit nuclear strikes against all countries except the 22 full parties to the Tlatelolco Treaty (an area not posing any security threats to France). Moreover, since the Chinese are undoubtedly aware that any Chinese nuclear attack upon a NNWS would probably draw in other NWSs to the detriment of China, they lose little in security terms by proffering non-use pledges to NNWSs.

Merits and Demerits of a Balkan NWFZ

The critical variables behind the implementation of a Balkan NWFZ thus appear to be political and military. The military acceptability of such an arrangement to NATO will depend upon the concessions that can be extracted from the Soviet Union on such issues as the exclusion of the Eastern Mediterranean from the zone, a reduction in the numbers and readiness of Soviet conventional forces near the Balkan region inside the Soviet Union, restrictions on Soviet deployments of MRBMs and the Backfire bomber, and superpower security assurances and verification procedures. Because the Soviets have been proposing a Balkan NWFZ for over twenty years, it is perhaps time for NATO to test the seriousness of these proposals by preparing a list of demands that could provide a basis for negotiation.

Political opposition to the NWFZ would be more likely to come from non-Balkan members of NATO rather than from the regional parties themselves, many of whom have supported a Balkan NWFZ in principle for decades. Parliamentary and Congressional opposition could be expected from political circles which would associate the establishment of a Balkan NWFZ with appeasement of Soviet interests in the area. Some European allies might oppose any such scheme on the grounds that it might symbolise a political 'decoupling' of American security policy from the defence of Europe.

While not minimising the substantial political obstacles associated with negotiating and implementing a Balkan NWFZ, the authors believe that the concept merits further analysis aimed at establishing a NATO position on the matter. If established, such a zone would break a long-standing pattern of limiting NWFZs to unpopulated areas and regions at the periphery of the international system. Summary dismissals, such as the American statement in 1959 that 'this proposal is similar to other Soviet proposals to accomplish piecemeal the design of rendering the Western nations incapable of deterring aggression',[37] serve no purpose other than the prolongation of a shaky *status quo*. And in the light of the rapid diffusion of nuclear technology and the numerous political crises brewing in the area, the *status quo* might ultimately prove to be more disruptive to regional security than alternative defence arrangements which are supplementary to NATO, including a NWFZ.

The major demerits of a Balkan NWFZ include the following: political obstacles from European countries fearful of any American decoupling from European security; difficulties in defining a range of collateral issues such as transit rights, nuclear-related installations, peaceful nuclear explosions, and sanctions for apparent violations; the likely difficulty in obtaining major concessions from the Soviet Union with regard to force deployments and capabilities within the Soviet borders; the lack of any consensus on security guarantees; and political problems associated with attempting to negotiate new nuclear arms control agreements in a climate of renewed superpower antipathy.

Conclusion

In its 1976 evaluation of NWFZs, the *SIPRI Yearbook* contained the following pessimistic assessment:

> Further fruitless consideration of the subject may even detract attention from the need to ensure the universality of the NPT and provide an excuse for certain countries to postpone indefinitely a decision on the renunciation of a nuclear-weapon option, as well as an alibi for the nuclear-weapon powers to eschew, also indefinitely, an undertaking not to use nuclear weapons against non-nuclear-weapon states.

At the other extreme, William Epstein has characterised the NWFZ as a potentially more effective means of controlling proliferation than the NTP.[38] This chapter does not advocate the immediate establishment of a Balkan NWFZ; its major goal has been neither to praise nor bury the notion of an NWFZ, but to analyse it.

As surveyed above, the politics of NWFZs have been most notably characterised by fragmented and tactical issue linkages. Most countries have shown considerable resistance to the idea of voluntarily relinquishing their sovereign right to acquire a national capability to make nuclear weapons. In the absence of a solid international consensus on the substantive linkages between NWFZs and world order and economic development, it seems likely that approaches to nuclear proliferation will continue to proceed on a piecemeal basis; yet another example of disjointed incrementalism. Grandiose schemes, like the international ownership of the entire nuclear fuel cycle, carry little weight in countries which already have more than their share of uncertainties and risks with which to cope.

A growing number of analyses of international regimes are

turning from globalist or holist approaches to intractable regulative and distributive problems of international society to more modest undertakings, especially those grounded on the basis of substantive issue linkage. As Robert Rothstein has argued:

> In an environment of conflict and uncertainty, separate systems with different but interlocking sets of rules may be more realistic than the quest for global rules . . . [this] should increase the possibility that problem solving and negotiation can be moved somewhat closer to the individuals, the sectors, or the countries most significantly affected by a decision.[39]

Further progress in the establishment of NWFZs is now stalemated by forces which are inherent in the nation-state system. Nationalism, simplistic cognitive images of national threats, an international preoccupation with state sovereignty, complex linkages to superpower politics and continuing strategic instability – all of these frustrate the establishment of NWFZs.

In sum, the future of NWFZs as a means of nuclear arms control rests upon two pillars. First, NWFZs will not be favoured in time of great strategic uncertainty. This is not to suggest a structuralist explanation for the creation of NWFZs. Indeed, the Tlatelolco, Outer Space and Seabed Treaties were all signed during a period of great strain between the superpowers. However, looking beyond the political problems associated with Czechoslovakia, Vietnam, and Cambodia, one must recall that this period was characterised by greater strategic stability than had previously existed between the superpowers. The Soviets had announced 'peaceful co-existence', a nuclear 'essential equivalence' had been reached, and the SALT process was ultimately under way. The Cuban missile crisis helped to forge Soviet–American support for a Latin American NWFZ and the NPT. Strategic stability would thus appear to be a necessary but not sufficient condition for the establishment of NWFZs. The second pillar consists of the emergence of a cognitive consensus on the definition of the central problems concerning the proliferation of nuclear weapons. There is little doubt, given the number that have already been established, that the *notion* of a NWFZ has widespread international support as a complementary means of pursuing nuclear arms control. Other areas of general agreement are: the acceptability of international safeguards, the undesirability of uncontrolled national stockpiles of plutonium, the need for an international repository of spent fuel, the desirability of multinationally controlled reprocessing centres (if large-scale reprocessing takes place), and the need for further controls and reductions of strategic arms. Furthermore, the superpowers now are in agreement about the undesirability of further proliferation and the importance of strict controls over nuclear technology. Since the larger problems of world order and justice will likely remain intractable, and since the diffusion of nuclear technology will continue apace, it is desirable from the standpoint of the current non-proliferation regime to pursue all alternatives for collaboration where substantive issue-linkage is possible. The authors believe NWFZs are one such area.

In the past NWFZs have been subjects of incrementalist bargaining associated with tactical and fragmented issue-linkage. At present substantive issue-linkage is increasingly evident in international fora where the prospects of further nuclear proliferation are deliberated. The future of NWFZs will ultimately rest on the extent to which they are believed by local parties and the NWSs to be in the interest of international security.[40]

Notes

1. *Random House Dictionary of the English Language* (New York, 1970).
2. Ernest Haas, *Tangle of Hopes* (Englewood Cliffs, New Jersey, 1969).
3. David Mitrany, *A Working Peace System* (Chicago, 1966).
4. Paul R. Viotti and Douglas J. Murray, 'International Security Regimes: On the Applicability of a Concept', paper presented at American Political Science Association Convention, Washington, DC, August 1980.
5. Ernest Haas, 'Why Collaborate? Issue-Linkage and International Regimes', *World Politics*, xxxii (1979–80); and idem, 'Is There a Hole in the Whole?' *International Organization*, xxix (1975).
6. Harry Eckstein, 'Case Study and Theory in Political Science', in Fred I. Greenstein and Nelson W. Polsby, *Handbook of Political Science*, vol. 7, (Reading, Mass., 1975).
7. John J. Weltman, 'Managing Nuclear Multipolarity', paper presented at a conference on 'The Future of Arms Control', Harvard University, Center for Science and International Affairs, 15–16 May 1980.
8. See Yolanda White, 'Working Paper for the Second Review Conference of the State Parties to the Nonproliferation Treaty', (New York, 1980); and Pugwash Council, 'Statement from the Pugwash Council on the Second NPT Review Conference', *Pugwash Newsletter*, Jan. 1980.
9. *Second Review Conference of the Nonproliferation Treaty*, NPT/CONF.II/9, 14 May 1980, Geneva (Latin American memorandum).

10. ibid., NPT/CONF. II/C. 1/9, 27 Aug. 1980 (Netherlands paper).
11. Haas, 'Why Collaborate?', loc. cit., p. 372.
12. See, *inter alia*, Articles 1 and 52 of the UN Charter. According to the provisions of Article 1, states undertake '. . . to take effective collective measures for the prevention and removal of the threats to the peace . . . to develop friendly relations among nations . . . and to take other appropriate measures to strengthen universal peace'. Also, the concept of the NWFZs is consistent with the provisions of Article 52 which envisages the existence of regional arrangements or agencies for dealing with matters relating to the maintenance of international peace and security as are appropriate for regional action.
13. UN, *Treaty Series* (New York, 1962), vol. 422, no. 5778, pp. 71–107; ibid., vol. 610, no. 8843.
14. US Arms Control and Disarmament Agency, *Documents on Disarmament, 1967,* (Washington, DC, 1968) pp. 69–83.
15. See Roderick Alley, *Nuclear-Weapon Free Zones: The South Pacific Proposal,* (Stanley Foundation Occasional Paper no. 14), 1977, pp. 40–3; Kathleen Teltsch, 'Iran Asks UN Action to Keep Region Free of Nuclear Arms', *New York Times,* 13 June 1974; Bernard Nossiter, 'Israel in Policy shift to seek Mideast Ban on Nuclear Weapons', *New York Times,* 8 Nov. 1980; UN General Assembly Resolution 3265B (xxix) on a 'Nuclear Weapon-Free Zone in South Asia', 9 Dec. 1974; Devendra Karshik, *The Indian Ocean: Toward a Zone of Peace* (Delhi, 1972); Betty Goetz Lall, 'On Disarmament Issues: The Polish Plan', *Bulletin of the Atomic Scientists,* June 1964; Jay C. Mumford, 'Problems of Nuclear-Free Zones: The Nordic Example', *Military Review,* March 1976; Statement by Soviet Government on Baltic Nuclear-Free Zone, 25 June 1959, US Department of State, *Documents on Disarmament 1945–1959* (2 vols, Washington, DC, 1960) ii, pp. 1423–6; and Bernard Feld, 'A New Look at Nuclear Weapon-Free Zones', *Pugwash Newsletter,* May 1977.
16. UN, *Special Report on the Conference of the Committee on Disarmament: Comprehensive Study of the Question of Nuclear-Weapon Free Zones in All its Aspects* (New York, 1976).
17. Haas, 'Why Collaborate?', loc. cit., p. 372.
18. NWFZs, in fact, can be thought of as selective demilitarisation. Here, the emphasis has been placed upon the absence of nuclear weapons instead of the absence of fortifications and troops. The underlying rationality, however, is almost the same as the following definition indicates: 'Demilitarization . . . denotes the agreement of two or more States by treaty not to fortify or station troops upon, a particular zone of territory; the purpose usually being to prevent war by removing the opportunity of conflict as the result of frontier incident or to gain security by prohibiting the concentration of troops on the frontier.' See L. F. L. Oppenheim, *International Law* (London, 2 vols, 1965 edn) ii, 24 n. l.
19. Norman Angell, *The Great Illusion* (New York, 1910); Philip Noel-Baker, *The Arms Race* (London, 1960); and Prince Kropotkin, *Memoirs of a Revolutionist* (Boston, 1899).
20. Nikolaos Stavrou, 'Greek–American Relations and their Impact on Balkan Cooperation', in Theodore Couloumbis and John Iatridis (eds), *Greek–American Relations* (New York, 1980) p. 150.

21. ibid., p. 151.
22. ibid., p. 151.
23. Stephen Larrabee, unpublished paper, Harvard University, Center for Science and International Affairs, 1979. Also see idem, *Balkan Security*, Adelphi Paper no. 135 (London, 1977).
24. *Nuclear News*, Feb. 1979.
25. ibid.
26. *Nuclear Proliferation Factbook* (1980 edn) p. 220.
27. Interview, April 1980.
28. The official Greek position on the Cyprus question is that this problem is essentially a matter for the two communities on the island and cannot be considered within the context of bilateral Greek—Turkish relations.
29. About Yugoslavia and nuclear weapons, see *Survival* xviii (1976), pp. 116—17; and xix (1977), pp. 127—9.
30. See, Andrew Wilson, *The Aegean Dispute*, Adelphi Paper no. 156 (London, 1980) p. 41 n.60; and SIPRI, *World Armaments and Disarmament: SIPRI Yearbook, 1976* (Cambridge, Mass., 1976) p. 389.
31. See UN, *Study of Nuclear-Weapon Free Zones*, p. 22.
32. See, '30,000 U.S. Nuclear Weapons', *Defense Monitor*, Feb. 1975; *Monitor*, Center for Defense Information, Mar. 1980, p. 6; and US Congress, Congressional Budget Office, 'Planning U.S. General Purpose Forces: The Theater Nuclear Forces', Jan. 1977.
33. US Congressional Budget Office, 'Planning U.S. General Purpose Forces: The Theater Nuclear Forces', Budget Issue Paper (Washington, DC, 1977).
34. Further details on the distinction between positive and negative security assurances can be found in Jozef Goldblat and Sverre Lodgaard, 'Non-Use of Nuclear Weapons', *Bulletin of Peace Studies* (1980).
35. See Cyrus Vance, 'Chinese Positions on Negative Security Assurances', in US Congress, House Committee on Foreign Affairs, Subcommittee on International Security and Scientific Affairs, Hearing on 'The Second Nuclear Nonproliferation Treaty Review Conference', 96th Congress, 1st Session, 16 July 1979, pp. 24—6.
36. Goldblat and Lodgaard, loc. cit.
37. Statement by the Department of State Regarding the Soviet Proposal for an Atom-Free Zone in the Baltic-Adriatic Region, 11 July 1959, US Department of State, *Documents on Disarmament 1945—1959*, ii, p. 1435.
38. William Epstein, 'Nuclear-Free Zones', *Scientific American*, Nov. 1975.
39. Robert L. Rothstein, *Global Bargaining: UNCTAD and the Quest for a New International Order* (Princeton, New Jersey, 1979) p. 272.
40. The authors wish to thank A. Carnesale, L. Eriksson, P. Katzenstein, J. Murphy, B. Posen, G. Poukamisas, R. Rainer, J. Sharp, D. Siotis and S. Van Evera for their helpful comments on an earlier draft of this chapter. All errors and opinions are of course the responsibility of the authors. The Ford Foundation and Cornell University Peace Studies Program have provided financial support during the preparation of this chapter.

7 Towards Security and Stability in the Balkans: the Role of Economic Co-operation

Nansen Behar

There hardly exists any more diverse area throughout the world in terms of varying nationalities and policies than the Balkans. Six continental countries and an island country are situated in a comparatively small area, and they all speak different languages and belong to different social systems, integrational communities or military alliances.

Historians have dubbed the Balkans 'the powder-keg' of Europe, on account of the fact that a number of small and large armed confrontations and wars have broken out here. Recently, however, the Balkans have been gradually turning into a zone of peace. Mutual trust and good-neighbourliness have been consolidated. The road towards this goal is full of diversions, sudden reverses or temporary increases of tension, either due to distrust accumulated throughout history or due to outside interference. 'We are realists, of course,' said State Council President of the People's Republic of Bulgaria, Todor Zhivkov, in his speech delivered at a National Assembly session. 'We do not shut our eyes to the difficulties coming both from the grave historical heritage of the Balkans and from the complexity of contemporary Balkan reality. We are aware also of the active attempts of certain reactionary forces to destabilize the situation in the Balkans.'[1] It can definitely be claimed, however, that the dominating tendency in the Balkans is one towards detente. Mistrust between the countries with different social systems is steadily being reduced and a new community of interests, promoted primarily by the aspiration to live in peace, is being set up. The Balkans can serve as an example to the whole world by promoting good-neighbourliness between countries with different social orders, in accord with the spirit of Helsinki.

Economic co-operation plays a key role in the realisation of this process. Each Balkan country has established bilateral relations with the other countries as an intermediary stage towards achieving reciprocal security through mutually advantageous economic, scientific and technological exchanges.

As a country lying in the centre of the Balkans, Bulgaria plays an active part in this process. Bulgaria's foreign policy is guided by the awareness that all the necessary prerequisites for understanding, security and co-operation are at hand in the existing situation on the Peninsula.

Thus Bulgaria has developed mutually advantageous economic relations with its southern neighbours, Turkey and Greece. The last decade has been particularly fruitful in this respect. Declarations on the principles of good-neighbourliness, understanding and co-operation were signed with Greece in 1973 and with Turkey in 1975. For the first time in the relations between Balkan socialist and capitalist countries the principles of peaceful coexistence were recognised by them on a state level. At the beginning of the 1970s Bulgaria's trade with Turkey and Greece ranged between 25 and 30 million dollars. In 1979 the soaring increase in trade with Greece amounted to 300 million dollars and with Turkey to 130 million dollars. The trade structure has also been changing: the relative share of industrial products is steadily growing, while the share of raw materials and agricultural products is decreasing. Some new forms of co-operation have also been launched, such as the export of truck spare parts and electric power exchange. Co-operation in transport has also been on the upsurge. Studies of the economic potential of these countries (Bulgaria, Greece, Turkey) have shown, however, that there exist still greater opportunities for future trade increase.

Bulgaria's economic contacts with Yugoslavia are still far below the trade potentials of both countries. Certain progress, however, has been registered recently. Co-operation in the fields of economy and transport has developed and a number of bilateral treaties for expanding economic, scientific and technological exchange was signed in May and June 1980.

Both bilateral economic relations and relations within the scope of the Council for Mutual Economic Assistance between Bulgaria and Romania are extremely good. The relations of Yugoslavia with Turkey and Greece and of Romania with the capitalist countries in the Balkans are developing along an ascending line. For a long time Albania had limited its economic ties with the other Balkan countries, but matters have recently been returning to normal.

Co-operation in the Balkans has been influenced positively by the general improvement of the political climate in Europe after Helsinki. On the other hand, economic co-operation itself has become a material impetus for detente. In his speech delivered at the Fourth Special National Assembly Session, President Zhivkov said:

> The Balkan countries are geographically connected, their national economies complement each other. The growing development of mutual ties among them is a necessity for the economic and cultural upsurge of all the Balkan countries, for the improvement of their peoples' welfare. Furthermore, we don't have any irreconcilable contraditions or difficult issues, which exist in some other parts of the world. Therefore, it is of mutual interest to take concerted steps towards improving the relations between the Balkan countries despite their different social orders and towards the establishment of the Balkan Peninsula as an area of peace, calm and security.[2]

Politicians from the Balkan countries with different social systems share a growing awareness that in today's world and particularly at a regional level, so-called security through armament (Balance of Terror) fails to bring lasting stability in international state relations. Turkish Government officials have repeatedly made statements on co-operation on the Balkans. A new 'concept for security' is being worked out in that country. It involves economic development and international co-operation as a basis for security. According to one writer, this concept, launched as early as 1978 by the Turkish Defence Minister, Hasan Isik, rejects the view that a country's security can be regarded only in terms of political and military notions. According to this concept, security is rooted in the 'capacity' of the country itself and this capacity is assessed by the optimal co-ordination of social, economic and internal political factors. The build-up of a stable and independent economy, in terms of the concept, is accompanied by the setting up of an independent military industry and the fighting capacity of every citizen for defence purposes must be provided. This is supposed to be in line with the principle of Kemal Atatürk: 'Peace at home – peace in the world.'[3] Here no attempt will be made to enter into a comprehensive analysis of this concept, but it is worth stressing, however, that it involves seeking some new elements of national security. Regarding economic co-operation with the Balkan countries, the Turkish Prime Minister, Suleyman Demirel, stated that Turkey will pursue a policy of perpetuating the process of co-operation during the 1980s also. Both the former long-serving Prime Minister of Greece Konstantin Karamanlis, now President of the country, and his successor as Prime Minister, Georgius Ralis, have made a number of similar statements endorsing the policy for good-neighbourliness and co-operation.

The vital necessity for economic co-operation, for detente and for the preservation of peace demands a search for new criteria and prerequisites for reciprocal security. Practical experience has shown that dominant among them are economic co-operation and the establishment of mutual interest in sustaining normal state relations among the different countries.

The need for a new approach towards the problems of security has not been sufficiently elaborated by political scientists. In this respect attention has to be concentrated on the interrelations between economic co-operation and detente. In the present writer's opinion, the components of a new approach to the problems of national security should be worked out, including economic co-operation and development as prerequisites for security. The following items might comprise this approach:

(a) Rejection of the view that armaments for the small countries and regions can guarantee stability in relations between the nations.

(b) The development of countries' own economic, scientific and technological potentials will establish the basis for broader equality in international relations. More advanced economies will naturally involve enhancement of international trade and more considerable participation in the international division of labour.

(c) Expanding civil scientific research and cutting down military research will increase the mutual advantage of broadening co-operation in science and technology. At present a number of the most advanced branches of science and technology are outside the range of international co-operation, on account of the extreme secrecy of military technology.

(d) Improving the volume of exports will entail more equitable and long-standing relations among the trading nations.

(e) From more extensive trading we may expect to see supplementary forms of co-operation. This could involve joint ventures, licence and patent exchange and concerted projects in a variety of countries. This in turn would increase the need for mutual trust, personnel exchange and other steps towards consolidating peaceful coexistence.

In the present writer's opinion, these components — and perhaps some others as well — should be elaborated and systematised with the aim of translating them from theory into the practice of international state relations. To achieve lasting peaceful coexistence in separate areas, an all-round firm balance in the world is indisputably needed first of all, and it can be achieved only within the framework of general and comprehensive disarmament.

Success in detente and stability in international relations cannot be achieved by the approach which the United States has been trying to impose on the economic relations with the Soviet Union in recent years. Although on a small scale, the Balkan countries with different social orders have given an example to be followed by other countries, namely that the policy of good-neighbourliness and economic co-operation, based on equitable and mutually advantageous relations, gives a better impetus along the road towards peace than the policy of military rivalry.

Notes

1. T. Zhivkov, *Internal and Foreign Policy of the People's Republic of Bulgaria* (Sofia, 1979) p. 27.
2. *ibid*, p. 29.
3. U. Steinbach, 'Perzpektiven der Türkischen Aussen und Sicherheitspolitik', *Europa Archiv* (1978) p. 435.

8 The Balkans: a Romanian Perspective

Ioan Mircea Paşcu

Introduction

For many years, the Balkans — once the 'powder-keg' of Europe — have been the source of frequent major crises. Besides the complexities of the region itself, this has mainly been due to long-standing great power active involvement and subsequent rivalry in the area.

Today the Balkans represent an important part of Europe, containing countries with a considerable human and material potential. Politically, there are four socialist countries (Romania, Yugoslavia, Bulgaria and Albania) and two capitalist states (Greece and Turkey). Militarily, there are two Warsaw Pact members (Romania and Bulgaria) and two NATO members (Greece and Turkey), plus a non-aligned country (Yugoslavia). Situated in the larger Mediterranean strategic context, the Balkans have an important position in the political—military picture of the continent and even beyond it (being located close to the Middle East and the Gulf). From the economic point of view, the Balkan states are, generally, developing countries, facing more or less the same problems. The ensuing complementarity of their national economies and their geographical proximity also provide an important basis for both bilateral and multilateral co-operation among them.

Under the circumstances, strengthening peace, security and co-operation in the Balkans — a constant objective of Romania's foreign policy — would make an important contribution to the similar European process and also to peace and stability in the world in general.

Traditions of Balkan Co-operation

In a larger sense, Balkan co-operation, or rather the co-operation among the Balkan peoples, has long traditions. Confronted with the Ottoman danger, the Balkan countries and peoples strengthened their links, helping one another in their mutual fight against the Turks. In such a context, Romania served on many occasions as a host for the revolutionaries from other Balkan countries, fighting for liberation from the Turkish yoke. In the last century, for example, many fighters for Bulgaria's independence were able to organise themselves and carry out their revolutionary activity aiming at the liberation of their homeland while based on the territory of Romania.

Closer to the present, more precisely in the period following the conclusion of the First World War, Balkan co-operation entered a qualitatively superior stage characterised mainly by the appearance of its first institutionalised forms. That was due to significant developments at the continental level. Thus a series of major events created a new European environment with a direct bearing upon the Balkan region. First and foremost was the disappearance of the old empires – Turkish, Tsarist and Austro-Hungarian – which were among the major competitors in the region. As a result, the external pressure upon the Balkans eased to a certain extent, creating new conditions allowing for a change of mood from conflict to co-operation. It is interesting that such co-operation included mainly the newly-created independent states from Central and South-Eastern Europe, which prized the same high values of national independence and sovereignty.

Following the conclusion of a number of treaties settling some conflicting issues among the Balkan states, the first interwar initiative for multilateral co-operation emerged: the Balkan conferences. There were four such conferences: Athens (1930), Istanbul (1931), Bucharest (1932) and Salonica (1933). Under discussion were many problems of common interest for the participating countries. Those conferences created the framework for the identification of fields prone to common action, such as labour legislation, communications, tourism, the creation of a Balkan

Postal Union, exchanges of professors and students and collaboration between Balkan intellectual institutions. As a result, in the
economic sphere too, there were agreed mutual preferential duties
and facilities, permitting an increase in commercial exchanges.

In general, the efforts were consumated in the establishment of
certain institutions for Balkan co-operation. For instance, in
December 1930 the representatives of the journalists from the
Balkan states decided to create the Association of the Balkan
Press. In April 1931 the tourist organisations from the participating countries decided to establish the Balkan Tourist Federation at
Istanbul. In February 1932 Athens became the host of the Balkan
Medical Union. In the same year Bulgaria, Greece and Turkey
created a Tobacco Office in Istanbul. By the end of 1932 a new
body — the Inter-Balkanic Chamber of Commerce — had started
to function in Salonica with a view to promoting economic and
commercial co-operation among the Balkan states. Last but not
least, Athens became the host city for the Balkan Mathematicians'
Union in 1934. Periodically, the activity of all those institutions
was reviewed in reunions held under the auspieces of 'The Balkan
Weeks', bringing together professors, scientists, politicians and
representatives of professional, youth and female organisations
from the Balkan countries.

Confronted with the increasing danger posed by the plans of
Nazi Germany and Fascist Italy with respect to their region, the
Balkan countries extended their co-operation in the political and
military field, too. As a result, the representatives of Greece,
Yugoslavia, Romania and Turkey signed the defensive Balkan
Pact in Athens on 9 February 1934. It is worth mentioning that the
pact was also originally intended to serve aims going even beyond
the purely political and military ones that underlay its negotiation.
It was also meant to serve as a basis for multilateral co-operation in
various other fields. For instance, there was an Economic Consultative Council (as an auxiliary to the Permanent Council of the
Alliance) performing an important part in recommending and
supervising problems resulting from the commercial, agricultural
and financial relations among the Balkan states. Its main objective
was to identify the most suitable ways of intensifying the commercial relations among the four members of the alliance as well
as with outside states, reflecting their level of economic development and the prevailing conditions in the Balkans at the time of
its creation and functioning. There were created Chambers of

Foreign Trade enlarging the ground for co-operation between the exporting institutions of member countries.

It is worth noting that the activity of the Council tended to extend the relations among the four members of the alliance to include all six Balkan states. In this respect, mention may be made of the Postal and Telecommunication Convention (concluded on 1 January 1936), the Permanent Committee for Tourism, and the Maritime Balkan Committee.

At the scientific–cultural level there was also a strengthening of co-operation as a result of the pact's conclusion. Thus there were organised two Congresses of Balkan Mathematicians (1934 and 1937), a series of Balkan Medical and Law Weeks and an increased exchange of professors and students.[1]

The outbreak of the Second World War and the subsequent Italian and German invasions led to the dissolution of the Balkan Pact and the interruption of Balkan co-operation. However, the experience of the interwar record of Balkan co-operation could be summarised as follows:

(a) Balkan co-operation was possible and prevailed over conflict when there was a genuine political will on the part of the Balkan states.

(b) Conflicting issues (which were largely settled at the end of the First World War) were not an obstacle to co-operation which was established first in the commercial, cultural and scientific fields; as a result, the general atmosphere improved, permitting a better understanding among the peoples living in the Balkans.

(c) Following such an improvement in the general climate and due to a genuine balance in the military potential of the Balkan states – there being no major centre of power to try to subordinate the others – it was possible to approach even the delicate political and military fields with notable results. In its turn, as is easily confirmed from the experience of the Economic Consultative Council, co-operation in these fields had a favourable impact on the extension of Balkan co-operation in general, and particularly in those fields in which it first started.

(d) As history repeatedly suggested, external interference and pressure represented a permanent obstacle to Balkan co-operation; when diminished – as was the case under the prevailing conditions at the end of the First World War — it permitted a mutually fruitful attitude towards problems of common interest, and when increased — as was the case under the conditions at the beginning of the Second World War — it could only lead to an interruption of contact between the Balkan states.

Following the defeat of Nazi Germany and Fascist Italy, and the victory of socialism in four out of six Balkan states (Romania, Yugoslavia, Bulgaria and Albania) new premises for resuming Balkan co-operation have appeared at the first signs of improvement in postwar international relations. Thus, the activity of the Balkan Medical Union was resumed in 1962, when Bucharest was the host city of the Sixth Medical Week, following a Romanian initiative. Bucharest was also the place where the Third Congress of Mathematicians was held after its postponement in 1939, marking the resumption of the activity of the corresponding Balkan Union. In general, besides resuming activity of the earlier institutions, Balkan co-operation was further extended by the parallel creation of new non-governmental organisations like the International Association for South-East European Studies (Bucharest, 1963) and the Permanent Conference of South-East European Engineers (Athens, 1972). The picture of present Balkan co-operation is completed with the existence of many other forms of collaboration in various fields. Among them one can mention the Conferences of National Red Cross and Crescent, the Folklore Festivals, the reunions of the UNESCO national commissions, of the representatives of Balkan architects, writers, film-makers, students, professors, lawyers and economists, and sporting gatherings of almost every kind.[2]

Romania's Relations with the Balkan Countries

Convinced that multilateral co-operation could be brought about on a bilateral basis, Romania has good and ample relations with all the other five Balkan countries, enjoying the absence of any conflicting issue with any of them. Romania's relationships are based on the principles of full equality of rights, respect for national sovereignty and independence, non-interference in internal affairs, mutual advantage and the non-recourse to force and the threat of force.

Romanian relations with Yugoslavia are friendly, based on mutual support and having long traditions. A decisive contribution to their continuous enlargement was brought by the frequent contacts between presidents, Nicolae Ceauşescu and Tito, and between other Romanian and Yugoslav leaders. Such meetings allow for broad consultation on a wide range of problems of common interest, identification of new fields of co-operation, and give a fresh impetus to those already existing. Politically, based on the common essence of their system, both Romania and Yugoslavia share similar views on a large spectrum of important issues including the democratisation of international relations, the New Economic World Order, European security and co-operation and disarmament. With respect to the situation in the Balkans, the two countries have manifested their resolution, on the occasion of their last summit in October 1980, 'to develop and intensify bilateral and multilateral co-operation between the Balkan countries . . . contributing to the strengthening of good neighbourly relations in this region, of peace and security in Europe'.[3] Economically, both countries share more or less the same level of development, reflected in the complementarity of their national economies. This is the cornerstone of large-scale bilateral co-operation in the fields of industry (steel, machine-building, electronics, chemicals, petrochemicals and mining) and of agriculture. Certainly, the most representative illustration of what can be achieved by two neighbouring and friendly socialist countries is the gigantic hydro-power system built jointly on the Danube: the Iron Gates I (completed) and II (under construction). This complex provides electric energy covering a large share of both countries' total consumption, permitting a better realisation of their human and material potential. Co-operation between the two countries also includes science, culture, education, health and tourism.

Romanian relations with Bulgaria are also friendly and have deep roots in history stemming from the common essence of their economic, political and social systems. They are being continuously enlarged, following the frequent contacts between Presidents Ceauşescu and Zhivkov. The relations between Romania and Bulgaria have a strong juridical background provided both by the Treaty of Friendship, Collaboration and Mutual Assistance renewed in 1970 and the Declaration regarding the Continuing Strengthening of Fraternal Friendship and Deepening of Collaboration between the Romanian and Bulgarian Communist

Parties, and between Romania and Bulgaria signed in 1977. Politically, with respect to the Balkan situation, the two states have recently affirmed their will 'to extend their multilateral relations with the other Balkan countries in the future, to transform the Balkans into a zone of peace, good neighbourly and mutually advantageous co-operation – which is in accordance with the interests of the Balkan peoples, the cause of peace and security in Europe and in the world'.[4] In the economic field, co-operation includes machine-building, chemical and metal industries, transportation and agriculture. In addition, there are some large common industrial projects of mutual interest, of which mention may be made of two: the Giurgiu-Ruse plant of heavy machinery and equipment and the hydro-electric complex of Turnu Măgurele-Nicopole, both on the Danube. Co-operation between the two countries also includes science, culture, education and tourism.

In general, Romania's relations with both Yugoslavia and Bulgaria are an example of relationships between friendly socialist countries, living in the same geographical context.

Romanian relations with Albania are, as in the previous cases, friendly and have long traditions based on both countries' fight for independence against external enemies. The exchanges between the two countries, and particularly the commercial ones, have been amplified recently, indicating an important potential for further large-scale co-operation.

Greece was the first non-socialist country from the Balkans with which Romania signed a Solemn Joint Declaration (on 27 May 1975). Mutual relations have led to co-operation in various fields such as animal husbandry and the industrial processing of meat. Romanian machinery equips some of the Greek industrial enterprises and Romanian assistance is involved in the railway linking Athens to Salonica. There are also two joint Romanian–Greek ventures – 'Elpex' and 'Terhellas' – with prospects for an increased number in the future. Politically, the two countries have recently decided (on the occasion of the last summit between Presidents Ceauşescu and Karamanlis held in Bucharest in September 1980) to resume common efforts towards both multilateral and bilateral co-operation in the Balkans, the former along the lines of the Greek initiative of 1976,[5] fully supported by Romania. In this respect, the parties 'have considered that strengthening confidence, trust, good neighbourliness, and peace in the Balkans represents a major contribution to security and co-operation in

Europe. The parties have expressed their will to maintain good relations with all other Balkan countries and to do their utmost to develop bilateral and multilateral contacts between the Balkan countries, in the interest of the Balkan peoples, with a view to the transformation of the Balkans into a zone of confidence, co-operation, good neighbourliness and friendship.'[6]

Romanian relations with Turkey have been steadily amplified and co-operation between the two countries includes oil and petrochemical industries (Romania and Turkey are building together the oil refinery of Central Anatolia in Turkey), agriculture and tourism.

The Balkans: Zone of Peace and Good-Neighbourliness, without Nuclear Arms

The present general picture of the Balkans is rather complex, including, as well as the evident trend towards co-operation which represents the main feature, some elements of confrontation stemming from a number of unresolved issues between some Balkan countries. However it is essential that the strengthening trend towards co-operation — illustrated among other things by the frequent contacts (including those at the highest level) between the representatives of the Balkan countries — creates the necessary framework to settle such issues which, otherwise, do cause concern, given the strategic environment of the Balkans and of Southern Europe in general.

Although, from the strategic point of view, the Balkans cannot be separated from the Mediterranean region as a whole, for analytical purposes we shall try to look at them as an area *per se*.[7] During the 1970s, Balkan states usually represented between a fifth and a quarter of the total military expenditure of the whole of Southern Europe (22 per cent in 1978, for instance).[8] Perhaps it would be interesting to employ a somewhat less-utilised indicator to illustrate the continuing increase in military expenditure of the countries we are referring to, that is the enlargement of the group of states spending more than 1 billion dollars (in 1973 US dollars, constant prices). Thus, if only France and Italy were spending more than 1 billion dollars in 1970, in 1978 there were six such countries, including three Balkan ones (Greece, Yugoslavia and Turkey), leaving Romania, Bulgaria and Albania below that threshold. The Balkan hierarchy of military expenditure shows the NATO countries (Greece and Turkey) in the first places, at between 42 and 52 per cent of the total, and Warsaw Pact countries (Romania and Bulgaria) as fourth and the fifth in the hierarchy, at around 33 per cent.[9]

At this point, one usually expects a comparative analysis between the forces of the two alliances, but the present writer does not wish to employ such techniques here largely because he thinks that their relevance in the Balkans is somewhat reduced. It is common knowledge that one of the main features of the whole Mediterranean region — including the Balkans — is the lack of a clear-cut East–West confrontation of the type we have, for example, in Central Europe. This is best illustrated by the pre-eminence of the Greek–Turkish conflict, the presence of the great powers in the surrounding seas, and the worsening of the situation in adjacent regions, all having a greater impact on the Balkans than the theoretical opposition between Greece and Turkey, on the one hand, and Romania and Bulgaria, on the other hand. During the last two years, for instance, the situation in the Middle East and the Gulf area has worsened. 'These circumstances', writes a Romanian specialist, 'increase the tendency of external factors to strengthen their presence in our region, multiply attempts on their part to create or reinvigorate spheres of influence, contribute to the involvement of the Balkan states in the present arms race, complicate and make difficult the settlement of disputed issues — inherited or recently created — between some of the Balkan countries.'[10] In fact, what we are witnessing is a 'contagious' process: a focal conflicting point generates waves of tension which increase the potential for conflict in the neighbouring regions. With the passing of time — the outburst of the Arab–Israeli conflict in 1967, war in the Horn of Africa, the revolution in Iran, the complex situation in Afghanistan, and the recent outburst of military hostilities between Iraq and Iran (all conflicting points surrounding the delicate oil supply region of the Gulf) — foreign military presence in the Eastern Mediterranean has placed the old strategic considerations with respect to the security of the great powers in a secondary position. Under those circumstances it is perhaps more difficult to reduce tension in the Balkan region, but the task becomes more imperative than ever.

Efforts to decrease tension in the Balkans have constantly been made during the postwar period. They reached a peak in the late

1950s and in the early 1960s, when no less than six proposals were advanced in respect to the transformation of this region into a nuclear-weapon-free zone (NWFZ) (either the Balkans only, or with some adjacent areas). It should be taken into account that two of those proposals were advanced by Romania. Thus, on 10 September 1957, Romania invited all Balkan countries to gather in one of their capitals to discuss issues referring to the transformation of the Balkans into a zone of peace, mutual understanding and collaboration. That first proposal, like the one to follow (6 June 1959), was a genuine effort to strengthen peace and security in the region, and to resume the old links severed by the Second World War and the ensuing Cold War.

One important aspect that should be stressed is that the Romanian proposals of 1957 and 1959 comprised both the political—military dimension (inescapable in any proposal for a NWFZ), and the economic, cultural and scientific ones.[11] This is a clear demonstration that Romania was genuinely interested in the achievement of the goals envisaged by the proposals, as a country which — being located in the Balkans — was, naturally, (and still is) interested in results beyond the simple creation of a NWFZ. On the other hand, the proposals once again stressed the necessary interdependence between security and co-operation, and the fact that those two goals are inseparable.[12] Under the prevailing conditions of the period which were dominated by the Cold War in general and the fact that nuclear competition was still in its unrestricted first phases, the Romanian proposals were not taken up. But we have referred to those two earlier proposals because they illustrate Romania's permanent interest in the creation of a zone of peace, co-operation and good-neighbourliness without nuclear weapons.

As can be seen, this is a complex concept, embracing three dimensions: political, economic and military. Politically, such a zone would be characterised mainly by the type of relationship to be established between the Balkan countries. They should be friendly relations based on mutual trust, mutual advantageous collaboration and co-operation, respect for sovereignty, independence and equality of rights, peaceful settlement of disputes, and respect for international law in general. In other words, these could be considered good-neighbourly relations.[13] It should be noted that such relations would require neither obligations of military assistance in case one of the countries involved would be the object of aggression nor renunciation of the membership of the alliances to which they currently belong.[14] Such relations would certainly improve coexistence between countries having different socio-economic and political systems and allow them to concentrate more on their development in the way they have freely chosen.

As has been seen, there is a large potential for co-operation, both bilateral and multilateral.[15] This potential is based mainly on the complementarity of the national economies of the Balkan countries, deriving from the fact that they all have more or less the same level of economic development, being faced with many similar problems, and on geographical proximity. Such co-operation would be mutually advantageous, allowing for a realisation of their human and material resources. At the same time, co-operation constitutes the necessary support for political and military initiatives of common interest for all Balkan countries. It is right to recall the lesson of the interwar period, namely that such co-operation has important traditions in the region, and that there are certain institutions which have proved their utility. However, their activity should be enlarged and new fields should be approached.

The military dimension of the concept is, naturally, very important. In this respect, there are some lines of action. First, the Balkans should be declared a NWFZ to be guaranteed by the obligations of the member countries not to produce or come into possession of nuclear weapons and of the nuclear countries not to introduce such weapons into the region and to respect its denuclearised status. Speaking in terms of feasibility, one of the main questions is: are there any special targets in the Balkans worthy of a nuclear attack? Of course there is no easy answer to such a question. But the present writer considers that among the targets most prone to a nuclear attack would be the foreign installations on Balkan soil or in its surrounding waters. With no such forces and installations in the region, the risk of a nuclear attack would certainly be reduced. And that brings us to the other line of action: foreign troops and installations which should be withdrawn from the Balkans, not only because the aim of a NWFZ would be thus better served, but because they represent in general a factor of tension and mutual distrust rather than an effective assurance against aggression. One must bear in mind, however, that these foreign forces are part of the strategic world equation – that is why they

are among the most likely targets for a nuclear attack — rather
than part of an exclusively Balkan equation. Besides, after exclud-
ing them, any simple analysis of the genuine Balkan military
balance would illustrate quite convincingly the rough equality in
military potential of the Balkan countries and the absence of any
major power centre within the region in a position to try to subordinate the other states. This major feature of the Balkan
strategic environment could play an important part in any subsequent disarmament efforts in the area, which are also a component of the concept itself, depending of course on achievements
in this direction at the continental level. In sum, the concept of the
Balkans as a zone of peace and co-operation and without nuclear
weapons, represents more than simple coexistence because it
requires certain behaviour in mutual relations — friendly and co-
operative, as between good neighbours. But it would be less than a
formal alliance — because it would not require any military
obligations in case of war and because, for instance, co-operation
between the Balkan countries does not require economic or any
other type of integration. 'We do not conceive', said President
Ceaușescu, 'a new bloc, of any sort, in our region, but on the
contrary, the development of such relations which should exclude
bloc politics, and base co-operation on full equality and respect for
independence, without recourse to force and the threat of force,
eliminating any outside interference in the internal affairs of the
Balkan countries.'[16] In other words, it would rather be a regional
arrangement meant to support efforts of the Balkan countries to
develop themselves and to live in peace. And if that is its major
aim, it is obvious that such an arrangement would not be directed
against any other country or group of countries, being a function
of the process of strengthening security and co-operation at the
continental level to which — in turn — it could considerably
contribute.

The Balkans and Europe

Today the interdependence of the Balkans with the continent as a
whole is more evident even than in the past, when the Balkans were
the area for the fiercest great power rivalry of Europe and were
considered the 'powder-keg' of the continent. And that is so
because one has to understand that, at present, it is impossible to

have a multilateral approach to European security: detente in some areas and conflict in others simply would not work. European security — including the Balkans — is a whole and should be approached accordingly.[17] Thus, strengthening security and co-operation, say in the Balkans, is both a function of and a stimulant to European security and co-operation in general. It is a function because a process of strengthening security through military disengagement and disarmament in the Balkans is possible when the general climate in Europe is favourable to such steps and some progress has been achieved at the continental level; subsequently, it is a stimulant because — as already stated — progress achieved in the Balkans would certainly have a positive impact on the European process as a whole. That is why any possible process with respect to military disengagement and disarmament in the Balkans should be examined in close connection with the process of European security and co-operation. But, above all, such an approach requires that the Conference on Security and Co-operation in Europe (CSCE) should start dealing more seriously in military matters. Perhaps it is just a matter of style to speak of military and political detente[18] as if they were two separate concepts. For in most cases, as Leo Mates of Yugoslavia has pointed out to the author, political tension is a direct result of an increase in the level of armaments of the potential adversaries. Reality shows that it is no longer possible, if one wants to achieve real progress, to continue to speak of political detente while simultaneously avoiding any concrete steps in the military field.

Although military disengagement and disarmament is a major component of the concept of the Balkans as a NWFZ of peace and co-operation, we would rather prefer here to address ourselves to a possible framework of discussion than to concrete steps. In respect to such a framework, at the European level it would certainly be a positive development to convene a General European Conference on Disarmament. The conference would deal with the military aspects of security in Europe and would require a common determination on the part of all 35 CSCE members to approach seriously military matters. It could analyse such material steps as freezing military budgets and their subsequent reduction, withdrawal of all troops from foreign territories and the dismantling of foreign military installations, halting of military demonstrations in regions close to the borders of other states and substantial reduction of forces and armaments. It could also provide the forum for the negotiation of a General Treaty for the elimination of force and the threat of force, which would certainly contribute to the reduction in the activity of the military blocs and their concomitant dismantling.[19] At the same time, such a conference could establish a network of subregional negotiating fora (for example, for the Balkans or for Northern Europe) with commissions on various types of forces (ground, naval and air) to discuss possible confidence-building measures, military disengagement and disarmament steps to be taken in the particular regions of the continent for which they had responsibility. In turn, the subregional fora could report to such a conference the progress achieved as well as the issues still under discussion. It would be of the utmost importance that business should be conducted in a democratic way and not on a 'bloc to bloc' approach (like the Mutual Force Reduction (MFR) talks in Vienna), allowing every participating country to contribute freely to the discussion. And for that purpose, the already-agreed-upon rules of consensus and rotation (now in force at the CSCE meetings) are essential. As for the matters to be discussed in the commissions, it would seem reasonable enough to proceed from the simple to the complex and to seize every chance as it appears; if it seems that it will be easier to get an accord on a disarmament measure before, say, disengagement then efforts should be intensified in spite of the fact that the disengagement spectrum would remain uncompleted. In short, an orderly but at the same time flexible approach would characterise work in those commissions.

Of course, this is just one of the wide range of approaches to military disengagement and disarmament in Europe and, perhaps, we still have a long way until we reach that stage. But the logic of life demonstrates that it would be much safer and materially rewarding to strengthen peace and security through military disengagement and disarmament rather than through the arms race.[20] And if the Balkans could set an example in this respect, that would certainly be in the interest of all Balkan countries and peoples, of Europe as a whole and of the world in general.

Notes

1. For a detailed analysis of Balkan co-operation in the interwar period see Cristian Popișteanu, *Romania și Antanta Balcanică: Momente și semnificații de istorie diplomatică* (*Romania and the Balkan Entente*) (Bucarest,

1971); Eliza Campus, *The Little Entente and the Balkan Alliance* (Bucarest, 1978); and Viorica Moisuc and Ion Calafeteanu *Afirmarea statelor naţionale independente unitare din centrul şi sudestul Europei (1821–1923) (Assertion of National Independence: Unitary States in Central and South-East Europe)* (Bucarest, 1979).

2. *Balcanii, zonă a păcii, cooperării şi bunei vecinătăti (The Balkans. zone of Peace, Co-operation, and Good Neighbourliness)* (Bucarest, 1976), pp. 273–6.

3. *Scînteia*, 25 October 1980.

4. ibid., 21 October 1980.

5. Following a Greek initiative, Athens hosted a reunion on economic and technical co-operation between the Balkan states during the period 26 January–5 February 1976. On that occasion, more than 200 fields suitable for multilateral co-operation were identified.

6. *Scînteia*, 6 September 1980.

7. In fact, the Balkan countries represent the core of the southern flanks of the two alliances, containing the bulk of forces and armaments earmarked for that region.

8. That is the six Balkan countries, France, Italy, Austria, Hungary and Spain. Portugal and the two superpowers were excluded from the calculation.

9. Based on data from the Stockholm International Peace Research Institute.

10. Vasile Şandru, 'Dezvoltarea colaborării în Balcani – parte integrantă a edificării securităţii în Europa' (Co-operation Development in the Balkans – integral part of security building in Europe), *Lumea*, 5 January 1978.

11. Interestingly enough, other proposals aiming at the creation of a NWFZ in the Balkans contained exclusively political–military aspects.

12. With respect to the necessary interdependence between the two dimensions the question is what should come first: co-operation in the economic, cultural and scientific field or co-operation in the political–military one. Of course, if one is not really interested in getting started one way or the other, there will be no way out of this dilemma. As far as the present writer is concerned, he would rather be inclined to think that co-operation is to be started with matters of a reduced political significance. If one could say that the political significance of the economic field is not high enough, that will eventually ease the tension, provide evidence of goodwill, and increase mutual trust, permitting, thus, a gradual approach to the more important problems of a political and military nature.

13. See *Dicţionarul Diplomatic (Diplomatic Dictionary)*, (Bucarest, 1979) p. 155.

14. This does not mean indifference to the existence of the two alliances. In fact, the establishment of such relations could be a major contribution to the elimination of the military blocs, reducing tension, increasing mutual trust, favouring co-operation to the advantage of the countries involved and in general creating an atmosphere allowing for the enlargement of mutual contacts. Once such relations were established, at the continental level, the chances for the concomitant dismantling of NATO and the Warsaw Pact – in favour of which Romania has repeatedly pronounced itself – would certainly be brighter.

15. One could raise the legitimate question of what kind of relationship is to be

worked out between the bilateral and multilateral aspects of co-operation. In our opinion, bilateral co-operation could offer larger opportunities for settling disputed issues between countries paving thus the way for the enlargement of multilateral (regional) co-operation. Conversely, multilateral co-operation could offer the framework for two countries having some disputed issues to reach a settlement in time. Logically, it follows that efforts should be directed both ways concomitantly, a path adopted, for instance, by Romania and Greece as with the visit of Karamanlis to Romania at the beginning of September 1980.

16. Nicolae Ceaușescu, interview for the Greek newspaper *Kathimerini*, 19 March 1979.

17. However, the Balkan countries have already taken steps towards integrating the process of strengthening security and co-operation in the Balkans into the all-European process. Thus in the period following the conclusion of the Final Act in Helsinki in 1975, the Balkan countries organised two multilateral renunions — Athens in 1976, already mentioned, and Ankara in 1979 in the field of communications and telecommunications — and some other reunions among which are the reunion of the Balkan Committee for interconnecting power grids (Bucharest, 1976), the conference of the official tourist bodies of the Balkan counries (Bucharest, 1976), and periodical reunions concerning the building of a North–South European highway. In general, the activity of some of the institutionalised forms of Balkan co-operation was already integrated within the process of strengthening co-operation at the continental level which placed the Balkans in a unique position within Europe in this respect. See Institute of Political Sciences, Stefan Gheorghiu Academy, *Romania and the Final Act* (Bucharest, forthcoming).

18. We have not mentioned the economic field because it is still a function of East–West political and military relations.

19. *Scînteia*, 2 August 1980.

20. The balance of forces which is often invoked in assuring security is in fact unattainable because, in reality, each country feels more secure when it has a margin of superiority over the potential enemy and not simply an equal level of forces and armaments. Thus the arms race is in essence a pure contest for superiority and the resulting 'security' is based on its own denial, that is on increased mutual suspicion and distrust.

9 Prospects for Mediterranean Security: a Yugoslav View

Radovan Vukadinović

Introduction

In any analysis of existing relations in the Mediterranean, the question of security figures prominently. This is because in that part of the world both Mediterranean and non-Mediterranean actors are important; and because global and narrow local objectives and influences come into play. A corollary, however, is that attempts are being made to reduce tensions in the region.

The extensive physical presence of the superpowers in the Mediterranean Sea and on its shores; the possibility of the superpowers exerting an influence on a number of countries which are either close to them in virtue of their socio-political development or simply in need of their friendship; the virtually permanent crisis in the Middle East; the existence of crisis points in the Mediterranean area; and the generally unstable situation − all these factors characterise developments in the Mediterranean and cause increased anxiety among Mediterranean countries and peoples. In a situation of this kind it is understandable that the Mediterranean countries should not be spared an intense arms race, that they should pile up arms and that, fearing greater complications, they should seek increased security within these parameters.

Looking at the Mediterranean against this background, which is unfortunately permanent, one can very well ask what possibilities there are of changing relationships in the Mediterranean region and of implementing measures which would at least whittle down the stockpiles of arms and lead up to a gradual improvement in the present general situation. It should be stressed at once that such an approach has to be based on assessments of long-term trends, it implies rational conduct and is based wholly on optimistic realism. Proponents of this outlook reject claims that this situation is insoluble and unalterable and that it does not depend on the actions of Mediterranean countries but only on external forces which have become deeply entrenched. Such claims are based on reality but a reality which is linked to the present moment and which can and must change as different conditions mature and as progressive, above all Mediterranean, forces embark upon organised activity.

The present writer believes that progress in the field of disarmament and in the quest for improved security in the Mediterranean should be sought in a number of directions:

1. the introduction of confidence-building measures into the Mediterranean region;
2. freezing and gradual scaling down of non-Mediterranean fleets;
3. freezing of military budgets in all Mediterranean countries;
4. halting the spread of military alliances and banning the establishment of new military bases;
5. turning the Mediterranean into a zone of peace.

These measures would not resolve the existing conflict situation nor would they dismantle the present military arsenals. But each can be seen as a contribution to a more stable climate, greater confidence and gradual disarmament.

Confidence-Building Measures

Confidence-building measures have been introduced into the practice of European politics through the Helsinki final document, and the development of European relations so far has demonstrated their full justification. In substance they boil down to a reduction in forces involved in military exercises, giving advance notice of military manoeuvres of specific scales, and exchanges of observers. The development of relations in Europe after Helsinki has produced concrete examples of how these measures can be realised in practice, both between the blocs and between neutral and non-aligned countries. All this certainly helps to improve relations in Europe.

These measures have not, however, been extended to the Mediterranean region where extra-Mediterranean countries have continued to stockpile arms and to strengthen their military presence which they want to be seen as a sign of their permanent interest in that part of the world. In view of their relations with alliances, considerations of their own security and the proximity of crisis points, the Mediterranean countries themselves have understandably become involved in the process of building up military forces. The increasing nuclearisation of the Mediterranean area poses a special danger as both sides are making use of an even greater number of aircraft armed with nuclear weapons, modernising their nuclear-rocket systems and deploying more and more nuclear submarines.

Of significance for the latest development of relations in the Mediterranean in the security sphere is that the region is excluded from efforts to reduce armaments because of the vested interests of the two superpowers. In contrast to the Indian Ocean or Central Europe, where at least the superpowers are trying to negotiate and somewhat scale down the level of their presence, the Mediterranean is completely excluded from these developments to such an extent that not even measures from the Helsinki final document have been applied to this region.

At the Belgrade follow-up meeting to the Conference for Security and Co-operation in Europe (CSCE) the Yugoslav delegation, precisely because of this state of affairs, proposed that the so-called naval component should be applied to the Mediterranean as a first step. This would mean that apart from mutual notification of military manoeuvres and movements by land forces, advance notice would also be given of naval manoeuvres in a way which would be acceptable to all countries.

It would pay handsome dividends if countries refrained from any form of military activity which could prolong or further aggravate tensions in that inflammable part of the world. Larger-scale military movements and manoeuvres, especially in the vicinity of the borders with other countries, might have serious consequences, particularly if forces of one of the superpowers take part in them.

In the meantime, it has been argued in many quarters that the confidence-building measures already adopted should be supplemented by the naval component of security. In this connection efforts should be made at the CSCE meetings to build these measures into the system of European security. It may be possible to achieve measures relating to the naval component on a broader European plane but the other possibility of approaching this question within regional frameworks should also not be ruled out. In that case, there would be a good chance of integrating these measures into the existing practice of relations in the Mediterranean. Their content might consist of:

1. the commitment of the coastal states to provide advance notice of any manoeuvres of their naval forces, or forces comprising naval units of a number of countries. This notification would have to be circulated to all states 21 days in advance and to contain such information as the purpose of the exercises, the number of states involved in them, the types of ships, the number of men involved and the duration of the manoeuvres;
2. exchanges of observers from coastal states, who would either board the ships of countries organising the manoeuvre or watch the progress of the manoeuvre from their own ships;
3. major movements of naval forces might also fall under the provisions of the Final Act so that in case a larger number of ships are replaced or new weapons introduced, the states would also be obliged to inform other countries of this;
4. the long-term objective of these measures would be gradually to limit the scale of manoeuvres and the area in which they are held.

These measures would apply to forces of individual countries and to the naval forces of the superpowers when they take part in manoeuvre-like missions together with members of their blocs. This would expand the scope of the measures and the number of countries helping to strengthen forms of confidence-building or, in a broader sense, security itself. If these measures were accepted, they should first of all constitute a commitment for all countries which participated in the CSCE. But immediately afterwards there should be an urgent need for strenuous efforts to extend these measures to cover all other Mediterranean countries. In this way an integral system of confidence-building measures would have been developed for the Mediterranean basin and the naval component of security would have become a basis for the working out of new solutions.

The Future of Non-Mediterranean Fleets

In view of the reality of interests and objectives of the superpowers and their objective involvement in the development of new relations which might lead to disarmament, a pacification of relations should certainly result in their freezing the size of their fleets. If such a freeze occurred in an initial phase, this would not threaten anybody's interests or positions since a rough balance has already been established. In a second phase, a gradual and balanced reduction in the military forces of the superpowers should also be embarked upon, which would have a decidedly positive effect on the totality of relations in the Mediterranean.

The Mediterranean countries, of course, are not in a position to make the superpowers freeze their fleets in one form or another. But they are at liberty to take every opportunity to canvas the idea of new relationships which will advance the security of all Mediterranean states, be they on the northern or southern shores of the Mediterranean. Moreover, it should not be forgotten that despite the increased strategic importance of the Mediterranean the two superpowers might in any case show an interest in scaling down their presence in the region or at least introduce a freeze for a specific period if the development of American–Soviet relations takes a favourable turn in the wider global context. Should progress be achieved in other areas of American–Soviet negotiations – for example, SALT, the Vienna talks on troop reductions in Central Europe and the negotiations on the Indian Ocean – the case for a new approach to the problems of the Mediterranean could be argued strongly. A balanced freeze on naval forces and possibly a mutual and balanced reduction in these forces at a later date would not alter the position of either side nor would it affect their effective capacity for action. Hence insistence on this idea, however much it may appear visionary and unfeasible at the present moment, can produce results provided it becomes part of a broader programme of action on the part of the Mediterranean countries. It is understandable that there can be no secure Mediterranean while foreign fleets are present and subject to no control as to size and strength. A freeze on the fleets of the super-powers, although not an end in itself, might move things significantly towards the real goal — the creation of a free Mediterranean where new relationships could be forged.

Freezing Military Budgets

A freeze on military budgets is a relatively old political proposal which has been suggested at various stages since the war. Although such a measure would be predominantly designed to be an initial step towards disarmament and even a way of halting the arms race, it would in itself be extremely positive.

On the eve of the Special Session of the UN General Assembly on Disarmament in 1978, a series of countries worked out proposals which placed emphasis on exactly this element of freezing military budgets. Many delegations put forward these proposals in New York, convinced that in the present situation of advanced military technology and a more or less firmly established balance of power it would be possible to keep spending at the present level.

In view of the persistence of the Middle East crisis, the Mediterranean perhaps presents a somewhat more complex problem in this respect. As a matter of fact, unlike many other parts of the world where a freeze might be more rapidly and easily introduced, the Middle East crisis opens new possibilities for military spending with neither side in the conflict trusting the other sufficiently to refrain from stockpiling arms. The Egyptian—Israeli Camp David Agreement may, however, have been a move in the direction of change.

Despite the particular difficulties arising from proximity to the Middle East, it may be confidently asserted that if a solution guaranteeing a freeze on military budgets was found on a universal plane, it would certainly sooner or later make an impact on the Mediterranean countries, even those involved in the Middle East crisis.

A freezing of military budgets would have to be conceived as an initial measure which would later lead to a scaling-down of arms stockpiles in the region as a whole. In this, naturally, all the general principles, primarily those of equal security, parity and equality, would hold good for the Mediterranean countries as well.

Halting the Extension of Military Alliances and the Establishment of New Military Bases

Although the Mediterranean shores are occupied by both non-aligned countries and those aligned with blocs, there is, understandably, sufficient scope in the areas of contact between the blocs and the principal non-aligned states to allow for the possibility that further countries may join blocs or permit an extension of the network of military bases. If the very volatile situation existing throughout the African continent is added to this, then it is quite clear that an agreement to ban the addition of new member countries to the blocs or to ban the setting up of new military bases would also be of great significance.

At the present time, for instance, certain Spanish political circles are going out of their way to make Spain join NATO, which coupled with its possible membership of the EEC should, in their opinion, ensure its peaceful development as a so-called Western democracy. Although such a step on the part of Spain would make no difference to relations in the Mediterranean militarily and strategically, Spain's membership of NATO would nevertheless have political repercussions and affect prospects for disarmament as a long-term and gradual process.

If the Mediterranean countries could start from their present positions, they would be given a sense of increased security. The non-aligned countries, in particular, would benefit from this as they would know exactly where they stood, what the possibilities were, what other countries intended to do and, no less importantly, what courses of action were open to the superpowers. On the strength of this they would be able to plan their future development with greater certainty.

Creating a Zone of Peace

The creation of a zone of peace and co-operation in the Mediterranean and the Middle East is a long-standing idea and could one day be of exceptionally great significance. The idea of nuclear-weapon-free zones (NWFZs) was born at the time when atomic weapons and later missiles began to be accumulated. It was hoped to provide guarantees to countries without atomic and subsequently nuclear weapons on their territories that in case of an attack no such weapons would be used against them. It is clear that two groups of actors would be involved: non-nuclear countries covered by NWFZs, and countries in possession of nuclear weapons. The obligations of non-nuclear countries boil down to a commitment not to permit nuclear weapons on their territory in return for guarantees from nuclear countries not to use nuclear weapons against them.

Immediately after the idea of creating an NWFZ in Central Europe and, then, also in the North of Europe had first been mooted, the possibility was mentioned of setting up such a zone in the Balkans. Later on, the Adriatic region was attached to the Balkans for these purposes and the year 1963 saw the emergence of the concept of an NWFZ in the Mediterranean. The idea gradually gained approval in a number of countries which became particularly interested in the possibility of creating such zones in the light of the results already achieved. The zone in Latin America had certainly led to the revival of the idea of a NWFZ in the Mediterranean and later of turning the area into a zone of peace. It is evident that political developments in that part of the world had exerted a decisive influence on efforts to push this concept through and on the chances of realising it.

The creation of a NWFZ in the Middle East area and its possible extension would be of great significance for the entire Mediterranean region. Just as it is impossible to separate positive development on an all-European plane from trends in the Mediterranean, so it is impossible to undertake partial solutions in the Mediterranean, which would apply only to some of the countries. This is why denuclearisation remains a very important measure of a political and military character, which might have a strong effect on the general development of international relations. The non-aligned countries, in particular, are aware of this and have for years been advocating the creation of a zone of peace and co-operation in the Mediterranean. This concept, which is certainly much wider in its effects, opens the possibility of developing new relations throughout the Mediterranean in addition to stipulating the denuclearisation of the area. On the other hand, it is based on the reality of the present state of affairs and requires the superpowers in the first place to respect such a zone. With the exclusion of their nuclear arsenals from the Mediterranean waters, the process of denuclearising other Mediterranean countries would be speeded up, and possibilities would be created for reducing armaments and turning the Mediterranean into a region of co-operation involving all countries and all nations. The documents from the fifth and sixth conferences of non-aligned countries refer specifically to the need to set up a zone of peace and co-operation.

Conclusion

In modern conditions, in which countries throughout the world are bound together by ever closer links of interdependence, new prospects are emerging for the Mediterranean countries to resolve the question of their security in a new way. Hence the question of armaments, or rather disarmament, presents itself in a different light. The positive development of international relations in the period of detente and the results achieved so far in this field are a clear indication of new possibilities for relations in the Mediterranean to take a different turn. In such conditions the Mediterranean countries are getting a chance to arrive at new forms of security and to reduce the huge burden of military expenditure which they have been forced to bear because of the abnormal state of international relations. To what extent the Mediterranean countries will succeed in these aims depends on the overall development of international relations but also on their own efforts.

10 Turkey's Problems and Prospects

Ciro E. Zoppo

The accelerated erosion of the American—Soviet detente and trends in military technology are changing the political and security dimensions of the Mediterranean. The changed political conditions in Iran and the Soviet invasion of Afghanistan have made Turkey, more than ever, a potential front-line country in the path of the hegemonial tendencies of the Soviet Union. These tendencies, already present in Tsarist Russia, have been increasing apace with the growth of Soviet military might and political influence.

One result of these changing factors is the emergent complementarity between Turkish and Spanish defence. Spain guards the Straits of Gibraltar and the Western approaches to the Mediterranean. Turkey, at the Dardanelles, is the Eastern gate to the Mediterranean. Political instabilities are greater in the Eastern Mediterranean — recall the continuing difficulties of Arab—Israeli relations, the unresolved Cyprus conflict and the fragile political conditions in Lebanon. Increasingly exposed in its security position, Turkey is also beset by internal political turmoil. This has increased the problematics of stability in the Mediterranean. Changing aircraft and missile technology is shrinking the East—West axis of the Mediterranean — whose North—South axis is already quite short — to the point where not only qualifications on the geographic features may lead to greatly-altered military missions,[1] but may lead also to a more instrumental political relationship between the countries of the Eastern and Western Mediterranean.

Consequently, the survival of Turkey's Western parliamentary system of politics and the condition of its defences have become important factors in the politics and security of the whole Mediterranean.[2] An analyst who surmounts the political passions aroused by the Greek—Turkish conflict would become aware that Turkey does not have to secede from the Atlantic Alliance, or abandon its military organisation, for the current Turkish crisis to result in conditions that would undermine additionally the East—West military balance in the Mediterranean and fault political alignments, further endangering detente and reducing Europe's foreign policy and defence options. The prospects for Turkish defence thus cannot be addressed out of context of Turkey's internal economic—political crisis and its linkages with foreign and regional politics. Especially important are the changed nature of US—Turkish relations. Moreover, the extensive weakness of the Turkish economy has reduced the contribution Turkey itself can make to rehabilitating its military postures and is bound to frustrate both its efforts to create an autonomous and self-reliant arms production, and NATO expectations about Turkish contributions to NATO defence. And the damage done by the Cyprus conflict, and the related US embargo on military aid to Turkey, to US—Turkish relations and Turkish force postures will shape, to an important degree, the adequacy of Turkey's defence for the foreseeable future. Hence a synthesis of the factors generated by the Turkish domestic crisis and the difficulties that arose in US—Turkish security relationships because of the Cyprus conflict constitutes a necessary framework for a discussion of the problems and prospects for Turkey's defence.

Turkey is in its worst crisis since joining NATO in 1952 and one of the worst in the history of modern Turkey. The crisis currently investing Turkey extends to all sectors of its polity: the political system, the economy, foreign policy and national security. A crucial aspect of the present situation in Turkey is psychological and relates to its national identity as a modern democratic nation, at the core of its European and Western vocation. The possible consequences for Turkey's foreign policy of this crisis in national identity could eventually have serious repercussions for East—West relations in the Mediterranean and the Middle East. The shifting nature of Turkey's relations with the Soviet Union and Eastern Europe and with the Arab states of the Middle East and the Maghreb are directly linked with this crisis of national identity.

Radical changes in Turkey's domestic political system would intensify trends and could bring into question or further emasculate Turkey's participation in NATO. The resulting situation would create a geopolitical imbalance in the Eastern Mediterranean and the Middle East not capable of being compensated for by Greece's military reintegration into NATO or by strengthening the security policies of other countries in the Mediterranean that are members of the Atlantic Alliance or allied with the West.

Opinions may differ as to the measure of success achieved in the attempt to Westernise contemporary Turkey. But there can be no doubt that in all important areas of the public life of Turkey − in the political system, the economy, national defence and foreign policy − the 'Westernising revolution' has been accomplished, and may be irreversible to an important extent. Nevertheless, Turkey is the only member of NATO whose political, cultural and social historical antecedents are not European. Commitment to the West is, therefore, more demanding psychologically and politically, and ultimately contingent. Given the geographical location, Turkey is also the only member of the Alliance in the Mediterranean exposed to a potential direct Soviet military threat by conventional warfare. The Soviet takeover of Afghanistan and Iran's fragile non-alignment has weakened Turkish defence, already hobbled by the US arms embargo. The attitudes and policies of Turkey's European and American allies toward the Turkish crisis are, therefore, uniquely crucial. They will have psychological impact of the greatest relevance for the political options available to Turkey in its domestic and foreign policies.

Turkey is not likely at this time to return to a neutralist foreign policy which, given the disparities in military and economic power between the Soviet Union and Turkey, would mean that it would have to be 'Finlandised' in important respects. Nevertheless, significant changes in Turkey's relations with the Soviet Union and Eastern Europe, with its Middle East neighbours, with Western European countries, and especially the United States, have been underway. Indeed, under present crisis circumstances, the Turkish ruling élites must revise their foreign and defence policies if they are to cope realistically with the pervasive effects of the crisis that exists in their national economy and their internal politics. Turkey faces the negative impact of the energy crisis and other restrictive changes in international economics experienced by its NATO allies but is simultaneously beset by internal political instabilities, including widespread terrorism and economic difficulties that, in the aggregate, are more grave than in any country of the Atlantic Alliance.

Short of a return to the non-alignment that characterised Turkish policy to the end of the Second World War, an agonising search for foreign policy alternatives in economic, diplomatic and military relations has epitomised Turkey's current national crisis. Its common denominator has been a deep sense of alienation from Western Europe and the United States widely shared by the Turkish political élites and their constituents. The policies of the United States are the most crucial referents in this search because it has been the bilateral relationship between the United States and Turkey that has set the compass for Turkish defence and foreign policy since the Second World War.

Although security considerations have been uppermost in US–Turkish relations, as they are the primary focus in NATO for all members, concerns about Turkey's economy and political system have now become a serious concern in the American and NATO outlook toward Turkey. Economic and political considerations have always played a part in American policies in the mutual relationship; being rationalised in terms of helping Turkey to develop a viable economy that could sustain its political system. This was the principal justification for American aid to Turkey under the Truman Doctrine, and once it had joined NATO, US military grant assistance was believed necessary to relieve the Turkish economy from the demands of military expenditures, since Ankara must procure all major weapons abroad. In 1969, for example, the amount given by the United States in military grant aid to Turkey was equal to the positive balance in Turkey's external balance of payments. Buying military equipment abroad represents a drain on foreign exchange reserves. For Turkey, a developing and not an industrial country, defence expenditures diverted from civilian to military use also tend to bring about larger negative economic effects. Today this is all the more crucial, except that the United States cannot now meet Turkey's requirements either in terms of economic, air or military assistance. It is not clear whether Turkish leaders fully understand this.

In Turkey, military and civilian sectors' expenses are especially fungible. The problem is, however, that Turkey's economic crisis is of such massive proportions that the United States would have to make Turkey one of the highest priorities in its foreign policy to justify the level of economic aid required to alter dramatically the present condition of the economy. Turkey is currently struggling under the weight of about $15 billion in foreign debt (of which $7 billion is short-term loans), and a $2 billion annual payments deficit. The rapid increase in crude oil prices has hurt Turkey's economy especially. In 1979 the value of imported crude oil and by-products practically equalled Turkey's total export revenue. Moreover, the annual inflation rate is well over 60 per cent and unemployment has reached 20 per cent. At the very least, direct American economic aid to Turkey would have to be comparable to the several billion dollars given to Israel and Egypt together, following the Camp David agreement. However, the inflationary trends, the other adverse effects in the monetary and trade fields on the American economy, together with ethnic constraints on US foreign policy, make such a posture toward Turkey unlikely. Of the other members of the Atlantic Alliance, only West Germany is in a position to offer economic aid to Turkey in useful amounts, yet not sufficiently decisively to correct Turkey's economic situation. Actually, recent and projected decreases in the number of Turkish workers in Germany will adversely affect Turkey's economy by increasing unemployment and reducing foreign income. The other European members of NATO do not have strong enough economies to aid significantly.

Turkey's international economic policies will of necessity reach out to the international system, and in particular toward those countries which can serve specific Turkish economic needs. The Soviet Union, Romania and the OPEC countries of the Middle East are among them. In terms of foreign trade the EEC occupies the most important place in Turkish economic policies. The United States has never been a major trading partner for Turkey. Only about 5 per cent of Turkey's exports go to the United States and Turkey's place in US foreign trade is low. Aid to Turkey has been overwhelmingly for purposes of mutual defence. The share of the EEC in Turkey's foreign trade, on the other hand, has increased steadily so that it now represents over 40 per cent of Turkey's total volume of trade. Clearly, NATO will not be the vehicle for solving Turkey's severe economic crisis any more than will the United States alone. As will be seen later, this situation will place nearly insurmountable constraints on Turkey's capability to modernise its defence establishment and meet the NATO missions assigned to its armed forces.

Concurrently, the Soviet Union has exploited Turkish political alienation from the United States and the Turkish economic crisis to effect a rapprochement with Ankara. This has had a direct impact on the economy and on the domestic politics of Turkey, an indirect influence on foreign policy options, and some effects on Turkish security calculations. In the decade immediately following the founding of the Turkish republic, credits advanced to Turkey by the Soviet regime — itself hardly installed in power — played a significant role in Turkey's industrialisation. Now Soviet economic assistance to Turkey is again playing a role in Turkish industrialisation. Turkish projects for the development of heavy industries and the expansion in raw materials manufacture subsidised by Soviet loans and aid generally fulfil a genuine need for the Turkish economy and are viable. Soviet aid and credit projects will in the short term exceed credits received from any single country, including the United States and West Germany. Because payments for these loans are generally made by Turkey through exports by barter arrangements, they are easier to repay than loans from Western countries. This is likely to lead to further expansion in Soviet–Turkish trade. An example is the Turkish–Soviet Trade Protocol for 1980. It stipulated a reciprocal trade volume of $600 million, reflecting a projected 40 per cent increase in trade volume over 1979. In addition, the Soviet Union is also increasing the volume of electricity it furnishes to Turkey. A similar trend has developed in Turkish economic relations with Eastern Europe, notably Romania.

Soviet economic assistance to Turkey has not only greatly increased during recent years but is also of the kind that strengthens public sector tendencies, while filling some of the gaps in Turkish industrial development created by Western reluctance to invest resources in areas viewed as either too risky or of dubious value for surmounting Turkey's economic problems. Hence their impact has also been political, and helpful to Soviet relations with Turkey. Since the late 1960s, efforts to develop the private sector of the Turkish economy — championed by Adalet Partisi (Justice Party) — have met with stubborn resistance from the other opposite mass party, the Cumhuriyet Halk Partisi (People's Republican Party) whose historical *étatisme* and present socialist tendencies favour development of the public sector instead. The People's Republican Party, whether in power or in opposition, is highly influential in the policies Turkey pursues domestically and abroad. Within its ranks and among the party's sympathisers are found the majority of Turkish bureaucrats, technocrats, journalists and a goodly number of the military. Soviet economic policies towards Turkey strengthen, therefore, public sector influence, creating vested interests in continued and expanding Turkish economic relations with the Soviet Union.

The Soviet Union and Eastern Europe cannot replace the United States and Western Europe as major sources of economic assistance, technology transfer and commercial partnership. But to the degree that Turkey is forced to become dependent for economic and development aid on the Soviet Union because of Western reluctance to help sufficiently, to that degree Turkish foreign policy will have to accommodate to the diplomatic positions of its powerful neighbour. Soviet diplomacy is engaged in an all-out effort to exploit Turkey's increasing sense of alienation from its Western allies by the promise of additional economic aid, especially development assistance to more than forty projects, and by structuring its economic aid to boost Turkish political forces favouring a predominantly public sector economy. This would further hobble Western aid efforts which are geared to a major role for private enterprise and the market economy.

This situation would be less worrisome were it not for the fact that the trauma of the US arms embargo has unprecedently eroded the US–Turkish alliance relationship. It has resulted in a firm commitment by the Turkish military and the political leadership to create alternate sources of military procurement to the United States and to the goal of developing a Turkish arms industry capable of producing some of the arms and equipment needed for an autonomous defence. In addition, Turkey's precarious economic situation has forced the Turkish Government to ask NATO to exempt Turkey from meeting the 3 per cent annual increase in defence expenditures and the requirements of NATO's long-range programme. The Soviet invasion of Afghanistan has strengthened Turkish incentives for co-operating with the United States in the common defence. But it would be imprudent to believe that US–Turkish relations can return to their pre-1974 condition. After the Soviet invasion of Afghanistan Turkey roundly condemned and supported all the United Nations' actions chastising the Soviet Union, but informed the United States that it would not join in active measures against the Soviet Union. Although the Afghan events did facilitate the conclusion on

10 January 1980 of the negotiations for a renewed US–Turkish Defence Co-operation Agreement, a careful reading of its provisions suggests that the acceptance by the United States of almost all major Turkish positions may have been even more responsible for their successful outcome.

The foregoing, then, are the political, economic and foreign policy referents that must frame the discussion of the prospects for Turkish defence postures. Turkish military forces in NATO belong to the operational command of LANDSOUTHEAST. This operational region has a common frontier with Albania, Yugoslavia and Bulgaria to the north, then along the coast of the Black Sea to the Soviet Union and Iran to the east, and in the south to Iraq and Syria. The frontiers with Albania, Yugoslavia and part of Bulgaria are assigned to the First Greek Army. But all the remaining frontiers of LANDSOUTHEAST are Turkey's responsibility. With the revolution in Iran, Turkey is now faced with all its neighbours being potentially hostile – including Greece, if viewed from Turkish perspective.

The terrain and the opposing ground forces would make it difficult for the Turkish armed forces to defend forward, with mobility, in most of this perimeter. In that part of Greece abutting Turkey, the north-east, there is a lack of defensive depth, so that a well-organised attack could reach the shorelines of the Aegean quickly, once the frontier positions were penetrated. Only a few kilometers separate Bulgaria from the Mediterranean. Hence a forward Turkish defence in Thrace would be of great assistance. But in Turkish Thrace, the open rolling terrain favours an attacker's mechanised and armoured forces. Estimates of Soviet and Bulgarian forces available for commitment against Greece and Turkey are from about sixteen to thirty division equivalents. Turkish and Greek forces facing this threat have been estimated at about twenty-three divisions. But the Turkish–Greek conflict over Cyprus hedges the cohesiveness of the defence. More important, Warsaw Pact forces are largely mechanised with a favourable combat tank ratio of at least three to one – their armour being more modern.

In eastern Turkey, although terrain is rugged and there are many narrow passes through which an attack must be mounted, the plains directly across the Soviet border in north-eastern Turkey favour military manoeuvrability. Moreover, Soviet forces available for this region consist of a minimum of twelve, possibly eighteen, motorised divisions. The Soviet invasion of Afghanistan has shown the technical calibre of these divisions, the air and armour support available to them, and the speed with which they can be augmented. Turkey has available for defence about seven division equivalents, six of them being primarily infantry. The jandarma formations that could back them up must also cope with serious public order requirements due to Kurdish unrest. The terrain advantage the Turks have could be negated by a Soviet airmobile assault. This sort of threat reinforces the urgency of a technological modernisation of the Turkish forces. But prospects for such modernisation are constrained, as will be explained later. In addition, Iraq and Syria, well equipped with Soviet, and in the case of Iraq, French, weapons could deploy about four divisions apiece against Turkey, with a four-to-one advantage in tanks — while retaining credible deterrence against Israel.

The air situation for Turkey is worse. Under COMSIXATAF, the operational forces available from Turkey are mostly obsolescent aircraft — F-84s, F-100 D/F and Cs, F-104G and Ss, manufactured in the 1950s. These represent the first and second Turkish Air Forces. The only improvement in Turkish air has been the adoption of 40 F-4Es and about 40 F-104Ss.[3] The vast size of the air space Turkey must defend makes this capability insufficient, even if both in-theatre USAF squadrons are available, and the Greek Air Force takes care of its air space on its own. Against this capability are arrayed Soviet long-range air forces composed of Backfire, Badger and Blinder aircraft, posing an all-weather, day or night, conventional and nuclear threat. Most of them are late models, well protected in their home bases. Warsaw Pact forces are generally more modern and better equipped for all-weather operations and electronic warfare. The Turkish Navy also faces a formidable threat in the Soviet Eskadra and the Soviet naval air forces. Surface-to-air missiles are also plentiful in Soviet and Bulgarian forces for combat zone protection.

In sum, Turkish weapon systems and equipment are in a state of serious obsolescence, and the military forces in being are inadequate for the defence of Turkey against a potential attack by the Soviet Union alone; certainly against a combined attack. In their present and their foreseeable state they do not constitute, therefore, a sufficient military deterrent. There have been, until very recently, no strong trends for effective changes in Turkish military capabilities — except that, following the US-imposed

1974 arms embargo, it was recognised that equipment and weapon systems, especially air and ground forces, had to be so severely cannibalised that a sizeable percentage of them might be beyond the stage where they could be repaired. But now it is generally agreed by Turks that the Turkish Army is inadequate for the performance of its NATO missions. At best, it could possibily defend Turkey against each of the countries it borders, one at a time, except the Soviet Union. On the ground, Turkish forces, it is widely recognised, are quite weak and obsolescent. The Turks believe that the major causes for this situation have been the US embargo and their deteriorated economy, in that order. In the air, the situation is equally discouraging. Because of widespread cannibalisation, a high rate of accidents and aged aircraft, the Turkish Air Force may have a greatly reduced combat effectiveness against the kind of aircraft it would have to face in combat. It could be questioned, therefore, whether the Turkish Air Force can defend Turkish air space against Soviet attack. The Turkish Navy too cannot fulfil its missions of controlling the Straits and protecting Turkish territorial waters, without NATO support.

Future prospects for Turkish defence, while showing some improvements in all three services, do not reveal possibilities for dramatic improvements that would make Turkish defence independently viable or capable of achieving their NATO missions within the foreseeable future. The state of the Turkish economy, the continuing serious consequences of the embargo, and the strong Turkish commitment to diversification of sources and autonomy in weapons and equipment procurement (itself a consequence of Turkish alienation from the United States caused by the embargo) make it unlikely that there will be dramatic improvements in Turkish defence: this notwithstanding a defence budget of a higher percentage of the total government budget than any other member of NATO. There has been limited improvement, reportedly, in the qualitative and quantitative weapons and equipment inventories. But the search for European alternatives for the ageing American equipment has been thwarted by Turkey's critical economic situation. Turkey's insistence on creating an autonomous armaments industry instead of aiding in the modernisation of its defence may, in fact, hinder it.

A Turkey that feels politically isolated from Western Europe and in economic competition with its European allies in the Middle East, that believes the American security guarantee to be strongly qualified by the conflictual relationship with Greece, and that must rely for critical oil supplies on the most politically radical, pro-Soviet Arab states, is more likely to accommodate itself to Soviet policies towards the Mediterranean and the Middle East. A consequence for Turkey's effective participation in NATO will be the perpetuation of the serious erosion in the Turkish relationship with the United States and its European allies. This process is likely to continue, gradually and probably without dramatic incidents, but with eventually telling effect on Turkey's participation in NATO. From a Western viewpoint, this cannot but be viewed with foreboding.

An underrated aspect of Turkey's participation in NATO has been Turkey's parliamentary democracy. Turkey is the only Muslim country of the Middle East that has been long committed to a West European model of parliamentary democracy. In the postwar period, except for short-lived military coups – intended not to overthrow the democratic system – Turkey has been also the only member of NATO's southern flank, besides Italy, to consistently practise liberal democracy. The same cannot be said of Greece or Portugal. The Turkish crisis has raised, in the minds of Turkish political leaders and especially the youthful electorate, some serious doubts about the long-term future of Turkish democracy. The major cause for these Turkish attitudes has been Turkey's alienation from Western Europe and the United States. But a contributing prior cause is to be found in the political left–right radicalisation and polarisation of Turkish domestic politics that has taken place following the 1960 military coup. The 1964, 1969 and 1974 Cyprus crises and the economic crisis have both contributed to this phenomenon and brought it to the surface.

The safeguards against revolution inherent in the Turkish political system – foremost among them the Turkish armed forces' patriotic cohesiveness, discipline and commitment to democracy as well as public order – can lead to the cautious conclusion that Turkey will not follow Iran's example. In light of the developments discussed above, however, Turkey's Western system of politics acquires essential importance for Turkey's relations with its NATO allies.

The common political ideology has been an important asset in the relations between Turkey, the United States and Western Europe. Without unduly oversimplifying, it may be said that shared political values have greatly aided in making it possible for the United States and Turkey to remain allies in the face of the acute policy differences that have afflicted their relations over Cyprus since 1964. Obversely, they have provided a buffer against Soviet influence in Turkey's internal politics. Thus Turkey's democratic system has not only functioned in a positive way in Turkish–US relations. It has also facilitated Turkey's political, economic and military relations with the democracies of Western Europe, especially West Germany. How critical the commitment to parliamentary politics is in the relations with members of the European Community has been illustrated by the experience of Spain, Portugal and Greece. The prolonged maintenance of a parliamentary democracy in spite of the vicissitudes Turkey has experienced since it joined the Western family of nations after the Second World War is a tribute to Turkey's commitment to Western democracy. If democracy should permanently fail in Turkey, the negative political repercussions for NATO and the West will reach beyond Turkey's frontiers to the Middle East, the Mediterranean and Europe.

Turkey's political prospects take meaning also in the context of Mediterranean security. Turkey, by virtue of its geography, is endowed with major significance for the security of the Mediterranean, including Spain, that goes beyond the limits of its economic and political status in the East–West political and military balance.

In the nuclear era, particularly for the Atlantic region which includes Western Europe and the Mediterranean, deterrence of East–West conflict is the only rational policy option. This is the case at conventional and regional, as well as strategic, nuclear and global levels. In fact, a NATO–Warsaw Pact conventional conflict that did not risk early escalation to nuclear war in the European theatre, and between the United States and the Soviet Union intercontinentally, is believed by most experts to be unlikely. Nevertheless, developments in recent years in the Soviet–American strategic balance and in the Eurostrategic balance have caused concern in the Atlantic Alliance including parties of the left in Italy, Socialists in France, and the Communist leadership of Yugoslavia, and have brought back into focus the importance of the East–West conventional military balance. With or without SALT II, the military and political risks for Western Europe appear to be increasing. Turkey is the forward and key location for NATO southern flank defence. Greece is not fully defensible without a Turkish forward defence in Thrace, for example. The emasculation of Turkey's defence capability would shift the NATO defence line to Italy and the 'choke points' between Sicily and North Africa. This would not only expose the Western Mediterranean to more direct Soviet pressure, but would also undercut the Western position in the Middle East and the Persian Gulf. A militarily strong and politically cohesive Turkey, not disaffected from the West, would reinforce deterrence at the conventional level and help maintain the East—West political equilibrium in Europe. It would also help sustain the non-aligned stance of Yugoslavia at a time when its future independence may be threatened by crisis in its leadership following the death of Tito.

The stakes for Europe and the Mediterranean countries in Turkey's crisis are high politically and militarily. A solution of the crisis is problematic at best.

Notes

1. The requirements of an expanded battle area, both surface and air space, are one illustration. Some have speculated that anti-ship and counterforce missile technology has increased the battle area tenfold. Missile-armed ships and aircraft can attack from any quadrant of the Mediterranean at long ranges.
2. This paper was presented to ISODARCO just weeks before the Turkish military coup of 1980.
3. All data on weapon systems on this and subsequent pages in this chapter are from the International Institute for Strategic Studies, *The Military Balance, 1978—1979* (London, 1978).

11 Greece and Nuclear Weapons

Kosta Tsipis

Introduction

Recently there has been considerable debate in Greece regarding the advisability of equipping the Greek defence forces with nuclear weapons. There has been much debate but little technical analysis of the costs, benefits and the scale of magnitude of the resources – natural, human, and manufacturing – required for such an effort.

This chapter will not address the advisability or not of nuclear weapons acquisition by Greece. It will only identify and discuss six technical and military issues involved in the process of accumulating a nuclear arsenal. First, the study will examine the circumstances under which Greece would want to acquire nuclear weapons. Secondly, it will deal with the methods of acquisition and their relative practicality. Thirdly, the study will identify the requirements in terms of manpower, facilities and materials implicit in some of the more realistic methods. Fourthly, the technical details of fabrication of nuclear warheads from uranium and plutonium will be examined. Fifthly, the costs, both direct and indirect, of such an effort will be estimated. Finally, the possible utility of nuclear warheads for Greece under several conditions will be examined.

Putative Circumstances Favouring Acquisition

There are several possible reasons, some logically founded, some not, for which Greece may want to accumulate a nuclear arsenal. These include:

1. deter a nuclear rival or neighbour from attacking Greece with conventional weapons;
2. deter an opponent from attacking Greece with nuclear weapons;
3. deter attempts of nuclear blackmail of Greece by an opponent that demands political, geographic or other concessions under the threat of nuclear attack;
4. use nuclear weapons to intimidate a non-nuclear rival or strengthen one's bargaining position in war or peace;
5. attempt to gain enhanced international status by exhibiting possession of nuclear weapons;
6. initiate a military–scientific technological base occasioned by the decision to acquire a nuclear arsenal;
7. follow the example of other nations of similar size and level of development;
8. create a nuclear deterrent following withdrawal from or collapse of existing military-alliance structures.

Although some of the circumstances listed here are dependent on external factors beyond the control of the Greek Government, and others are implicitly matters of internal political decision, this chapter does not seek to evaluate them or rank them in any order either of importance or of probability of occurrence. The occasion for such a decision may be triggered by a number of events including:

1. nuclearisation of neighbours or potential adversaries;
2. breakdown of international constraints of nuclear proliferation;
3. diminution or elimination of the technological and feasibility gap that separates use of nuclear energy for production of electric power from use in the manufacture of weapons;
4. reduction in perceived protection afforded by an alliance;
5. rise of hostile or imperialistic tendencies in neighbouring countries.

The rise of unforeseen circumstances that may add weight in domestic arguments in favour of the acquisition of nuclear weapons is an ever-present possibility that should not be neglected or overlooked.

Methods of Acquisition of Nuclear Weapons

There are, of course, a number of methods by which Greece could in principle at least acquire one or more nuclear weapons. They can be broadly divided into three classes:

1. illegal acquisition, either overt or covert;
2. purchase of weapons or of essential components requiring only final assembly;
3. manufacture them from their constituent raw materials.

Clearly, illegal acquisition (for example, overtly to capture weapons based on Greek soil, or covertly to become the recipient of weapons that somehow have been stolen from existing arsenals) is a conceivable but not a probable mode of acquisition. This is in part because of the enormous security, diplomatic and political costs, and in part because most probably only a token number of weapons could be acquired in this fashion. Consequently, this method of acquisition will not be considered acceptable in the context of this chapter and will not be pursued further.

Under the present international circumstances purchase of nuclear warheads or of essential components of warheads is impossible. It is, of course, conceivable that a complete breakdown of the NPT some time in the future will result in an international market in nuclear weapons. However, the trend is certainly moving in the opposite direction: the United States, certainly until the defeat of Carter, has vigorously pursued efforts to restrain as much as possible the opportunities for additional countries to acquire nuclear weapons or the capacity to manufacture them. The French and West German Governments tacitly agreed with American proposals and future diplomatic activity among the supplier countries will tend to strengthen the NPT and minimise or postpone for considerable periods of time the probability of emergence of additional nuclear-armed countries. In conclusion, then, it can be asserted that purchase of nuclear weapons will remain impossible until at least the end of this century.

The only method for acquisition remaining is to manufacture nuclear warheads, either from uranium or from plutonium. Throughout this chapter it will be assumed that as a matter of fact the fabrication of fusion weapons (colloquially but inaccurately known as the 'hydrogen bomb') both requires the possession of, and is one technological level more sophisicated than the fabrication of, fission weapons. Therefore this chapter will not address at all the question of fusion weapons, and will concentrate only on analysing the requirements for the assembly of fission weapons based on uranium or plutonium. This basic assertion is supported by historical fact, since all countries in possession of fusion weapons (the United States, the Soviet Union, Great Britain, China and France) first mastered the technology of fabrication of the simpler fission weapons that subsequently can be used either as the trigger device of a fusion explosive or as part of a fission-fusion fission device based on the 'booster principle'.

Fabrication of Warheads from Uranium or Plutonium: Fissile Material Requirements

There are only three materials suitable for the production of nuclear fission weapons. Uranium-235 (U_{235}), Uranium-233 (U_{233}) and plutonium-239 (Pu_{239}). The first two are found in nature as isotopes of the much more abundant, but not fissionable U_{238}. Plutonium is a man-made element generated in nuclear reactors by the absorption of one neutron by U_{238} that becomes U_{239}. This isotope decays immediately to Neptunium 239 which after a few days is spontaneously transformed to Pu_{239}, a relatively stable element. U_{233} has never been used in nuclear weapons because its presence in uranium ore is negligible. It can be produced in reactors containing thorium 232 by a neutron capture and the subsequent rapid decay of the formed Protactinium into U_{233}. The fission properties of U_{233} vary little from those of U_{235}. Therefore in all subsequent discussion only U_{235} and Pu_{239} will be considered. These two elements possess three properties that make them suitable materials for a nuclear explosive device:

1. They can be fissioned by a neutron, releasing in addition to energy several neutrons capable of splitting other nuclei. Therefore they can sustain a chain reaction.
2. The neutron generation time (the average time between the creation of a neutron by fission and the time this neutron produces another fission) is small compared to the time it takes for a pressure wave to travel through the core of fissile material inside a warhead.

3. The critical mass (the minimum amount of material needed to maintain a chain reaction and therefore produce an explosion) is small, about 50 kg for U_{235} and 8 kg for pure δ-phase metallic Pu_{239}. Since these materials are on the average 18–20 times more dense than water, a critical mass of uranium occupies the volume of an ordinary orange while that of plutonium is about the size of a table-tennis ball.

In assembling a nuclear weapon it is useful to surround the uranium or plutonium with a material that reflects neutrons back into the core of the weapon, thereby reducing the necessary amount that constitutes a critical mass: if U_{235} is surrounded by a lining of several centimetres of U_{238}, a good neutron reflector, the critical mass is reduced to about 12 kg. The corresponding critical mass of plutonium surrounded by 10 or more centimetres of beryllium is 4 kg. Consequently it is here assumed that 12 kg of U_{235} or 4 kg of Pu_{239} are enough for criticality. It must be noted that the advanced nuclear technology of the United States has reduced these values considerably. Thus a modern American weapon with an explosive yield of 20 000 tons of TNT has a nuclear core that weighs about 10 kg. It will be assumed, however, that any country such as Greece will be obliged at least *ab initio* to use nuclear explosives technology that will require considerably larger amounts of Pu_{239} or U_{235} for a 20 kiloton weapon. Thus it is here assumed that a weapon of this explosive yield will require at a minimum 20 kg of plutonium or *50–60 kg* of 93 per cent pure U_{235} with a 7 per cent U_{238} admixture. These figures will form the base of all subsequent calculations concerning methods of production of U_{235} and then of Pu_{239}.

1. U_{235}

Natural metallic uranium contains 0.7 per cent of U_{235} and 99.3 per cent of U_{238}. Since each ton of average uranium ore as extracted from the ground contains about 1.5 kg of metallic uranium, one requires roughly 6000 tons of metallic uranium which contains 50 kg of 93 per cent U_{235} needed for one weapon. Each kg of uranium metal costs $20–40 to extract from the ore. It is expected that the $40/kg (1976 dollar) price must be taken as the lowest limit of the cost of uranium metal extraction for the case of Greece, if the country were in possession of uranium deposits. Probably the actual cost will be considerably higher because of royalties and licensing costs of imported technology and know-how. Thus the price of uranium metal per weapon will be at least

$$(0.93 \times 50/0.7 \times 10^{-2}) \times 40 = 2.7.10^5\$.$$

Since, however, metallic uranium contains only 0.7 per cent U_{235} it is necessary to subject the natural uranium to a process that would enrich it to the necessary 93 per cent U_{235} concentration suitable for weapons fabrication. It takes about 300 separation work units per kg of 0.7 per cent U_{238} natural uranium to be enriched to the necessary 93 per cent U_{235} suitable for weapons fabrication. The current cost of a separation work unit is \$100. Therefore the separation cost per weapon is $50 \times 300 \times 100 = 1.5 \times 10^6\$$. There are four known methods for the enrichment of natural uranium: gaseous diffusion, gas centrifuge, the Beckler nozzle and laser separation. The gaseous diffusion enrichment method is the only proven working method for producing weapons-grade material. It requires extensive facilities with capital cost exceeding US \$1 billion (1965) for a plant that processes about 10 000 tons of natural uranium per year. A smaller plant would cost less, but the capital investment does *not* scale with the size of throughput; therefore even a small gaseous diffusion plant with a capacity of a few hundred tons per year would cost several hundred million dollars. In addition, gaseous diffusion consumes large amounts of power. For 10 000 tons throughput the annual power consumption is 6 million kW, and the annual operating cost about \$1 billion (1976). Thus even if the complex technology of gas diffusion enrichment were completely at hand such a facility would be prohibitively expensive for Greece. The gas centrifuge method is more suitable for production of smaller quantities of enriched weapons-grade uranium. However, the process is still in the stage of early development and no firm costs can be quoted. The Urenco/Centec group has a pilot plant in operation that can produce enough U_{235} for ten weapons per year. The estimated capital cost is about $200 \times 10^6\$$ and the operating expense of the order of $15-20 \times 10^6\$$ per year. At this cost, and without investment amortisation, the cost of U_{235} per weapon will be between \$1.5 and 2.0 million (1976). Gas centrifuge technology is also highly classified and requires the ability to produce light but very strong cylinders and very low friction bearings. Neither of these two metallurgical technologies is developed in Greece. Their development will require additional investment and a considerable period of time. On the other hand, it may be possible at some future date to purchase key centrifuge components from France, the Netherlands, Great Britain, the United States or Japan. The Beckler nozzle isotope separation method is still in its preliminary stage of development and it is unlikely that any significant quantities of uranium will be separated by that method for a number of years. The costs of this method are expected to be roughly the same as the gas centrifuge method.

Laser isotope separation is in principle possible but not a single atom of uranium has been separated by this method as yet. It is expected that the method will not be in practical application (if it ever succeeds) for at least another ten years. Several serious technical difficulties remain to be practically resolved and as a result it is impossible at this time to predict the capital investment and operating costs of a uranium enrichment facility using laser separation.

To summarise: the total cost of 50 kg of 93 per cent enriched U_{235} enough for one 20 kiloton weapon is 2.7×10^5 for natural uranium + 1.5×10^6\$ for enrichment $\simeq 2$ million dollars (1976). The cheaper of the two enrichment facilities that would produce enough U_{235} for a few weapons per year is expected to cost \$200 million (1976) to construct and between \$15 and \$20 million to operate. (The latter number divided by the number of weapons produced per year is the per weapon enrichment cost listed above as 1.5×10^6\$ per weapon assuming a production of enough U_{235} for ten weapons per year.) This figure is in complete agreement with the cost estimate derived independently on the basis of the necessary separation work units. Both methods of enrichment involve highly secret advanced technologies unavailable to Greece at this time. Therefore to the above costs one must add an indeterminate amount for technology acquisition.

2. Pu_{239}

Pu_{239} is produced in reactors when U_{238}, the abundant isotope of uranium, is irradiated by neutrons. This process can take place in any type of reactor, power, research, or the pool type available at Democritos Research Center. The annual Pu_{239} production (in kgs per MW electric energy per year) for various types of reactors is given below:

Boiling water	0.23 kg/MWe/yr
Pressurised water	0.23 kg/MWe/yr
Pressurised heavy water	0.29 kg/MWe/yr
Gas-cooled	0.25 kg/MWe/yr

A 1000 MW power reactor then would produce of the order of 250 kg of plutonium per year at 75 per cent load factor. Under these circumstances the plutonium produced will be a mixture of Pu_{239} and Pu_{240}. The latter isotope does not fission, is more likely to capture a neutron and become Pu_{241} and therefore both increases the neutron generation time and raises the critical mass value necessary for an explosive device. In addition, Pu_{240} fissions spontaneously with the emission of several neutrons, one of which may start the chain reaction before the plutonium core has reached its supercritical state and therefore may cause the untimely predetonation of the nuclear charge. This, aside from the obvious risks of an accident, has two undesirable effects: first, it makes the explosive yield of the weapon unpredictable and second it may reduce it by a factor of 10 or more, that is instead of the expected 20 kT yield the device may 'fizzle' and yield 1 or 2 kT TNT equivalent. In order to keep the proportion of Pu_{240} small in the fuel rods of a power nuclear reactor these rods must be burnt only to 10 per cent of their useful uranium content. This, however, is extremely uneconomical. Accumulation of Pu_{239} from the operation of power reactors entails a very large economic penalty.

Instead of a power reactor one could install a dedicated plutonium production reactor similar to the Dimona facility in Israel or the proposed Osiris metallurgical research reactor of Iraq. Such a reactor, if it would be possible to acquire it from one of the supplier countries, would cost approximately $50 \times 10^6$$ (1976) and would have an annual operating cost of $4 million. This figure does *not* include the cost of fuel or amortisation of capital investment. For a reactor that could produce about 100 kg or plutonium a year, this cost would be about $340 000 per kg. For a reactor that would produce 40 kg of Pu_{239} a year the cost per kg would be about $650 000. A heavy water moderated reactor of 20 MWe power rating would produce about 10 kg of plutonium per year. This reactor would have to be imported from Canada but Ottawa does not license the export of such reactors as part of the NPT efforts.

Finally, it is worth considering the capabilities of the small experimental reactor at Democritos. The time needed to produce 10 kg of plutonium with this reactor under several operating conditions varies between five and thirty-five years. The five-year time span requires 90 per cent enriched uranium fuel that the US government exports with great difficulty and the proviso of on-site inspection of its use. Needed alterations of the core of the reactor will require one—two additional years and about $1.5—2.0 million. The times listed imply continuous irradiation of the rods excluding any other use of the reactor at Democritos.

A complete plutonium production facility with an output of 40 kg plutonium per year will require, in addition to the reactor, a uranium ore-processing and refining plant, a fuel element fabrication facility, a plutonium separation plant (reprocessing) in which the plutonium produced by irradiation in the fuel rods will be separated from the uranium by chemical means, and a plutonium metal reduction plant. The total complex is estimated to cost about $50 million and requires about five years to install *given the technological know-how*. The annual cost will be about $25 million.

Plutonium is a highly toxic and radioactive substance and its handling and processing requires special remote-handling and sealed facilities. The cost estimate for a complete plutonium-handling complex assumes less than completely safe installations in the plutonium (fuel element) reprocessing plant. It is therefore to be expected that accidents or fatalities of workers by radioactive or toxic exposure may occur. A completely safe facility may cost an additional $5—10 million. The overall costs of a plutonium production reactor cum the complete plutonium-handling facility result in a price per kg of plutonium roughly the same as would result from using a power reactor somewhat inefficiently to produce Pu_{239} in its fuel rods, if the annual plutonium production is about 40 kg. For smaller quantities a power reactor appears more economical while for larger quantities a dedicated plutonium production reactor results in lower costs per kg of plutonium. Assuming that 20 kg of 90 per cent or better Pu_{239} metallic plutonium is necessary for a 20 kT weapon, one arrives at a price per plutonium weapon of about $10—20 million. This is sharply higher than the cost of a similar warhead in the United States. The difference is due both to the economies of size and the advanced nuclear warhead technology of the United States.

Weapon-fabrication Manpower and Facilities Requirements

The fabrication of a weapon, given adequate supplies of suitable fissile material, requires a number of activities such as design and fabrication of the explosive core itself, design and fabrication of the arming and fusing mechanisms, measurement of the properties of the fissile material at hand, some testing of this material, design and fabrication of fail-safe mechanisms to protect the device from unauthorised or premature use, and design and installation of protective measures that will protect the device from catastrophic events such as accidental release from an aircraft in flight, fire, earthquake or other extreme environments. The explosive core will usually consist, in an implosion-type weapon, of the fissile material, the surrounding neutron reflector (tamper) and the necessary explosive shaped charges and associated electronic and fusing components necessary to render the mass of the fissile material supercritical. Considerable expertise is needed for the design and manufacture of this assembly. Once the assembly is ready it has to be integrated into the weapon which will presumably be an air-droppable bomb that must weigh no more than 1000 kg and preferably half of that if it is to be carried by an F-4 fighter-bomber or other aircraft of that type. The entire weapon must then be tested in underground facilities and careful and extensive instrumentation is necessary in order to evaluate its performance. Considerable know-how in diagnostic physics will be necessary for that task. Finally, storage facilities for the weapons must be designed and constructed. These facilities must be both readily available to suitable aircraft, and safe from unauthorised entry, surprise attack and accidents.

The fabrication of a nuclear weapon using plutonium is additionally complicated by the complex metallurgical processes involved, the toxicity, chemical reactivity and radioactivity of the material. The capital investment in a facility that could assemble ten warheads a year would be about $15 million, and the annual operating costs about $2 million. Three to five years at the very minimum will be required for the design and initial assembly of a device *once the necessary personnel is assembled*. Longer periods of time must be contemplated if anything less than a massive effort is made to acquire nuclear-weapons capability. The number of scientists and engineers required for a total programme for the production of fissile material, and the design, initial assembly and testing of a fission weapon, is estimated by several independent analysts to be about 500 scientists, of which 50 at least must be at the doctoral level, that includes physicists, chemists, metallurgists, electronics, computer and explosives experts. In addition, the effort will require 1500 engineers, mainly nuclear, chemical and electronic. If Greece will have to train twenty to thirty PhD scientists (four–eight years needed) and 300 other scientists (four–five years needed) the total cost for *training* alone is $30 million over a period of four–eight years. In addition, assuming that 1000 engineers are to be trained, the cost will be approximately $90 million over a period of four–eight years. Most of this money will have to be in foreign currency since the majority of the training will have to take place abroad. In addition, a fraction of the scientists and engineers currently gainfully employed in the Greek industrial sector will have to be siphoned off into the nuclear-weapon effort, drastically reducing both the productivity and the rate of growth of Greek industry. This will represent an unknown cost in lost opportunities and retardation of the further industrialisation of Greece.

The task of designing a weapon will require extensive computational capability for calculations and simulation studies. This computational capability does not exist today in Greece and will have to be imported. Several million dollars will be required for that.

The testing of the device will cost between $11 and 20 million, depending upon the availability or not of a suitable mine for the test. This figure includes the cost of instrumentation but not of the device tested.

Direct and Opportunity Costs of the Programme

In addition to the direct costs of the programme outlined in the last two sections that amount, for a plutonium device, to a capital outlay of nearly $250 million, there are several other types of costs that can only be briefly outlined.

One, namely the loss of the services of a sizeable portion of the Greek scientific and engineering potential to the nuclear-weapons programme for periods up to ten years, has already been hinted at. While Greece is in the process of becoming increasingly industrialised in order to better fit in the EEC, such a diversion of scientific and technical manpower will have serious economic and perhaps political side-effects. Additionally, any overt attempt by Greece to acquire a nuclear arsenal will result in immediate retaliatory measures from the supplier countries such as the United States, France, West Germany, and Great Britain. These measures will no doubt involve embargoes of essential technological imports to Greece, economic penalties such as loss of most-favoured trade status in the United States, and loss of privileges in the EEC. But, most importantly, such an attempt at nuclearisation will deny Greece access to nuclear technology and nuclear fuel essential for its nuclear power reactor programme. A nuclear reactor is such a vastly complex and massive engineering system that Greece simply cannot construct it. Fuel elements for this reactor could be in principle fabricated in Greece *if* the country had enough uranium ore to support it for the thirty-year normal lifetime of the installation. But Greece does not, and even if such ore were available it would cost much more to fabricate the fuel elements locally rather than to purchase them from a supplier country. Thus the per kilowatt cost of power from the reactor would become prohibitively high. It is a fact that further industrialisation of Greece to the end of the century will require the installation of a nuclear power reactor, and therefore the reactor cannot be abandoned in favour of acquiring a nuclear arsenal. Once the reactor is in operation, it would in principle be possible to divert a number of 10 per cent burnt fuel elements and extract the plutonium from them. That, however, would jeopardise further supplies of fuel for the reactor and therefore it would be equivalent to shutting down the reactor permanently for the sake of diverting plutonium for weapons fabrication.

Diplomatic and security costs must also be considered. Abrogation of the NPT, of which Greece is a signatory, is bound to evoke the most profoundly negative response both from supplier countries and from the community of nations such as Sweden that have been championing the NPT. Diplomatic isolation may in the end erode the position and security of the country more drastically than the acquisition of nuclear weapons could restore (to say nothing of the five–ten-year hiatus during which Greece will not have nuclear weapons, but will be known to be developing them).

By far the most serious indirect cost of the initiation of development of nuclear weapons in Greece will be the actual diminution of its security that will result. Such development will undoubtedly force neighbouring countries to initiate a counter-development aimed at eventually providing them also with a nuclear arsenal. Greece then will become involved in a regional nuclear arms race that will end with the country having one or more opponents possessing nuclear weapons, a threat that it does not face now.

Thus the long-term security of the country will be diminished drastically. On the other hand, the situation is symmetrical: if a putative adversary of Greece launches a nuclear weapons development programme, Greece would have to re-examine the entire issue in a new light.

Finally, expenditure of sums, mainly in foreign currency, for a nuclear weapons development programme is bound to affect the economic ability of the country to support and improve the conventional armed forces. Thus it may well be that the several hundred million dollars necessary for the development of a nuclear arsenal could buy more security for the country if spent procuring high-technology conventional weapons or strengthening the industrial and technological base of the economy, than buying nuclear weapons that, as the experience of all the existing nuclear countries has shown, cannot be used for political or military ends other than deterrence. Thus possession of nuclear weapons did not prevent the defeat of American forces in Vietnam or improve the political or military ability of the British to impose their will in Rhodesia, Ireland and elsewhere. Neither has any of the nuclear powers parleyed the possession of nuclear weapons into successful coercion or military advantage.

Utilities of a Nuclear Arsenal

A nuclear arsenal consisting of a modest number of tested, air-deliverable weapons could prove quite useful under certain circumstances. These circumstances, however, have at this time and in the foreseeable future very small probability of occurrence, and therefore the overall utility of nuclear weapons should be viewed in that frame of reference. For example, possession of nuclear weapons could prove an effective deterrent against a nuclear adversary bent at blackmailing or coercing Greece. They would in all probability dissuade him from attacking Greece, although it is not certain that, if in possession of superior conventional forces, such an adversary could not attack and occupy a portion of Greek territory. In the last analysis, then, a nuclear arsenal can only deter nuclear attack or nuclear blackmail from another nuclear power. It will also most probably, but not certainly, discourage a non-nuclear adversary from attacking Greece. It must be borne in mind that to date nuclear weapons have not proved helpful in resolving favourably conventional conflicts.

A useful by-product of a programme to develop a nuclear arsenal in Greece will be the establishment of a strong nuclear-technology base and the rapid improvement and expansion of the scientific and technological potential of the country. The decision to build nuclear weapons in France resulted in a rapid development of nuclear and electronics technology in that country. On the other hand, it must not be forgotten that France already possessed an advanced technological base at the time the nuclear weapons programme was initiated. Finally, if the Greek Government decided to improve the scientific and technological potential of the country, it can certainly do so without the initiation of a nuclear-weapons project.

Air-deliverable nuclear weapons may find in some cases battlefield applications such as against concentrations of hostile forces. They could be used with impunity, however, only if the adversary did not possess nuclear weapons. In addition, it must be remembered that use of nuclear weapons on the battlefield requires dedicated units for delivery, and extensive training of all forces that would be involved in such use. These conditions tend to abbreviate the conventional capabilities of the armed forces, and as NATO has already experienced, this proves to be a costly effort both financially and in terms of combat units and equipment available for conventional operations. At any rate, before one can decide on the cost-effectiveness of nuclear weapons for battlefield use, one must carefully examine all alternative munitions and systems that could perform the same mission with similar, or better, results.

Conclusion

This brief analysis tends to confirm that, if for any reason Greece decided to develop a nuclear weapons arsenal, it would be possible to do so. The fabrication of deliverable, tested nuclear weapons does not present in principle any insurmountable technical obstacles. If Greece were ready to pay the costs, both in finance and in political, diplomatic and security disadvantages, she could eventually acquire a nuclear arsenal. This study has pointed out that if Greece is in possession of useful uranium ore deposits, that is of deposits that yield above 1.0 kg of uranium metal for every ton of ore, in enough quantity to provide not only the necessary fissionable material for weapons, but all the necessary fuel for the nuclear power reactor needed for energy production, then Greece could contemplate abrogating the NPT and charting a course of nuclear technology development independently of the supplier countries. Such action could postpone acquisition of a power reactor until the beginning of the next century, and fabrication of nuclear weapons until the mid-1990s. If Greece wants to avail herself of technology and fuel necessary for the projected power reactor, she has *no alternative* in the foreseeable future but to remain a signatory of the NPT. Diversion of fissionable material from an operational power reactor is both a dangerous violation of treaty obligations that Greece has signed and does not in itself make nuclear weapons available. The processing and fabrication of this purloined material into weapons *cannot be performed secretly*. At any rate, any credible nuclear weapon requires testing which will obviate all previous secrecy.

The development of the facilities for the production of weapons-grade fissile material, of the weapons' assembly plant, of the design, testing and fabrication of the weapon and of assorted subsidiary activities will require 10 000−15,000 man-years and the expenditure of more than $250 million over a period extending between five and eight years. Subsequent to this initial investment, it is expected that the established facility will be able to produce two 20 kT nuclear weapons a year at a cost of roughly $10 million each (1976). A higher rate of production will require more fissile material but will affect the overall cost in manpower and funds only marginally. Finally, while there are serious costs of opportunity in excess of the direct manpower and monetary costs that may in effect amount to a sum larger than the direct costs mentioned above, the utility of a nuclear arsenal for Greece appears for the foreseeable future confined to marginal circumstances that have small probability of occurrence. The disutilities, on the other hand, that stem mainly from the connection between nuclear weapons and nuclear power, and the explicit desire of the supplier nations to discourage and penalise proliferation of nuclear weapons, are immediate, certain, and enormously threatening to the economic and industrial development of Greece.

12 The Foreign Policy of Albania After the Break with China

György Réti

The Three Principal Enemies

In his statement at the UN General Assembly in October 1979 Foreign Minister N. Nase of Albania summed up the view taken of the world situation by the makers of Albanian foreign policy:

> the world situation is very complex and fraught with great dangers. This is the result of the intensification of the expansionist and hegemonistic policy pursued by the superpowers and their efforts to exercise their dictates, their arbitrariness and their interference in the internal affairs of all countries . . . The rivalry between the United States and the Soviet Union for domination and hegemony in the world has been and remains the main source of tension and conflict between different countries, as well as local wars, and is the greatest danger to the peace and security of the peoples . . . In the shadow of and in collaboration with the United States, social-imperialist China is seeking to create spheres of domination, to become the principal military power in that zone [the Far East], to establish its domination in Asia and throughout the Pacific.[1]

The above assertions contain the most enduring and the newest elements of Albanian foreign policy. The most enduring element of Albanian foreign policy, and at the same time its greatest fault, is that for about twenty years now it has lumped together US imperialism and the main force of socialism and peace, namely the Soviet Union. Accordingly the manifestations of Albanian foreign policy make no distinction between the blocs of alliances of the two world systems — between NATO and the Warsaw Treaty, as well as between the EEC and the CMEA. Albanian foreign policy position statements also emphasise that Albania is not willing to establish diplomatic relations with either the United States or the Soviet Union.

The most important new element of Albanian foreign policy is that is has also put its earlier 'great ally', China (now described as 'social-imperialist' like the Soviet Union) in the same class as its two principle enemies.

The Albanian–Chinese Differences

Considering that the break between Albania and China is a recent event and marks the end of an era in Albanian foreign policy, it is appropriate here to deal in greater detail with its antecedents, causes and consequences. As is well known, it was in collaboration with China and the Communist Party of China that from 1961 onwards Albania waged its struggle against the majority of the international working-class movement and its main force, the Soviet Union, and its allies. In this struggle Albanian and Chinese leaders were united by their rejection of the corrective ideas formulated at the Twentieth Congress of the Communist Party of the Soviet Union: condemnation of the criticism of the personality cult, denial of peaceful coexistence of countries with different systems, as well as rejection of the possibility of a peaceful transition to socialism. The Albanian leaders qualified as 'revisionist' the countries and parties which had accepted the principles endorsed at the Twentieth Congress and asserted that 'capitalism was restored' in those countries. Albania suspended its participation in the CMEA and withdrew from the Warsaw Treaty. It broke off all relations with the Soviet Union and reduced to a minimum its contacts with the other countries it considered 'revisionist'.

In Albanian–Chinese relations which had seemed undisturbed in the 1960s increasing troubles cropped up from the early 1970s onwards. The root cause of this was that the Albanian leadership was unable, and unwilling, to follow the changes in the internal power structure in China and still less China's prompt overtures to the United States, NATO and the EEC, as well as its unprincipled relationships with several fascistoid regimes. The Albanian leadership felt offended also by the fact that China, having emerged from its international isolation, gave less and less heed to its little ally in the Balkans. Reduction of political and economic assistance from the Chinese leadership engaging in great-power politics induced the Albanian leadership to try, by expressing its criticism first through confidential channels and later more and more openly, to bring the Chinese leadership to take increasingly into account the points of view and interests of Albania. Since these attempts had failed and since in the Chinese power struggle the 'Radicals' displaying greater understanding towards Albania had been defeated by the 'Pragmatists', the Albanian leadership decided to make public its differences of opinion with the Chinese leadership.

The first manifestation of this was the publication, on 7 July 1977, of an article criticising the Chinese theory of 'three worlds'.[2] This article – still without naming China – accused the advocates of the theory of 'three worlds' of having betrayed the theory and foreign political practice of Marxism-Leninism, as well as the national liberation struggle of the peoples. The publication of the article was followed by a year-long campaign by the Party of Labour of Albania (PLA) and its foreign supporters who, still without naming the 'accused', attacked more and more vehemently this 'anti-Marxist and counter-revolutionary' theory. Simultaneously a rapid deterioration of Albanian–Chinese relations could be observed in all fields. This process culminated in the note of 7 July 1978 from the Chinese Government to the Albanian Government announcing the stopping of economic and military aid to Albania and the recall of the Chinese experts working there.[3] Next, the PLA and the Albanian Government gave publicity to their 'bill of indictment' against the Chinese leadership in a long letter dated 29 July 1978. With the publication of these two documents the Albanian–Chinese confrontation which had so far been partial and covert became total and open and was further intensifying. In 1979 Albania published, in a number of worldwide languages, Enver Hoxha's work *Imperialism and the Revolution* and two volumes of his political diary, which summarise and systematise the criticism of Chinese policy.

The essence of the criticisms formulated in Hoxha's works and in other Albanian documents can be summed up as follows:

1. The Chinese side had exaggerated and magnified its economic assistance to Albania and the size of credits, the value of which between 1954 and 1975 was not 10 000 million yüan, as stated in the Chinese note, but only 3000 million yüan (1 yüan = about US $0.50). By making public the provision of military aid China did harm to the defence of Albania. The Chinese experts committed to the flames or carried off the documentation of the constructions they had built in Albania, and left a number of investment projects unfinished. By doing so they caused immeasurable damage to the Albanian national economy. The aim of economic assistance had been to make Albania a vassal state of China.

2. In a comradely way, through confidential channels, the PLA several times informed the Chinese leadership of its disagreement with China's great-power chauvinistic policy, but Mao and his successors departed from the Leninist norms of inter-Party relations, because 'they knew no other way than the dictate of their own views and the enforcement thereof upon others, particularly upon smaller parties and states'.

3. The Communist Party of China has always maintained a wavering attitude in the struggle against revisionism.

4. The PLA condemned the Chinese claims to Soviet territories because, on the one hand, this action 'harmed the cause of the struggle against Khrushchevite revisionism' and, on the other, it 'implied a manifestation of great-power chauvinistic spirit and the fomentation of a European war'.

5. The Chinese leadership, instead of providing Albania with appropriate defensive weapons, advised that country to conclude a military alliance with Yugoslavia and Romania. Thereby 'it intended to entangle socialist Albania in the meshes of a war-mongering conspiracy' being woven by China in the Balkan area.

6. The 'Maoist thought' guiding Chinese policy is, as was stated by Hoxha, 'a hotchpotch of views in which principles borrowed from Marxism were mixed with idealistic, pragmatic and revisionist principles of different philosophical systems'. During the Chinese revolution Maoist conceptions were substituted for the Marxist-Leninist doctrine. In the policy of the Chinese leadership great-power chauvinism was substituted for proletarian internationalism. Anti-Leninist practice was adopted with regard to

the organisation and leading role of the Party. The army has always played a decisive role in the struggle between different factions in China. This is what happened also in the 'great proletarian cultural revolution', which 'was not a revolution, was neither great nor cultural, but especially was not proletarian'.

7. Albanian documents expose to murderous criticism the Chinese theory of 'three worlds', which means 'negation of the theory of Marx, Engels, Lenin and Stalin'. The division of the world into three parts is based on a racialist and metaphysical world-view. The theory of 'three worlds' negates the decisive role of class criteria, the existence of the socialist world, and sees the driving forces of history in the extremely heterogeneous 'third world'. The Chinese leadership proclaims a 'holy alliance' of the so-called second and third worlds, as well as the United States, against the Soviet Union.

8. In the opinion of Albania the primary aim of Chinese foreign policy is 'to change China into an imperialist super-power as soon as possible'. Since the designs of the Chinese leaders are in sharp contrast to China's backwardness from the economic and military points of view, they have resolved to rely upon US imperialism and other developed capitalist countries. They intend China to dominate over the developing countries. 'They have based Chinese strategy and foreign policy on the fomenting of wars between the imperialists.' The most ardent desire of the Chinese leadership is to see the Soviet Union and the United States run into frontal collision 'while China, sitting a comfortable distance off, would be warming its hands at the nuclear fire which would annihilate its two principal rivals and make it the all-powerful, exclusive master of the world'. The Chinese leadership is on a common barricade with the US imperialists, the barricade of counter-revolution. In the strategic plans of American imperialism the US—Japan—China alliance is to play the same role in Asia as NATO does in Europe. 'Having stood all tests, China has demonstrated that it is the keenest champion of American interests in Europe, the Near East, Africa and Asia alike.'

9. Albanian statements have branded China's aggression against Vietnam as 'a barbarous act of the fascist type', being 'a logical consequence of the social-imperialist policy of the Chinese leadership'. China attacked a harmless country and a heroic people. As the Chinese could support 'the barbarous and fascist clique of Pol Pot', in the same way 'Vietnam can also support the

revolutionaries and the people of Cambodia in building their free, independent and sovereign country'. The peoples of Asia have to be on their guard because 'what China now does in Vietnam, it can tomorrow do to them as well'. 'He who now fails to support Vietnam is helping the warmongers', is stated in the Albanian communiqué condemning the Chinese aggression against Vietnam.

Growing Activity of Albanian Foreign Policy

Since the deterioration of Albanian–Chinese relations a certain increase in the activity of Albanian foreign policy is perceptible. Since 1977 Albania has established diplomatic relations with ten countries, mostly developing ones, thus raising to eighty-four the number of countries with which it maintains diplomatic relations. (Albania has embassies in twenty-two of them, while sixteen countries have diplomatic missions in Tirana.)

In his election speech delivered on 8 November 1978 Hoxha summed up the principles of Albanian foreign policy in these words:

> In our relations with the foreign world, our Party and Govern-ment have pursued and are pursuing an open and correct policy. When our partners are genuine Marxist-Leninists, then our relations with them develop on the road of friendship, fraternal collaboration and mutual aid. With the capitalist and revisionist states, we develop trade and cultural relations of mutual benefit, on the condition that equality, sovereignty and non-interference in internal affairs are respected.[4]

Both from this speech and from other statements, however, it appears that at present the Albanian leadership regards only some diminutive parties which follow the PLA as 'genuine Marxist-Leninist' and puts all other parties and countries of the world in the 'capitalist and revisionist' category. In connection with countries of this category Hoxha had the following to say:

> We have clearly defined our political and ideological stands towards the capitalist and revisionist states — we fight their ideology, policy, methods and acts, just as they fight Marxism-Leninism, the revolution, and socialism . . . In our relations

with the capitalist and revisionist states, the concrete attitudes of these states with regard to our country are taken into account. Proceeding from these attitudes we distinguish between those which are well-intentioned towards us, which are for friendly approaches and normal trade and cultural relations with our country. With such states as the Scandinavian countries and Austria, Belgium, France, Holland, Switzerland and others, the possibility exists for the trade relations of our states to develop with mutual benefit, and for cultural relations with them to develop better.[5]

The Albanian leadership thus continues not to count among its 'well-wishers' those socialist countries regarded as revisionist, although these countries have, on a number of occasions in the past few years, given expression to their good intentions towards Albania and to their readiness to develop bilateral relations in many a field. Consequently the statement included in the report to the Seventh Congress of the PLA that 'with revisionist countries' Albania main-tains only 'restricted relations on a very low level' continues to be valid. Indicative of this low level is that with these countries Albania maintains, at variance with general diplomatic usages, diplomatic missions headed not by ambassadors but by chargés d'affaires, although the socialist countries have on several occasions proposed the raising of these relations to embassy level. In default of political and cultural relationships Albania's relations with the majority of the European socialist countries are accordingly restricted practi-cally to the field of foreign trade. And following the Albanian—Chinese split there has been a slow increase in the foreign trade of Albania with the European socialist countries.

It does no good to the development of relations between Albania and the socialist countries that the Albanian communications media systematically conduct a campaign of subtle and rude propaganda against the majority of the socialist countries of Eastern Europe.

Since the early 1970s Albania has paid greater attention to the improvement of mutual relations with its neighbours in the Balkans. Although the Albanian leadership is opposed to multi-lateral co-operation among the Balkan countries, it is definitely inclined to develop bilateral relations. This goes particularly for the two neighbouring countries with which Albania's relations were most strained in the 1950s and 1960s, namely Yugoslavia and

Greece. In the early 1970s Albania resumed diplomatic relations severed two decades before, and this step entailed a relatively rapid development of economic and cultural exchanges.

The Albanian foreign policy principles concerning Yugoslavia were summed up by Hoxha in his above-mentioned election speech as follows:

> With the Yugoslav revisionist leadership we have irreconcilable ideological and political contradictions . . . Nevertheless . . . we are for the continuation of normal commercial and cultural relations with Yugoslavia. With the peoples of Yugoslavia we want to live in friendship and within our rights.[6]

The last sentence referred to the nearly one and a half million Yugoslav citizens of Albanian descent. For two decades the lot of these people has been one of the pivotal issues of Albanian–Yugoslav conflicts. Simultaneously with the improvement in the situation of the Albanians living for the most part in Kosovo Autonomous Province, Kosovo has come to fill the part of a bridge in the relations between the two countries. The regular and increasingly developing political, economic and cultural relations which have taken shape between Albania and Kosovo contribute to the general development of Albanian–Yugoslav relations. As a result, Yugoslavia has become the most important economic and cultural partner of Albania.

A prerequisite for the development of Albanian–Greek relations was that official Greek quarters should renounce their previous territorial claims against Albania. Thereafter relations between the two countries began to develop. The improvement of political relations was indicated by the fact that Greece was the first capitalist country with which Albania established regular consultations on a ministerial level. Albanian–Greek foreign trade is also undergoing rapid development. Cultural groups often stage guest performances in each other's country. In 1977 Greece started a regular airline to Tirana.

Even though in a less spectacular manner, Albanian–Turkish relations are also developing. A manifestation of this was the first visit to Tirana by the Foreign Trade Minister of Turkey in 1979. In addition to the development of economic relations, talks were conducted on the establishment of an air traffic service between the two countries.

Less undisturbed are Albania's relations with two other states in the Balkans, namely Romania and Bulgaria. In earlier years Albanian propaganda left Romania out of its campaign against the 'revisionist countries'. This is why it came as a surprise that Hoxha's book *Reflections on China* contained violent attacks against Romania too. Bulgaria, on the other hand, had also earlier been one of the main targets of Albanian attacks.

The development of Albanian–Italian relations was demonstrated in 1979 by the fact that, for the first time since its liberation, Albania received a visit from an Italian Cabinet Minister in the person of the Minister of Commerce. Italy is at present the most important capitalist trading partner of Albania. Cultural relations are confined chiefly to those areas of southern Italy where Italians of Albanian descent (Arberes) are settled. It is worth noting as a point of interest that every evening the Italian television newscast is amplified and thus made receivable in Albania. (At the same time the broadcasts of Yugoslav television which can be received without amplification are jammed in Albania.)

The relations of Albania with the Western European countries qualified as 'well-intentioned' in Hoxha's aforementioned speech, owing to the relatively feeble interest taken by those countries, develop at a slow rate.

In relation to West Germany and to Great Britain Albania consistently takes the stand that it will refuse to establish diplomatic relations until the former pays compensation for the losses caused to Albania in the Second World War, and until the latter makes restitution of the unlawfully-withheld Albanian stock of gold. From time to time the world press gives news of confidential talks about these matters with representatives of the two states. Despite the absence of diplomatic relations, West Germany is one of the most important economic partners of Albania.

As regards the Near East Albania assured the Palestinian people of its support in their struggle, condemns the Camp David deals, but – presumably in view of its relations with Egypt – it has not criticised openly President Anwar Sadat's policy.

In connection with recent events in the Middle East the Albanian statements of foreign policy greeted the Iranian Revolution with enthusiasm while indiscriminately condemning intervention by the United States, China and the Soviet Union in the internal affairs of the countries of the Middle East.

Albanian statements on the situation in Indochina pledged

support to the peoples struggling against Chinese aggression. Similarly they express solidarity with the peoples of Africa, Asia and Latin America fighting for their independence and against neo-colonialist intervention. At the same time much is detracted from the value of such statements by the fact that they always contain anti-Soviet phrases inviting those peoples to be vigilant in face of their natural allies, the Soviet Union and the other 'revisionist' countries.

The efforts to ease international tension were played down by Hoxha in his election speech:

> We say openly . . . that the beautiful words about the problems of disarmament that are spoken at the United Nations Organization, at the Conferences of Helsinki, or Belgrade and elsewhere, are sheer demagogy.[7]

The keynote of the foreign policy statements made after the Albanian−Chinese split was that Albania would not alter the line it had followed before. Hoxha talked of this in his election speech in these words:

> Our enemies are mistaken when they think that in following an independent policy, our country is allegedly isolated and 'abandoned on the streets', that 'it will hold out its hand to somebody who will pull it out of the mire', etc. The People's Socialist Republic of Albania has never been, and never will be isolated, it has never been and never will be left on the streets. It is advancing confidently, relying on its own strength, building, creating, training and defending itself fearlessly and, with its heroic example, it is inspiring and will continue to inspire the oppressed masses of the world. The unwavering stand of Albania in its policy is resolute and correct, because it is guided by the theory of Marx, Engels, Lenin and Stalin.[8 and 9]

Notes

1. United Nations Document A/34/PV.19, pp. 4−5.
2. 'Theory and Practice of the Revolution', *Albania Today*, no. 4 (1977) pp. 20−9.
3. *Peking Review*, 21 July 1978.
4. 'Albania is Forging Ahead Confidently and Unafraid', *Albania Today*, no. 6 (1978) pp. 6−25.

5. ibid.
6. ibid.
7. ibid.
8. ibid.
9. The present article is a translated excerpt from György Réti, *Mit kell Tudni Albániáról?* (Kossuth Könyvkiadó: Budapest, 1981). Drafted in 1980, it does not take account of important later events such as the disturbances in Kosovo and the Eighth Congress of the PLA.

13   The Cyprus Crisis

Daniele Moro

The difficulty in reaching a workable solution of the Cyprus crisis is not due only to intercommunity relations having reached a point where they have become almost impossible. It arises also out of the international implications of the Cyprus question. In other words, very strong external pressures have been and are increasingly being exerted on the island. While it is true that the Cyprus crisis involves directly only Greeks and Turks, the crisis *for Cyprus* involves powers of various sizes, not all of which are close to the conflict area.

It is thus possible to approach the Cyprus crisis in various ways. One is by the study of the history of the island and of the inability of the Greek majority and the Turkish minority to live together peacefully. Another approach is to look at the way the island's fate has been affected from the outside by Greece and Turkey. But to assume that the problem is restricted to a clash between Athens and Ankara is equally wrong: no analysis can be limited to these two NATO countries even though they have come very close to a direct confrontation and have thus been diverted from their basic NATO role with a resulting worsening of both countries' relations with their main ally, the United States. For an attempt has been made by the Soviet bloc to exploit the Cyprus crisis. In addition, many Arab countries have been and are concerned with the question. In fact the Cyprus Government has had a large measure of success in finding wide Arab support for its position. Many explanations have been offered. For example, it has been claimed that the Arabs 'recall how they were treated by their Turkish masters during the Ottoman Empire, and world public opinion is finally being informed about the way Turkey treats the Kurds living in the eastern regions of the country and who are themselves Muslims'.[1]

Consequences deriving from the Cyprus crisis have recently been growing. The Western countries are facing increasing problems: the Middle East conflict does not look close to a peaceful solution; the Lebanese conflict continues; the Iraqi–Iranian War is still raging; the Soviets still occupy Afghanistan; and there are growing fears concerning Balkan stability. All these elements combine to concentrate increased attention on Cyprus. It is in the American interest, of course, to see that troops, above all those of Turkey, deployed in Cyprus, are utilised on the Soviet front. Much more important, however, is the American right to continue to use facilities both in Turkey and in Greece; and this has been brought into question, at various stages, because of the consequences of the Cyprus crisis. If, for example, the United States should be prevented from using facilities in Crete, the Soviets would be greatly helped in case of war taking place in the wider Mediterranean.

From the Soviet point of view it is quite obviously preferable that Cyprus be an island formally reunified, as in Archbishop Makarios's time, and neutralised,[2] accompanied by the closing down of the British Sovereign Bases, or at least with strong limitations on their use. But although the Soviet Union has generally taken sides with the Greek Cypriots, it should be remembered that in certain periods Moscow has tried to get onto better terms with Turkey (the Soviets were particularly successful during Bulent Ecevit's term in office). Nevertheless recent events show that the Soviets are not wavering in their support for the creation of a federalised and neutral regime for the whole island. For example, in *Pravda* on 12 December 1978 the following appeared:

> It is to partition that behind-the-scenes efforts of the enemies of the sovereignty and independence of Cyprus are turned. As the Republic's progressive forces note, imperialist manoeuvres are now increasingly evident. The main aim of these activities is to 'solve' the Cyprus problem within the framework of the North Atlantic coalition and to convert the island into a NATO base and stepping-stone into the Middle East — *an area which is in close proximity to the socialist states.*[3]

Rude Pravo, the Czechoslovak newspaper, was if possible even more explicit on 27 March 1979:

> The only solution that would satisfy the imperialists is partition and double union with the countries which are NATO members;

it is the dissolution of the Cyprus Republic, the crushing of the progressive movement in Cyprus and the changing of the island into an unsinkable aircraft carrier of imperialism.[4]

It may also be observed that the Soviet Union, despite having made no attempt to be directly involved in reaching a solution to the Cyprus problem, has exploited the situation, even while claiming a sincere wish for a peaceful settlement. Doubts exist, in fact, as to whether Moscow has a real interest in seeing a workable solution to the conflict. For it should be remembered that intercommunity problems are present not only in Cyprus: Athens and Ankara are also still concerned about the situation of the Greek minority in Istanbul and of the Turkish minority in Western Thrace.

The only clear result of the crisis has been a weakening of the southern flank of NATO and an increase in anti-American feeling on both sides. It is also interesting to note that Greece and Turkey have been the only NATO countries to see the establishment by coups of military regimes. One recalls, too, the charge of American sympathy with the Colonels' coup in Athens in 1967. In due course the same Colonels supported the EOKA B takeover in Cyprus which provided the 'justification' for the Turkish invasion of Cyprus in 1974. None of this served to improve relations between Turkey and the United States. But matters went from bad to worse as a result of the US Congress's decision to impose an arms embargo which lasted from 5 February 1975 to 4 September 1978, even though in practice it was not strictly enforced. On 5 February 1975 the British Broadcasting Corporation (BBC) in London clearly summarised the position:

the decision by the American Congress to cut off military aid to Turkey from today has been described by the Turkish Prime Minister, M. [Sadi] Irmak, as a very grave mistake. He said that Turkey would now review its military contribution to NATO. A correspondent for the BBC in Ankara says that diplomatic sources here believe the Turkish Government will probably dismantle the twenty or so bases in the country. The arms embargo has been strongly opposed by President Ford and Dr Kissinger, as set by Congress, unless there is substantial progress towards a settlement of the Cyprus question. Our correspondent says the feeling in Ankara is that the American cut will have an adverse effect by hardening Turkey's attitude.[5]

On 13 February 1975 the Turkish Federated State of Cyprus was established in the North. In October 1975 there was an initial partial lifting of the ban. And other Western countries provided some alternative arms supplies. The result of American policy was thus that both Greece and Turkey were totally dissatisfied.

Another very embarrassing question relates to the British role in the crisis. The Greek Cypriot side charged Great Britain with being 'blind' as regards the Turkish invasion and the need to stop it. A report from the British House of Commons Select Committee on Cyprus did not in fact accept the official version of British alleged inability to intervene effectively because of ignorance that the EOKA B coup and the Turkish retaliation were to take place. A spokesperson for the Foreign Office said, however,

> even had we chosen to take part in some military enterprise we did not within the island have the resources to make a viable military proposition . . . we did not possess on the island at any time troop levels which would have enabled us meaningfully to intervene either in the invasion or before or during the [Nicos] Sampson coup.

Even the United Nations' efforts have not been very useful in reaching a workable solution. While the deployment of UN troops has been effective in physically dividing the two sectors of the island, the UN-sponsored meetings have been judged by many observers as quite inconclusive.

The worsening of the international situation in recent years has certainly complicated the task of those seeking a peaceful solution. There have been direct and indirect consequences. The international air space over the Aegean has been closed; clashes over ownership of the continental shelf have occurred; and the question of Turkish access to the open sea has arisen. Another negative result of the Cyprus crisis has been Greek threats to leave the military wing of NATO. In general, Turkish and Greek reactions have caused the weakening of the southern flank of NATO just at a time of a large expansion of the Soviet presence in the Mediterranean. The United States, moreover, has been seriously affected, having military bases in both countries. After serious difficulties, however, Turkish—American relations have improved. On 29 March 1980 a Turkish—American agreement was signed concerning US facilities on Turkish soil. Under this agreement the two most important sites, at Sinon on the Black Sea coast and at Pirinclick in south-eastern Turkey, will continue to monitor Soviet nuclear and military developments untrammelled, though these sites and others will be under nominal Turkish control. The Americans may not use the bases for other than NATO purposes, that is not for those relating to the Gulf or South-West Asia.[6] (The Iranian crisis and the closing of the American bases there have, of course, served to increase American interest in Turkey, in Greece and in Cyprus.)

According to East European sources, the Americans are in fact planning to use or have just started to use the British Sovereign Base Areas' facilities for monitoring the southern border of the Soviet Union. For example, the following appeared in *Izvestia* on 7 April 1979:

> The notorious U-2 spy planes will be based in Cyprus at the British Air Force Base in Akrotiri. They will make flights over the areas located on the Soviet—Iranian border, i.e. approximately in the place where the American spy bases were located not long ago. It has been reported that American radio-electronic equipment has possibly been already moved from Iran to the British bases in Cyprus. Several hundred American servicemen are taking up quarters on the bases . . . At the same time radio-technical facilities are being set up for uninterrupted communication with the American Mediterranean fleet.

A similar charge was made by the Communist Party of Cyprus. After the British Government had denied it, the Communist Party of Cyprus reiterated it and recommended that the Government of Cyprus should prevent non-British forces from using the bases and should ultimately abolish them.[7]

During 1980 there were some signs of an improving situation with respect to Cyprus. Greece rejoined NATO's military structure; the civil international air space between Greece and Turkey was reopened; and, last but not least, Greece joined the EEC on 1 January 1981.

Formally the Government of Cyprus has received and is still receiving plenty of support from abroad. For example, the Meeting of Commonwealth Heads of Government held in Lusaka, Zambia, in August 1979, expressed 'full support' for the Cypriot struggle and asked for full implementation of UN resolutions to promote a settlement of the island's problems. Cyprus was also one of the items on the agenda of the Sixth Summit of Non-Aligned Countries held in Havana, Cuba, in September 1979. In its declaration the summit reaffirmed its solidarity with the Government of Cyprus, a founding member of the non-aligned movement.

Despite signs of detente, many problems still exist. First, there is the lack of a definition of a new formula for the re-establishment of the all-Sovereign State, with arguments revolving around terms such as 'binational' (mixed population), which is Greek-sponsored, and 'bizonal' (divided population), which is Turkish-sponsored. There is also the problem of prisoners who have 'disappeared'. The Greek side claims that 2129 people have vanished in the north. The Turks have claimed, at different times, that there are between 240 and 800 missing Turkish persons. Both sides reciprocally reject these charges. The fate of Varosha, the Famagusta tourist resort, sealed off since the Turkish occupation, has also been a cause for great concern. Apart from some *de facto* links − for example, electric energy is supplied to the Turkish zone in Nicosia in return for drinking water − the island looks completely divided. There are many suspicions on the Greek side that Turkey is secretly proceeding towards an annexation of the north. There are also strong allegations regarding the immigration of about 40 000 to 50 000 people from the Turkish mainland. Turkey rejects this charge by affirming that there has been only an influx of technicians to rebuild the occupied area. But, in any case, there is little doubt that in fact a process of immigration has occurred either as part of a possible annexation plan or just to modify the ethnic balance of the area. The first problem to be solved, according to the Greek side, is the reopening of Varosha; and there are growing rumours of an impending agreement. If this materialises some thousands of refugees could then return to work in one of the most developed tourist resorts.

While the division of the island could in any event become a definitive partition, the Government of Cyprus seems to have strengthened the traditional role of Cyprus as an ideal bridge between Europe and the Arab world, as a melting-pot of different pressures and influences. The old dream of Makarios to maintain

the island in a precarious equilibrium between East and West,
North and South, seems still to be workable, in spite of the conflict. The problem is whether this equilibrium will apply to all of
the island or just to part of it.[8]

Notes

1. Public Information Office of the Government of Cyprus, *Answers to Questions usually asked by Foreign Journalists* (Nicosia, 1980) p. 50.
2. The following view on Soviet attitudes to neutralism is of interest:
   the Soviets have pursued their policies in all different Mediterranean
   countries and situations . . . they have exploited instability in Turkey and
   in Greece and the disputes between the two . . . they have preached non-
   alignment for Cyprus, Malta, Tunisia, and Morocco in order to draw these
   states from the West, while trying to undermine non-alignment in Belgrade
   and pull Yugoslavia back in the Soviet camp. (John C. Campbell, 'The
   USSR and the Cyprus Situation', *Problems of Communism*, May–June
   1979).
3. *Pravda*, 12 Dec. 1978 (translation supplied).
4. *Rude Pravo*, 27 Mar. 1979 (translation supplied).
5. Public Information Office of the Government of Cyprus, *The American Arms
Embargo against Turkey* (Nicosia) pp. 8–9.
6. *The Economist*, 5 Apr. 1980.
7. *Yearbook on International Communist Affairs, 1980* (Stanford, 1980) p. 125.
8. For further reading see Andrew Wilson, *The Aegean Dispute*, Adelphi Paper
no. 155 (London, 1979–80); and Duygu Bazoğlu Sezer, *Turkey's Security
Policies*, Adelphi Paper no. 164 (London, 1981). The present chapter was
written before the change of government in Greece in 1981.

Index